TENTH EDITION

OFF THE BEATEN PATH®
GEORGIA →

A GUIDE TO UNIQUE PLACES

JANICE MCDONALD

travel

Guilford, Connecticut

Editor: Kevin Sirois
Project Editor: Lauren Brancato
Layout: Joanna Beyer
Text Design: Linda R. Loiewski
Maps: Equator Graphics © Morris Book Publishing, LLC

ISSN 1541-6615
ISBN 978-0-7627-8124-9

Printed in the United States of America
10 9 8 7 6 5 4 3

To my mother, Dorothy McDonald, who traveled with me via phone.

Contents

Introduction ix

Metro Atlanta 1

Southwest Georgia 41

Southeast Georgia 76

Northwest Georgia 98

Middle Georgia 120

Coastal Georgia 148

Northeast Georgia 179

Index 217

About the Author

Janice McDonald has traveled the world producing videos and writing books and articles. Even though she's traveled all seven continents, she still gets a kick out of what she discovers in her own backyard in Georgia. A native of Myrtle Beach, South Carolina, Janice has called the Atlanta area home for more than half her life. She has spent much of that time exploring and getting to know her adopted state. A favorite rule of hers in any country is to avoid the main roads and take the road less traveled. She invites you to do the same as you explore Georgia with her.

Acknowledgments

This book was great fun to do and I would like to thank all of those who went along with me both physically and via phone and computer. My mom, Dorothy McDonald, and sisters, Paula Miles and Anna Boyce, are always great to travel with. Offering suggestions and companionship were Barbara Lynn Howell, Steve Green, John Vlahakis, Karen Rosen, Sandee LaMotte, Ben Chappell, Kathleen Saal, Denyse Brackett, and Sandra Holmes. There is not enough room on the page for everyone who spoke to me along the journey, but I particularly want to mention Kim Hatcher of the Georgia Department of Natural Resources and Stephanie Paupeck of the Georgia Department of Economic Development for their insight and guidance.

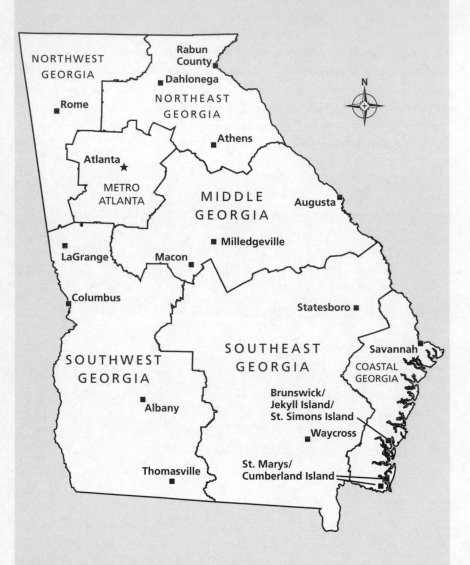

NORTHWEST
GEORGIA

Rome

Rabun
County

Dahlonega

NORTHEAST
GEORGIA

Athens

Atlanta

METRO
ATLANTA

MIDDLE
GEORGIA

Augusta

Milledgeville

LaGrange

Macon

Columbus

Statesboro

SOUTHEAST
GEORGIA

Savannah

COASTAL
GEORGIA

SOUTHWEST
GEORGIA

Albany

Brunswick/
Jekyll Island/
St. Simons Island

Waycross

Thomasville

St. Marys/
Cumberland Island

N

Introduction

Having grown up exploring Georgia's neighbor to the north, this South Carolina girl wasn't sure she could be wowed by Georgia. She was wrong.

Getting off the beaten path to explore and discover those out of the way treasures has opened my eyes and many doors. It was a blast, and I would share each new discovery with friends and family. Soon I was getting calls from friends and even strangers asking for ideas of what to do on a weekend. It was a little early to retort, "Buy the book." As tempting as it was to send them off based on their interests, I would tell them—and you—to open up to new things. The places you think you may not be interested in may turn out to be the places that leave the best lasting impressions.

Georgia is blessed to have such history and diversity within its borders. Its coastal beaches, islands, and marshes take me back to my Coastal Carolina roots, but no amount of describing can prepare you for the beauty. The Spanish moss–laden trees are hauntingly beautiful and the saltwater marshes change color with the sun. Passing through the midlands while farmers were plowing their fields caused me to pull over and watch them turn the red Georgia clay. Driving white-knuckled on the winding highways north of Helen during a foggy morning paid off as the sun burst through to reveal the mountains ahead. Georgia's State Park system throughout is amazing, but the scenery in those parks in North Georgia can be breathtaking. If you can go one place, make it Anna Ruby Falls, especially after a rain.

As you get away from the main highways, you will see that every stop on the road has a story and offers a unique draw. A covered bridge may offer a great photograph, but what if you learned it was built by a freed slave who taught his craft to four sons who also built bridges across the state? Or the large mound of earth you're looking at holds the key to an ancient Indian tribe? Even a trail or stream is connected to the people who came through centuries ago and holds some sort of natural wonder worth diverting from the main road.

But not all there is to see deals with the past. There are people to meet who are currently making their mark on Georgia and there's much to see and do for the active. From canoeing down the Suwannee River to hiking the Appalachian Trail, combing the beaches of barrier islands, or just kicking back and fishing. Try it all!

Researching and living this book has been more fun than you could imagine. I would encourage you to get out and explore as well. Maybe you'll find something I and the original author did not. If you do, please let me know by writing to me c/o Globe Pequot Press, PO Box 480, Guilford, CT 06437.

Restaurant cost categories refer to the price of entrees without beverages, desserts, taxes, or tips. Those listed as inexpensive are $10 to $12 or less; moderate, between $12 and $19; and expensive, $20 and over. Places to stay listed as inexpensive are up to $100 per double per night; moderate, $101 to $200 per night; and expensive, $201 and up per night.

Before you launch your off-the-beaten-path adventures, gather information from these sources: **Georgia Dept. of Economic Development, Tourist Division** (75 5th St. Northwest, Suite 1200, Atlanta, 404-962-4000, www .georgia.org) and **Georgia Department of Natural Resources, Parks and Historic Sites Division** (1352 Floyd Tower East, 2 Martin Luther King Dr., Atlanta, www.gadnr.org). For general information call (800) 869-8420 from anywhere in the United States; in Metro Atlanta call (404) 656-3530.

The Parks Division's Reservation Resource lets you make one toll-free call for campsites, cottages, picnic shelters, and lodge rooms throughout the system. Rates vary at different parks. Campsites, with electrical and water hookups, range from $20 to $30 a night. Completely furnished 1-, 2-, and 3-bedroom cottages are $80 to $200. Rates are higher on weekends and in certain seasons. Double rooms at state park lodges are $75 to $225. Call individual parks for exact rates. In metro Atlanta call (770) 389-PARK; anywhere else in the United States call (800) 864-PARK or go to www.georgiastateparks .org or www.gastateparks.org.

In 2000 the Georgia Department of Transportation changed the numbering system for interstate highway exits. The old sequential system, in which numbers are in chronological order, has been replaced by a mile log system, in which exit numbers correspond to mileposts. For instance, exit 2, on I-75 in southeastern Georgia, is 2 miles from the Florida border. Exit 353, near the Tennessee border in northwestern Georgia, is 353 miles from the Florida border. For a brochure of the new numbers, contact Georgia Department of Transportation (2 Capitol Sq., Atlanta, (888) 419-4368, www.dot.state.ga.us).

If you're interested in a particular area, contact the local convention and visitors bureau or chamber of commerce.

Facts about Georgia

State tourism toll-free phone number: (800) VISIT-GA (847-4852)

MAJOR NEWSPAPERS

Atlanta Journal-Constitution, Augusta Chronicle, Macon Telegraph, Savannah Morning News, Columbus Enquirer, Athens Banner Herald, Rome News Tribune

POPULATION

Georgia has 9.8 million people and is the nation's ninth most populous state.

MAJOR METRO AREAS

Atlanta, 5.5 million   Augusta, 196,000
Savannah, 350,000   Macon, 323,000
Columbus, 300,000

SIZE

With 57,513 square miles, it is the largest state east of the Mississippi, 21st in the nation.

FAMOUS PEOPLE

* 39th President Jimmy Carter

* Juliette Gordon Low, founder of the Girl Scouts

* Dr. Martin Luther King Jr.

* *Gone With the Wind* author Margaret Mitchell

* Television and radio host Ryan Seacrest, from Dunwoody

* Rock bands Widespread Panic, R.E.M., and the B-52s, all from Athens

* Academy Award–winning actress Julia Roberts, born in Atlanta and raised in Smyrna

* *The Help* author Kathryn Stockett lives in Atlanta

* Milledgeville novelist Flannery O'Connor *(The Violent Bear It Away, Wise Blood)*

* Columbus novelist Carson McCullers *(The Member of the Wedding, The Heart Is a Lonely Hunter)*

* Eatonton Pulitzer Prize–winning novelist Alice Walker *(The Color Purple)*

* Eatonton folk story author and humorist Joel Chandler Harris *(Uncle Remus: Tales, Uncle Remus: His Songs & His Sayings)*

* Moreland novelist Erskine Caldwell *(God's Little Acre, Tobacco Road)*

- Popular performers Ray Charles, Lena Horne, Otis Redding, Little Richard Penniman, bandleader Harry James, opera superstar Jessye Norman, songwriter Johnny Mercer, comedian Oliver Hardy

- Danielsville's Dr. Crawford W. Long, who performed the world's first painless surgery with ether in 1842

- Baseball's "Georgia Peach" Ty Cobb, from Royston

- Actress Joanne Woodward, from Thomasville

- Actor Burt Reynolds, born in Waycross

- Folk artist Howard Finster, from Summerville

- Western legend John "Doc" Holliday, born in Griffin

- Two-time Oscar–winning actress Jane Fonda, an Atlanta resident

- Media mogul Ted Turner

- Pop singer Elton John, a part-time Atlanta resident

- 1940s movie actress Miriam Hopkins, born in Bainbridge

PUBLIC TRANSPORTATION

Atlanta has a rapid rail and public bus system, Metropolitan Atlanta Rapid Transit Authority (MARTA). Other cities with public transportation systems are Macon, Savannah, Augusta, Athens, and Columbus.

READING FOR KIDS

Joel Chandler Harris's *Uncle Remus: Tales and Uncle Remus: His Songs & His Sayings.*

CLIMATE

Summers are hot and humid, especially in the southern half of the state and the coast; spring is beautiful and balmy; winters are usually mild, with some snow accumulation in the northern mountains; fall, especially in the northern areas and the mountains, is brisk and cool, with colorful foliage.

GEORGIA TRIVIA

Georgia has 159 counties, more than any other state except Texas (which is four times larger), and more than twice as many as almost-the-same-size

Florida and Alabama. There'd be even more, but two counties went bankrupt in the 1920s and merged with Atlanta's Fulton County.

ELEVATIONS

Georgia's highest point is Brasstown Bald Mountain, 4,784 feet above sea level; lowest point is sea level on the Atlantic coast.

Georgia's hottest recorded temperature was 113 degrees Fahrenheit on May 27, 1978, at Greenville; the coldest was 17 degrees below zero in Floyd County (Rome) on January 27, 1940.

INTERESTING INFORMATION

You can travel around the world and never leave Georgia. Towns include Vienna (called VIE-enna), Cairo (KAY-ro), Berlin, Boston, Bremen, Hamburg, Rome, Milan, Athens, Arabic, and Sparta. You can shop at Bloomingdale and try to solve the secret of Enigma. Like Scarlett O'Hara, you'll never be hungry in Peach, Bacon, Baker, and Coffee Counties. Don't stub your toe on The Rock, and don't Bogart that joint, my friend.

METRO ATLANTA →

Atlanta & Fulton County

With a population of 5.8 million, Metro Atlanta is one of the nation's fastest-growing and most diverse urban centers. New suburbs with cookie cutter subdivisions and shopping malls, threaded by perpetually clogged freeways, sprawl in all directions. In the city of Atlanta—population 420,000—an energetic young population is busily reviving many older neighborhoods. Downtown is also experiencing a rebirth.

Centennial Olympic Park, created for the 1996 Summer Olympic Games, is surrounded by new high-rise condos, hotels, retail shops, restaurants, and major new visitor attractions. In the 21-acre park, at Marietta Street and Andrew Young International Boulevard, you can sit in the sunshine and admire downtown's striking skyline. If the weather's warm, shuck your shoes and splash in the park's *Five Rings Fountain* and perhaps look for your name on the 467,000 bricks that pave the walkways. The *Quilt Plaza,* made of brick and marble, tells the story of the largest games in Olympics history. You can play on a life-size chessboard and enjoy artworks from quirky to classical.

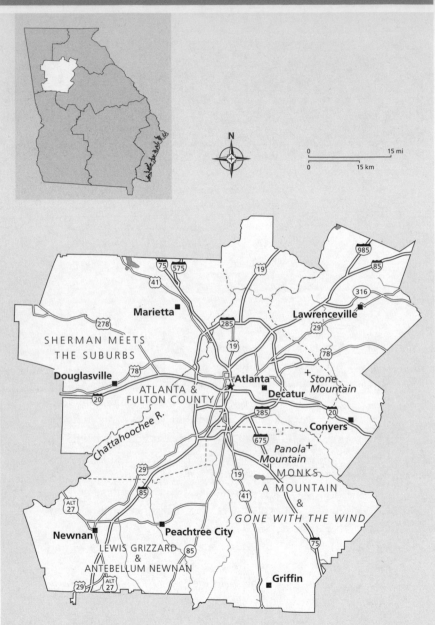

N

0   15 mi
0   15 km

985
85
75   575
19
41
316

Marietta
Lawrenceville
278
285
29
19
78

SHERMAN MEETS
THE SUBURBS

Douglasville
78
+ *Stone Mountain*
Atlanta
Decatur
20
ATLANTA &
FULTON COUNTY
285
20
Conyers
Chattahoochee R.
675
Panola +
Mountain
MONKS
A MOUNTAIN
&
29
19
GONE WITH THE WIND
41
85
ALT 27
75

Newnan
Peachtree City
LEWIS GRIZZARD
&
ANTEBELLUM NEWNAN
85

29
ALT 27
Griffin

Attractions include the **Georgia Aquarium,** opened in November 2005. It's the world's largest fish tank, holding more than 8 million gallons of water. It's home to the world's largest fish, whale sharks destined to reach the size of school buses, and a supporting cast of over 120,000 fish and mammals from around the world. The ark-shaped aquarium is at 225 Baker St., (404) 581-4000, www.georgiaaquarium.org. Open daily. Adults $29.95, seniors 55 and over $25.95, children ages 3 to 12 $23.95, and under 3 free. The nearby **Imagine It! The Children's Museum of Atlanta** (275 Centennial Olympic Park Dr., 404-659-5437, www.imagineit-cma.org) has scores of interactive ways to keep energetic youngsters busy. Open daily. Age 3 and up $12.75, 2 and under free.

The **World of Coca-Cola** attraction opened in summer 2007. For details, see the "I'll Have a Co-Coler" sidebar, page 22. Get information on area attractions at the Atlanta Chamber of Commerce on the edge of the park (235 Andrew Young International Blvd., 404-880-9000).

For quick eats, step across Marietta Street to the food court and sit-down restaurants in the **CNN Center** atrium. You can take the **Inside CNN Tour** of the Cable News Network Studios and Turner Broadcasting Network and see news broadcast around the world. Fifty-five-minute tours begin every ten minutes. Adults $15, seniors and ages 12 to 18 $14, ages 4 to 12 $12, under age 4 admitted free. For information and reservations phone (404) 827-2300 or visit www.cnn.com/tour.

Castleberry Hill is an up and coming arts district, downtown off the beaten path, but only a short walk west of Centennial Olympic Park and its numerous attractions. The neighborhood, a pie-shaped wedge bounded by Peters, Walker, and Nelson Streets, was once a bustling industrial area with packing plants, warehouses, and livery stables. In the early 1980s artists and other urban pioneers discovered the rundown buildings and commercial storefronts and began converting them into galleries and spacious loft apartments.

Now more than a dozen art galleries and studios call Castleberry home. Loft conversions and new residential buildings are home to more than 600 permanent residences. Among the galleries that keep regular hours are Marcia Wood Gallery (263 Walker St., 404-827-0030, www.marciawoodgallery.com), Krause Gallery (291 Peters St., 404-522-6205, www.krausegallery.com), Besharat Gallery (175 Peters St., 404-577-3660, www.besharatgallery.com), Emerging Art Scene (321 Nelson St., 404-890-0532, www.leitchfineart.com), Liana Delgado Studio (161 Mangum St., 770-366-5893, www.lianadelgado.com), ZuCot Gallery (333 Nelson St., 404-343-6977, www.zucotgallery.com), and Romo Gallery (309 Peters St., 404-222-9955, www.castleberryhill.org/romo.html). It's best to call in advance. The **2nd Friday Art Strolls** held each month from 7 to 10 p.m. are the best way to take in all the galleries, including ones opened only for the stroll. Check the website, www.castleberryhill.org.

As the number of galleries and residents increases, restaurants and other services are also developing. *The Elliott Street Deli and Pub* at 51 Elliott St. (404) 523-2174, www.elliottstreet.com, has become a local hangout and often hosts events like the annual Chili Cook-off or hot dog eating contest. Other restaurants and bars include *No Mas! Cantina,* a spacious 2-level Mexican

METRO ATLANTA'S TOP HITS

Centennial Olympic Park

Georgia Aquarium

The Fourth Ward

Martin Luther King National Historic District

Ansley Park

Atlanta Botanical Garden

Piedmont Park

Atlanta History Center

Little Five Points

Zoo Atlanta

Atlanta Braves Baseball

Chattahoochee River National Recreation Area

Chattahoochee Nature Center

Roswell

Atlanta Preservation Center

Oakland Cemetery

Wren's Nest

Center for Puppetry Arts

Herndon Home

The Big Chicken

Michael C. Carlos Emory University Museum of Art and Archaeology

Fernbank Museum of Natural History

Fernbank Science Center

Stone Mountain Village

Norcross's Historic Old Town

Southern Museum of Civil War and Locomotive History

Yellow River Wildlife Game Ranch

High Museum of Art

Imagine It! The Children's Museum

Panola Mountain State Conservation Park

Antebellum and Victorian Newnan Driving Tour of Homes

Lewis Grizzard Memorial Museum

Kennesaw Mountain National Battlefield Park

Decatur Court Square

Marietta Town Square

Lawrenceville Courthouse Square

Pickett's Mill Battlefield Historic Site

World of Coca-Cola

CNN Center studio tours

eatery with loads of art and handicrafts and a big outdoor patio. An adjoining store with the same name sells handmade Mexican furniture and quality crafts (180 Walker St., 404-574-5624, www.nomascantina.com). A number of bars with late-night music are among the restaurants and galleries.

The food court and tablecloth restaurants in the **Peachtree Center** office building and hotel complex, on Peachtree Street between Andrew Young International Boulevard and Baker Street, have a wide selection of cuisine to take out or enjoy in. Pick up a souvenir T-shirt with your burger and fries at the **Hard Rock Cafe** at Peachtree and Andrew Young International (404-688-7625).

Downtown Atlanta's **Woodruff Park** doesn't have a lot of greenery, but on weekdays this open space at Peachtree, Marietta, and Decatur Streets is a prime people-watching location. At weekday lunch, the benches and small patches of grass fill up with Georgia State University students, office workers, street preachers, politicians, freelance musicians, and entertainers. Pick up a sack lunch at one of the numerous eateries around the park and sit back and watch the water wall and fountain at the north end of the park. *Phoenix Rising,* the large bronze sculpture at the park's south end, symbolizes Atlanta's rebirth after its Civil War destruction.

The Historic Fourth Ward Neighborhood just east of downtown is one of the city's trendiest places to visit. It helps that the **Martin Luther King, Jr. National Historic District** and the **Martin Luther King, Jr. Center for Nonviolent Social Change** are both located at its heart at Auburn Avenue and Boulevard. The Fourth Ward was Dr. King's neighborhood, and no doubt he'd be surprised to see the host of new restaurants and bars that now line Edgewood Avenue. The National Historic Site is run by the National Park Service and is open daily 9 a.m. to 5 p.m. and is free to the public. The King Center is independent of the historic site and operated by the King family, but it is across the street at 449 Auburn Ave., (404) 526-8900, www.thekingcenter.org. It is also open daily from 9 a.m. to 5 p.m. and is free to the public.

North of downtown, the **Midtown neighborhood,** along Peachtree Street between Ponce de Leon Avenue and 16th Street, is one of Atlanta's liveliest and most eclectic areas. Straight, metrosexual, and gay bars and dance clubs, restaurants of every stripe, hotels, shops, live theaters, and sleek high-rise condos line Peachtree, Tenth, and Juniper Streets and Piedmont Avenue.

The **Woodruff Arts Center** (home of the **Atlanta Symphony Orchestra** and **Alliance Theater**) and **High Museum of Art,** at 1280 Peachtree St., are the city's cultural temples. In 2005, the High tripled its exhibition space with 3 new buildings and a central piazza, designed by Italian architect Renzo Piano. Make sure to check the schedule because the museum's collections in general are world class and the limited-engagement exhibits draw large crowds. Past exhibits included one featuring hundreds of pieces of art from the Louvre, previously never seen outside of France. The High is open Tues to Sat 10 a.m. to 5 p.m., Thurs 10 a.m. to 8 p.m., Sun noon to 8 p.m. Closed Mon and holidays. Adults $18, age 65 and over $15, ages 6 to 17 $11, students with ID $5. Contact the museum at (404) 733-4400 or www.high.org.

The *Margaret Mitchell House and* Gone With the Wind *Museum* (999 Peachtree St., 404-249-7015, www.gwtw.org,) includes 2 attractions associated with the bestselling novel and 1939 movie. Mitchell wrote her novel on the battered typewriter in her basement apartment in the restored Victorian boardinghouse she called "The Dump." There's a video about her life and her book, as well as letters, photos, and memorabilia. Opened in 1999, the *GWTW* Museum adjacent to the house is devoted to the movie, which premiered in Atlanta in 1939. Exhibits include movie scripts, props, costumes, set design sketches, the front door of the O'Hara family's fictional Tara plantation house, and a portrait of Scarlett O'Hara (Vivien Leigh) in a blue dress, still showing a stain from a whiskey glass an angry Rhett Butler (Clark Gable) threw against it in the second half of the movie.

Although Mitchell wrote only one novel, she was a prolific letter writer. In a letter to her mother-in-law in 1936, she describes the day she frantically gathered the *GWTW* manuscript to deliver to the editor of Macmillan Books: "For years [the manuscript] has been knocking about the house in about twenty very dirty manila envelopes. Some were under the bed . . . some were in the pot and pan closet. I had sixty first chapters, each worse than the other. So, I sat down and took off my garters and tore off a new first chapter. . . . It wasn't until I got to the lobby of [the editor's] hotel that I realized what I looked like, hatless, hair flying . . . my hastily rolled up stockings coming down around my ankles."

The museum is open Mon through Sat from 10 a.m. to 5:30 p.m., Sun noon until 5:30 p.m. Admission for the house and museum is $13 for adults, $10 for seniors and students, and $8.50 for children ages 6 to 17. Mitchell was struck and killed by a taxi on her beloved Peachtree Street, 4 blocks from the house, in 1949. She's buried under a simple gravestone, with her married name Marsh, in downtown Atlanta's historic Oakland Cemetery.

One of the most interesting ways to delve into the city's history is on a tour led by the *Atlanta Preservation Center* (404-688-3350, www.preserveatlanta .com). The center's 9 walking tours from Mar through Nov focus on the city's architectural and cultural heritage. The *Fox Theatre* tour (held throughout the year) takes you backstage at one of America's last surviving 1920s "picture palaces." Adorned with minarets, Moorish arches, Egyptian hieroglyphics, and a blue-sky ceiling that twinkles with electric stars, the Fox (404-881-2100) hosts a full schedule of touring musicals, concerts of all sorts, and a summertime classic movie festival. It's at 660 Peachtree St. at Ponce de Leon Avenue.

MARTA, the Metropolitan Atlanta Rapid Transit Authority, is an up-to-date way to get around the city. The clean, 2-line rapid rail system intersects at Five Points Station downtown and is a swift way of getting to the **Woodruff Arts Center/High Museum of Art,** Hartsfield-Jackson International Airport, and other attractions. If you are downtown, you may want to take advantage of MARTA's new streetcar system built in 2012. The 2.5-mile loop connects Centennial Park to the Martin Luther King, Jr. National Historic site as well as most major tourist attractions in the downtown area. The MARTA bus system is a more comprehensive but much slower way of getting about. Fare for either is $2.50 one way, including transfers; for information call (404) 848-4711. Fares are lower with a long-term BreezeCard, available at rail stations.

For an ear on what's happening, check *Access Atlanta* online at www .accessatlanta.com or pick up the "Go Guide" section in Friday's *Atlanta Journal-Constitution*. The alternative weeklies *Creative Loafing, Sunday Paper,* and gay-oriented *Southern Voice* are all available in sidewalk boxes free.

Ansley Park, a lovely neighborhood dating to the 1920s, is a quiet place to walk, drive, or ride a bike. On Peachtree Street at the Woodruff Arts Center/ Colony Square area, turn east onto 15th Street and north onto Peachtree Circle and follow the meandering byways past sumptuous lawns and gardens skirting homes in a spectrum of styles. Stop for a picnic, a walk, or a giddy ride on a swing at Winn Park, at Peachtree Circle and Lafayette Drive. Follow a street called The Prado to Piedmont Avenue.

Cross this busy street and you're at the **Atlanta Botanical Garden** (404-876-5859, www.atlantabotanicalgarden.org). Take your time strolling through 30 acres of formal gardens, rose gardens, a Japanese garden, and a 15-acre hardwood forest with a marked walking trail or better yet, walk high above it all with the canopy walk. The concrete walkway built in 2010 climbs up to 40 feet, allowing you a bird's eye view of the hardwood trees. Many state, regional, and national flower shows are held in the Day Building at the entrance. The Botanical Garden's centerpiece is the Dorothy Chapman Fuqua Conservatory, with 16,000 square feet of tropical, desert, Mediterranean, and endangered plants. The Fuqua Orchid Center displays tropical orchids from around the world in their natural habitat. There's also a gift shop and small restaurant. Open Tues through Sun 10 a.m. to 6 p.m. Admission is $18.95 for adults, $12.95 for ages 3 to 17; under age 3 free.

After the Botanical Garden, wander into adjoining **Piedmont Park.** Dating back to 1887, the 189-acre park has tennis courts, a swimming pool, softball fields, playgrounds, and paved, auto-free roadways for jogging, hiking, biking, and rollerblading. In summer, the park's lawns and hillsides fill up with tanning bodies. You can rent skateboards, in-line skates, roller skates, and bikes at **Skate Escape** (404-892-1292), across from the park at 1086 Piedmont Ave.

The **Virginia-Highland neighborhood,** about 1.5 miles east of Piedmont Park, is one of the city's favorite dining, shopping, and entertainment areas. It's divided into 3 parts: From Ponce de Leon Avenue, a lively strip of restaurants, bars, coffee shops, and offbeat shops extends about 3 blocks north on North Highland Avenue; after a 3-block residential break, it comes back to life around the Virginia Avenue–North Highland Avenue corner; after another residential break, you'll find more fun stuff at North Highland and Amsterdam Avenues and at another strip at North Highland and Morningside Drive.

The **Buckhead neighborhood,** off Peachtree Street/Road about 6 miles due north of downtown, has long been Atlanta's most splendid residential enclave. West of Peachtree Road, follow the green-and-white scenic drive markers past Spanish and Italian villas, French chateaux, Old English Tudor homes, and white-columned Greek Revival, Georgian, and even Japanese-style showplaces that preside over immense lawns and great stands of trees and flowering shrubbery. Some of the most beautiful homes are on West Paces Ferry, Andrews, Habersham, Blackland, Valley, and Tuxedo Roads.

The neighborhood also has some of the city's finest restaurants. Lenox Square and Phipps Plaza, tony malls at the Peachtree Road/Lenox Road intersection, offer the treasures of Gucci, Saks, Neiman Marcus, and other upscale retail chains.

Famous part-time resident Elton John lives in the penthouse at Park Place, a high-rise condo at Peachtree and East Wesley Roads. Pop singer Janet Jackson also lives part-time in Elton's building.

You'll have a better understanding of what makes Atlanta the kind of city it is after a day at the **Atlanta History Center** (404-814-4000, www.atlanta

How Buckhead Got Its Name

Buckhead, Atlanta's most affluent, most fashionable neighborhood, owes its unique name to an early settler. In 1838, Henry Irby paid a few dollars for a small piece of wilderness near the modern-day intersection of Peachtree, Roswell, and West Paces Ferry Roads. He put up a tavern and a general store that became a meeting place for farmers, hunters, and tradesmen. One day while hunting in the dense woods, he shot a buck, posted the deer's impressive head on his door, and christened the establishment The Buck's Head Tavern. In time, the tavern gave its name to the entire neighborhood. Irby Avenue remembers the founding father.

historycenter.com). The tree-shaded, 30-acre sanctuary at 3101 Andrews Dr., includes 3 fascinating attractions: the insightful and very well done Museum of Atlanta History; the circa 1836 "plantation plain" Tullie Smith Farmstead; and the Swan House, an opulent Italian-Palladian villa, built in 1926 and appointed with European and Asian furnishings and set among formal gardens and terraced fountains. Open daily. Admission is $16.50 for adults; $13 for seniors 65 and older and students ages 13 to 18 and over with ID; $11 for youths 4 to 12; children under 4 are free.

The center has 6 signature exhibits, the largest of which is the **Centennial Olympic Games Museum.** The 27,500-square-foot, 3-story museum traces Atlanta's dark-horse bid for the 1996 games, the building of venues, and a timetable of events at the 16-day games. Exhibits include medals dating to 1896, a collection of Olympic torches, and gifts to the city from the 197 participating teams. An interactive Sports Lab lets kids and adults test their skills against Olympic athletes.

If you still pine for the flower-child days of the 1960s or feel like dyeing your hair electric blue or orange and skateboarding on the sidewalk, **Little Five Points** is your kind of place. You can be totally mainstream and still enjoy an outing at this Southern-style East Village/Soho area. Around the intersection of Moreland and Euclid Avenues, across Ponce de Leon Avenue from Virginia-Highland and about 3 miles east of downtown, you'll find a cluster of good, inexpensive restaurants—Indian, Caribbean, Mexican, Italian, Cajun—coffee bars, bars with and without music, and funky shops selling vintage clothing, new and used CDs, and books on astrology, herbal medicine, and other esoteric subjects. Just like the good old days, street musicians perform for your pleasure and spare change.

East Atlanta Village, off I-20 and Moreland Avenue about 10 minutes south of Little Five Points, is one of the more hidden old neighborhoods to get the Lazarus treatment. Young entrepreneurs have turned vacant storefronts around the Flat Shoals Avenue–Glenwood Avenue intersection into kicky shops with unique and offbeat gifts, art, antiques, and imports. The resurgent old neighborhood's newfound diversity is reflected in inexpensive to moderately priced eateries that serve French, vegan, Italian, Australian, Caribbean, and contemporary American fare. Hot local bands draw the young and sleepless to The Earl (488 Flat Shoals Ave., 404-522-3950, www.badearl.com); **Mary's** (1287 Glenwood Ave., 404-624-4411, www.marysatlanta.com) is a popular gay bar. For a quick pick-me-up, find a sofa at **Joe's East Atlanta Coffee House** (510 Flat Shoals Ave., 404-521-1122). The anti-corporate java and dessert shop is the unofficial "living room" for urban pioneers, who meet for jolts of espresso while they read, study, and revel in the urban slacker lifestyle.

Zoo Atlanta, in Grant Park (800 Cherokee Ave., 404-624-5600, www .zooatlanta.org), a few blocks from the Village and 2 miles from downtown, is a fun place to spend a day. A top attraction is the growing giant panda family. On loan from China, Lun-Lun and Yang-Yang are proud parents to sons Xi-Lan (Chinese for Atlanta's Joy), born August 30, 2008, and Po (named for the lead character in the movie *Kung Fu Panda*), born November 3, 2010. Their first daughter, Mei Lan (Chinese for "Lovely Atlanta") returned to China in 2008. They spend a lot of time sleeping and munching bamboo, but when they move around and climb trees in their lavish habitat, you'll wish you could rush in and give them a big bear hug. The zoo's other big attraction is the Ford African Rain Forest, a natural habitat for families of silverback mountain gorillas. In early 2000, Willie B., the zoo's beloved 41-year-old silverback—the king of the zoo since his childhood—died of old age. A life-size statue of the world-famous silverback is at the zoo entrance. Other zoo habitats house more than 1,000 tropical birds, big cats, bears, giraffes, reptiles, and other exotic creatures from around the world. Open daily. Admission is $20.99 for adults, $16.99 for seniors and students, and $15.99 for children 3 to 11.

Also in historic Grant Park and just next door to the zoo, the *Cyclorama* is a colossal painting in the round capturing a crucial hour in the Civil War Battle of Atlanta. Open daily 9:30 a.m. to 4:30 p.m. Phone (404) 658-7625 for information. Admission is $10 for adults, $8 for seniors and children ages 4 to 12.

Atlanta has many other off-the-beaten-path attractions. Here are a few:

Your suspicions that the government "has money to burn" will be confirmed when you visit the *Federal Reserve Bank of Atlanta's Monetary Museum.* During your prearranged guided tour, you'll see millions of dollars worth of damaged paper bills being shredded. You'll receive a complimentary bag of Uncle Sam's "confetti" and see "live" currency counted and sorted and sent out to Southeastern banks. The tour also takes you through the Visitors Center, where interactive and multimedia exhibits give in-depth lessons in the US economy. The Federal Reserve Bank is at 1000 Peachtree St., across from the Margaret Mitchell House, in Midtown Atlanta. To arrange a free tour, phone (404) 498-5500, or visit www.frbatlanta.org and search for "tours."

The *Robert C. Williams American Museum of Papermaking,* on the Georgia Tech campus (500 10th St., 404-894-6663, www.ipst.gatech.edu/amp), takes you on a self-guided tour through thousands of years of paper and paper technology. "Pre-paper" exhibits include tree leaves from India, Egyptian papyrus, Indonesian bark, and other substances that ancient peoples used before the invention of the real thing, in China around AD 105. Contemporary exhibits feature North America's first paper mill in 1690 and mills that produce paper in the 21st century. Papermaking workshops are held periodically. Open Mon through Fri 9 a.m. to 5 p.m. Free admission.

William Breman Jewish Heritage Museum (1440 Spring St., Midtown Atlanta, 678-222-3700, www.thebreman.org), explores the history of Judaism and Atlanta's own rich Jewish history. In addition to 2 main galleries, the museum offers a genealogy center, extensive archives, a resources library, and changing exhibits such as "Shalom, Y'all," a history of Judaism in the South. Open Mon through Thurs 10 a.m. to 5 p.m., Fri 10 a.m. to 3 p.m., and Sun 1 to 5 p.m. Admission for adults is $12; seniors 62 and over $8; students $6; children ages 3 to 6 $4. Age 3 and under free.

Children as well as adults will enjoy the **Center for Puppetry Arts** (404-873-3391; www.puppet.org), on the northern edge of downtown at 1404 Spring St. The converted redbrick school building houses a fascinating puppetry museum and puts on a year-round program of puppet theatricals, some aimed at youngsters, others tailored for adults.

Oakland Cemetery (248 Oakland Ave. at Memorial Drive, 404-688-2107), offers a look toward Atlanta's past, right behind the ultramodern King Memorial MARTA Station. Established in 1850, Oakland's redbrick walls enclose a wealth of architectural and cultural heritage. Victorian aristocrats are entombed in temple-like mausoleums, embellished with stained glass, gargoyles, and marble busts. You can walk through Confederate and Jewish sections; see the graves of the city's firstborn child and other celebrities, such as *Gone With the Wind* author Margaret Mitchell, golf champion Bobby Jones, governors, mayors, and beloved pets; and spread a picnic lunch under the magnolia trees. Open daily. Free tours are conducted on weekends.

A MARTA train to West End Station and a bus connection or 3-block walk will bring you to the **Wren's Nest,** the Victorian home of Joel Chandler Harris, creator of Br'er Rabbit, Br'er Fox, the Tar Baby, and other delightful critters who roam through his 1880s book, *Uncle Remus: His Songs & His Sayings.* Rooms are filled with furnishings and mementos of Harris and his family, editions of his book in many languages, and re-creations of his beloved characters. The house got its name when a mother wren decided that Harris's wooden mailbox would be perfect for her brood. The mailbox now has an honored place among the Wren's Nest's treasures. Especially if you have children, try to visit when storytelling sessions are scheduled, which is every Sat at 1 p.m.. Wren's Nest (1050 Ralph David Abernathy Blvd., 404-753-7735) is open Tues through Sat 10 a.m. to 2:30 p.m. Admission is $8 for adults, $7 for senior citizens and teens, $5 for children ages 4 to 12.

West of downtown, **Herndon Home** (587 University Place) is a landmark of black achievement. The dignified Beaux Arts-style mansion was built in

AUTHOR'S FAVORITES

Atlanta Botanical Garden	Oakland Cemetery
Georgia Aquarium	Chattahoochee River National Recreation Area
World of Coca-Cola	
Centennial Olympic Park	Court Square entertainment area in Decatur
Atlanta Braves baseball	Stone Mountain Park
Virginia-Highland neighborhood	Zoo Atlanta

1915 by Alonzo Herndon, a former slave who founded Atlanta Life Insurance Company, the nation's largest black-owned insurance firm. Herndon called the mansion "Diamond Hill" and it's easy to see why. The 15 rooms showcase his remarkable life. Most of the antique furnishings and family photos are original. The Herndon Home is open Tues through Thurs 1 to 4 p.m., other days by appointment. Free admission. For more information call (404) 581-9813.

Georgia's 19th-century poet Sidney Lanier sang the praises of the Chattahoochee River in his idyllic "Song of the Chattahoochee." The river rises in the north Georgia mountains and flows through metropolitan Atlanta on its way to the Gulf of Mexico.

The *Chattahoochee River National Recreation Area,* a 48-mile stretch of river and gentle rapids flowing between wooded palisades, is the focus for recreational pursuits of all sorts. From spring through fall, Atlantans love to set their rafts, canoes, and kayaks loose in the river for a lazy day of relaxation. Sturdy 4-, 6-, and 8-person rafts may be rented from Shoot the Hooch at the Chattahoochee Outdoor Center (1990 Island Ford Pkwy., 770-395-6851). If rafting isn't your pleasure, you can also spread a picnic, hike, bike, jog, bird-watch, and exercise on the 22-station fitness trail. The park's main entrance is at US 41 and the Chattahoochee River bridge. Contact the Park Superintendent at 1978 Island Ford Pkwy., (770) 399-8070, www.nps.gov/chat. There is a $3 entrance fee.

The river's fauna and flora are celebrated at the *Chattahoochee Nature Center* (9135 Willeo Rd., Roswell, 770-992-2055, www.chattnaturecenter.com). The private, nonprofit natural-science center's exhibits of plants and wildlife, special programs, and workshops are in a tranquil 50-acre setting by the riverbank, about 20 miles north of downtown Atlanta. Guided walks on Sat and Sun at noon and 2 p.m. weave through 20 acres of nature trails and along a

1,400-foot boardwalk over the river. You can also pick up a brochure and take a self-guided tour. Make a full day of it with a picnic lunch. Check the schedule, because there is almost always something special planned for families and kids. The center is open Mon through Sat from 9 a.m. to 5 p.m. and Sun from noon to 5 p.m. Adults $5, seniors and ages 3 to 12 $2.

On December 22, 1853, Mittie Bulloch, a **Roswell** debutante, married New Yorker Theodore Roosevelt in the dining room of **Bulloch Hall,** her family's Greek Revival showplace. The happy couple, of course, had no inkling of the far-reaching consequences of their union. After the nuptials, they moved to New York and in 1858, had a son, Theodore, who became our 26th president when William McKinley was assassinated in 1901. Their other son, Elliot, had a daughter, Eleanor, who married her cousin Franklin.

In 1905, President "TR" made a sentimental journey to his mother's ancestral home. If he came back today, he'd find Bulloch Hall looking pretty much as it was when his mother was a blushing bride.

Mittie's father, Maj. James Stephens Bulloch, grandson of Georgia's Revolutionary War Gov. Archibald Bulloch, built the house in 1839, the same year Roswell King, a Connecticut Yankee, founded the town and built textile mills on the Chattahoochee River.

One of the South's rare examples of pure temple-form architecture, with a fully pedimented portico, Bulloch Hall is one of more than 100 Roswell structures on the National Register of Historic Places. In 1978, the city of Roswell purchased the house and 16 acres and opened it to the public. A few of the Bulloch family's original furnishings are complemented by period pieces. Modern brides say their vows in the same dining room where Mittie said hers. A reenactment of Mittie and Theodore's wedding is a highlight of "Christmas in Roswell," which also includes Victorian holiday decorations, high teas, parades, seasonal storytelling, and the lighting of the town square.

Bulloch Hall (180 Bulloch Dr., Roswell, 800-776-7935, 770-992-1731), is open Mon through Sat from 10 a.m. to 3 p.m., Sun 1 to 3 p.m. No tickets are required to tour the grounds, but for the home, adult admission is $8, seniors $7, students 6 to 18 $6, under 6 are free. Another noteworthy historical site is **Archibald Smith Plantation,** an 1845 cotton farm, with 12 original buildings, at 935 Alpharetta St., Roswell, (770) 641-3978. The farm is probably one of the best examples of historical and cultural interpretation of 19th century farm life in the region. Open Mon through Fri from 11 a.m. to 2 p.m., Sat from 11 a.m. to 1 p.m. Adult admission $18, $15 for students.

Teaching Museum North, in a former elementary school at 791 Mimosa Blvd., Roswell, (770) 552-6339, is a good place to learn about the history of Roswell, the state of Georgia, and the United States. The Roswell Room's

Where's the Olympic Stadium?

If you'd like to visit Atlanta's Olympic Stadium, you'll have to attend an Atlanta Braves baseball game at Turner Field. The stadium where the 1996 Summer Games opening and closing ceremonies and track and field events were held was ingeniously constructed so that about half of the 85,000 seats could easily be taken out after the games and the stadium converted to a new high-tech, 50,000-seat home for the Braves. The giant brick pillars on the outside of "The Ted's" courtyard were part of the Olympic stadium and will give you a sense of its original size. If you get bored with the game, the stadium has plenty of other bells and whistles. You can play a host of virtual reality games, test the speed of your pitch, shop, visit the Braves Museum, and have dinner and drinks in food courts and the center field restaurant and bar.

TV screens all over the stadium let you enjoy the game just as you would in the comfort of your own living room. It was renamed for former Braves owner Ted Turner, whose TBS Superstation put the Braves in living rooms from coast to coast during the 1990s.

exhibits depict the town's antebellum homes and other buildings spared by the Civil War. A mural traces the region's history from Native Americans to the present. Georgia's many authors, including Pat Conroy, Flannery O'Connor, Sidney Lanier, Alice Walker, Margaret Mitchell, James Dickey, Eugenia Price, and Erskine Caldwell, are honored in the Writers Corner. Other rooms showcase Georgia's economic, political, and social history; US presidents; transportation; and the changing role of women in America. Open Mon through Fri 8:30 a.m. to 3:30 p.m. A $3 per person donation is requested, but not required. Study guides are available through their website: www.teaching museumnorth.org.

Roswell King laid out the Town Square in New England fashion, with a park in the center and a bandstand where "TR" spoke to townsfolk in 1905, surrounded by brick shop buildings. An original general store that once sold everything but liquor now houses *J. Christopher's* (605 Atlanta St., 770-640-5548), which serves breakfast, brunch, and lunch, and still nothing more potent than sweet tea.

A town as old as Roswell naturally (or supernaturally) has plenty of rumored ghosts. Ghost Talk, Ghost Walk (770-649-9922, www.roswellghosttour .com) every Friday evening takes you on a stroll through the Historic District, where you'll hear legendary tales, ghost stories, scandals, and very likely an outright fabrication or two. The biggest mystery is the fate of 400 women and children textile workers, charged with treason by the Union army in 1864 and taken north, most of them never heard from again. The Lost Workers of Roswell Monument, in Old Mill Park on Sloan Street, is their memorial.

Antiques shops and galleries are foremost on many visitors' minds. Canton and Alpharetta Streets are chock-a-block with cozy shops and mammoth collectibles malls. If your art preferences lean in the folk and whimsical direction, stop in **Matilda's Enchanted Cottage** (377 South Main St., Alpharetta, 770-754-7831, www.matildascottage.com). You'll find a magical complex of imaginatively decorated cottages crammed with folk art, pottery, paintings, hand-painted furniture, quilts, weaving, and glassware made by local and nationally recognized artists.

Just around the corner at 1160 Canton St. is even more to try and take in. The **Raiford Gallery** (770-645-2050) could keep you busy for hours exploring the one-of-a-kind works from more than 400 artists, including 50 jewelers, in the gallery's beautiful open wooden structure.

To arm yourselves with information on what to see and do, stop first at the **Roswell Visitors Center** on the square (617 Atlanta St., Roswell, 800-776-7935, 770-640-3253, www.visitroswellga.com) for a video overview, historical exhibits, and walking/driving maps. Guided walking tours with a docent from the Historical Society are available by appointment, but audio tours of the Civil War Walk and the Roswell Mill Village Walk are available for free download through their website.

With a population of 666,000, **DeKalb County** is the Metro area and Georgia's third most populous county and one of Georgia's most ethnically diverse. You'll find many off-the-beaten-path attractions among the county's busy streets and freeways, shopping malls, and subdivisions.

There's an Andrew Young International Boulevard in downtown Atlanta, but the metro area's real "international" boulevard is **Buford Highway** (GA 23). A 10-mile stretch of multilane urban roadway from Lenox Road in the city of Atlanta north through the DeKalb towns of Chamblee and Doraville to Jimmy Carter Boulevard in Gwinnett County is lined with more than 700 businesses and services run by Asian and Hispanic immigrants. Since the early 1980s, old strip shopping centers and newly built malls have filled up with supermarkets where shoppers come from around the Southeast for Korean, Thai, Chinese, Vietnamese, Caribbean, Mexican, Central American, and South American produce, seafood, rice, spices, and other staples. The area is nicknamed "Chambodia" for Chamblee and Cambodia.

Dozens of restaurants offer a selection of authentic cuisines you might expect to find only in Seoul, Bangkok, and Lima (or in Los Angeles, San Francisco, and New York). Some of the major hubs include Plaza Fiesta, at the busy Buford Highway–Clairmont Road intersection (4166 Buford Hwy.,

404-982-9138), where you can buy *hecho en Mexico* (made in Mexico) shoes, sandals, Western wear, apparel of all kinds, religious items, DVDs and CDs, candy, breads, pastries, and cakes; get your hair styled; see a doctor; have your taxes prepared; and explore dozens of stores and kiosks. Walk-up eateries serve inexpensive Mexican and Latino fast food.

Farther north, Asian Square (5150 Buford Hwy.) is anchored by the mammoth Ranch 99 supermarket stocked with Asian and Hispanic goods and about a dozen Taiwanese, Malaysian, Chinese, and Vietnamese restaurants. You can also find jewelry, books, videos, clothes, toys, and gifts, as well as an Asian bank, accountants, and other services.

While you're in northeast DeKalb, you can explore an assortment of antiques shops and flea markets around the Peachtree Road–Broad Street Junction in "old" downtown Chamblee. You're bound to find something you can't resist and didn't realize you needed at **Moosebreath Trading Company** (770-458-7210), **Broad Street Antique Mall** (770-458-6316), and **Whipporwill Co.** (770-455-8357).

Since the Olympics, **Decatur,** the DeKalb County seat, has enjoyed an ongoing renaissance. Vacant storefronts on **Court Square,** across from the historic county courthouse, are now filled with upbeat restaurants, taverns, coffeehouses, and shops.

In a cul-de-sac off East Ponce de Leon Avenue there is a choice of popular American and ethnic eateries and bars, including the much acclaimed **Brick Store Pub** (404-687-0990, www.brickstorepub.com). The Brick Store is considered to have one of the top beer collections in the country, featuring an entire cellar devoted to Belgian brews. With the quaint setting and diverse selection of places, you'll probably have to wait for a table on weekends. In warm weather, you can sit at outdoor tables that line the sidewalks. Restaurants are right outside the Decatur MARTA rail station, with a spacious open plaza with benches and a fountain, about a 15-minute ride from downtown Atlanta. On summer Saturday nights, Decaturites spread blankets and picnic suppers on the courthouse lawn and enjoy live music at the bandstand.

Emory University's **Michael C. Carlos Emory University Museum of Art and Archaeology** (571 South Kilgo St., 404-727-0516) holds a trove of antiquities from around the world. Treasures in this beautifully planned building on the Emory Quadrangle include Greek and Roman coins, statuary, and amphorae; an Egyptian mummy with a gilded face; and European, pre-Columbian, and Asian art objects. Floors are inlaid with diagrams of ancient temples and palaces. Special exhibitions are held regularly. An $8 donation is requested. Open Tues through Fri 10 a.m. to 4 p.m., Sat 10 a.m. to 5 p.m., and Sun noon to 5 p.m. The museum is on the Emory Quadrangle, near the university's main entrance at North Decatur and Oxford Roads. On-campus paid parking is available.

Across from the campus on North Decatur and Oxford Roads, you'll find a row of popular student-oriented eateries, including Everybody's Pizza, Doc Chey's Noodle House, Starbucks, Chipotle Mexican Grill, smoothie and sub shops, and Saba Pasta. If you're into vegetarian and organic foods, check out **Rainbow Grocery** (North Decatur Plaza, 2118 N. Decatur Rd., 404-636-5553). The compact store stocks organic and nonorganic fruits and vegetables, cheese, frozen food, bread and other staples, and herbal remedies. Help yourself to the salad bar and carryout sandwiches, desserts, and prepared dinners. The cafe in the rear of the store serves delicious vegetarian burritos, lasagna, chili, sandwiches, and soups. Open daily.

What can you do on a rainy day in Atlanta? Rain or shine, you can spend all of it at the **Fernbank Museum of Natural History** and the companion **Fernbank Science Center.** Both are operated by the DeKalb County Board of Education. The natural history museum's attractions include the hands-on "A Walk through Time in Georgia," "Sensing Nature," and "The World of Shells," children's discovery rooms, towering dinosaur skeletons, and an IMAX theater. Located at 767 Clifton Rd. between downtown Atlanta and Decatur (404-929-6400, www.fernbankmuseum.org), the museum is open Mon through Sat 10 a.m. to 5 p.m. and Sun noon to 5 p.m. Adults, $17.50; students and senior citizens, $16.50; ages 3 to 12, $15.50. IMAX theater: adults, $13; students and seniors, $12; ages 3 to 12, $11. Combination museum-IMAX: adults, $23; students and seniors, $21; ages 3 to 12, $19. Each Fri from Jan to Nov, Fernbank hosts Martinis and IMAX, an adult cocktail party complete with live band, cash bar, and food. You can come for the music for $7 and not take in the movie; otherwise, adults are $12 and students and seniors $11.

Fernbank Science Center, in a 65-acre hardwood and pine forest threaded with walking trails, has a 500-seat planetarium offering seasonal looks at the heavens. You can also look at far-flung galaxies through the Southeast's largest telescope. Other exhibits focus on Georgia's varied plant and animal life. Open daily, charges only for planetarium shows: $4 for adults, $3 for students. Find it at 156 Heaton Park Dr., (678) 874-7102, www.fernbank.edu. Gates to the forest are locked at 5 p.m.

A granite monolith 825 feet high and 6 miles around, with numerous attractions and 6 million visitors yearly, is hardly off the beaten path. However, many **Stone Mountain Park** visitors include a visit to **Stone Mountain Village.** Outside the park's gates, the village's 19th-century Main Street is flanked by covered sidewalks and 3 blocks of stores stocked with vintage books, arts and crafts, Civil War artifacts, antiques, geodes, apparel, jewelry, and oddities.

You can get a haircut in an old-fashioned barber shop and buy an ice cream, a sandwich, or a full meal at several cafes and restaurants. **Mama Mia's** (961 Main St., 770-469-1199) has been serving hearty Italian cooking for more than three decades.

Housed in the old trolley station, **ART Station** (5384 Manor Dr., just off Stone Mountain's Main Street, 770-469-1105) exhibits paintings, sculpture, and other works by local and regional artists. You can also sign up for classes.

Clayton County, south of downtown Atlanta, was the fictional setting for Tara, Twelve Oaks, and other *Gone With the Wind* landmarks. Appropriately, the **Road to Tara Museum,** in Jonesboro's Depot Welcome Center (104 North Main St., Jonesboro, 770-478-4800, 800-662-7829, www.visitscarlett.com), houses one of the largest collections of *GWTW* memorabilia in the world. Exhibits include re-creations of some of the movie's most famous costumes, first editions of the book in many languages, posters, continuous showings of the film, and souvenir items. If you look closely at a mural, you'll see the familiar face of Elvis Presley, carrying the Confederate battle flag. The mural's artist, Del Nichols, includes Elvis in everything he does. The museum is open Mon through Fri 8:30 a.m. to 5:30 p.m., Sat 10 a.m. to 4 p.m. Adults, $7; seniors and students, $6.

If that's not enough Scarlett and Rhett for you, you can hop a bus at the center for either the **Southern Belles & Whistles Tour** or **Peter Bonner's Gone With the Wind Tour.** You'll be treated to a full array of *GWTW* connections to Jonesboro. Tour reservations can be made at (800) 662-7829. Adults are $24.95, $21.95 for seniors, and $12.85 for children 12 and under.

Margaret Mitchell's childhood playhouse is located behind **Pope Dickson & Son Antique Funeral Museum** (168 N. McDonough St., Jonesboro, 770-478-7211, www.popedickson.com). The playhouse was originally at the Fitzgerald Plantation, which belonged to Mitchell's grandparents. Pope Dickson's Antique Funeral Museum is believed to be America's only drive-by museum. It's open daily 9 a.m. to 5 p.m.

Exhibits in a glassed-in, lighted room include a horse-drawn hearse that led a double life: In 1883, it carried the body of Georgia governor and former

Buster, Hero Dog

Buster, a heroic police dog, is remembered with a granite tribute in front of the Jonesboro police headquarters on North McDonough Street. The inscription reads: NOT JUST A DOG, BUT A POLICE OFFICER, A PARTNER, A FRIEND, ONE WHO MADE A DIFFERENCE. Buster's fellow officers put up the monument bearing Buster's image after bad guys brought down the fearless, 5-year-old crime fighter in 1990.

On the Trail of Mark

If you're a fan of the comic strip *Mark Trail*, you may be interested to know that it had its origins in Sandy Springs. Mark, Cherry, and all of the other characters were based on the friends and neighbors of cartoonist and naturalist Ed Dodd. Dodd's studio was in his Frank Lloyd Wright–designed home in a 130-acre enclave called the Lost Forest, located off Brandon Mill Road on Marsh Creek. As a staunch conservationist, Mark Trail would have no doubt been upset to know that after Dodd retired in the late 1970s, the forest was sold and developed. The original Lost Forest home burned to the ground in 1996. Most of the homes of the Lost Forest subdivision are located on large lots so you might be able to imagine the neighborhood as undeveloped forest. It's easy to find. The roads have names like Marsh Creek, Hidden Falls, and even one called Mark Trail.

Confederate vice president Alexander Hamilton Stephens to his resting place at Crawfordville, 70 miles east of Atlanta. "Little Alex," as he was affectionately known, would have been amazed to learn that during the Civil War, this same hearse smuggled runaway slaves over Northern lines and returned Confederate soldiers across Southern lines. The smugglees hid in a secret compartment and escaped by a trapdoor. Other exhibits include a Civil War iron casket, Victorian funeral jewelry, and embalming equipment. It's lighted until 11 p.m. nightly.

Monks, a Mountain &
Gone With the Wind

Like other Metro Atlanta counties, **Gwinnett** (population about 805,000) has grown so rapidly the past 30 years, it seems to be one vast, unbroken landscape of mammoth shopping malls, subdivisions, and apartment complexes. It's now Metro Atlanta and Georgia's second most populous county. But if you peek behind the "new" Gwinnett, you'll find that many of its old towns and cities have become walkable havens with unique shops, restaurants, and art galleries.

Norcross's Historic Old Town is a pleasant throwback to yesteryear a few minutes off traffic-crazy I-85 and Jimmy Carter Boulevard. Take N. Norcross–Tucker Road off Jimmy Carter and follow the Historic Norcross signs to South Peachtree Street. Antiques and gift shops include **Taste of Britain** (73 S. Peachtree St., 770-242-8585), with imported teas, biscuits, jams, china, and gifts. There are also an old-fashioned barbershop, a vintage hardware store, and other small businesses in the well-preserved 19th-century buildings grouped around the old wooden train depot. *Norcross Station Cafe,* in the done-over depot, and *Dominick's Little Italy* across the street, are detailed in "Places to Eat in Metro Atlanta," at the end of this chapter.

Not to be outdone by other Gwinnett County cities, *Lawrenceville,* the county seat, has done a vibrant renovation of its Courthouse Square. The centerpiece is the majestic 1885 redbrick courthouse with the tall white turret and clock tower. No longer the seat of county government since a modern courthouse was built in the early 1990s, the historic building, with its manicured lawns, brick-paved sidewalks, benches, retro streetlights, and memorials to soldiers who died in the Civil War and Creek Indian War, has historical displays and meeting rooms. Around it is a lively mix of shops, galleries, and eateries. Shoppers have a choice of *Scotland Yard Antiques* gifts and accessories, (678) 407-1010; the Paper Fairy, (770) 513-0400; and *Red Hat Lane,* with one of north Georgia's biggest selections of Red Hat Society accessories, (770) 338-2165. *Just What I Like!* is a jumble of contemporary watercolors, acrylics, prints, metal wall sculptures, wood furniture, and accessories, (678) 985-5506.

The *Aurora Theatre* (1128 E. Pike St., 770-476-7926) is Lawrenceville's most popular attraction. Located in a renovated historic church, a professional repertory company performs in the 200-seat main auditorium year-round. The Aurora is also home to a performance academy and hosts dances when performances are not underway.

The food is as much fun as the Lawrenceville shops. Choices include Flying Saucer Retro Cafe and Bakery (770-339-9930), with sandwiches, salads, soups, and delectable sweets; and the ever-popular McCray's Tavern (770-407-6745, www.mccraystavernlawrenceville.com). McCray's has a huge beer selection and its menu ranges from pub fare to shrimp and grits or a garlic rib eye.

For a look at Gwinnett County "when," take a walk through the *Lawrenceville Female Seminary.* Built in the 1850s after the original burned, the 2-story brick Greek Revival building was a finishing school that tutored antebellum young ladies in reading, writing, and etiquette. Over the years the old school building taught boys and hosted civic clubs, the United Daughters of the Confederacy, and a radio station. In the 1970s, when Dairy Queen coveted the site, the county government purchased it, had it placed on the National Register of Historic Places, and made it the home of the Gwinnett County History Museum's collections of farm implements, textiles, historic photos, and exhibits on schools, religion, music, and other aspects of the county's life. Imagine the blushing bride coming down the aisle in a wedding gown fashioned of cotton and flour sacks. It's at 455 S. Perry St. in downtown Lawrenceville. Open Mon through Thurs and Sat by appointment. No admission charge. Phone (770) 822-5178 for information or visit www.gwinnettcounty.com.

In the mood for authentic Mexican tacos and moles, Ecuadorean and Salvadorean empanadas, pad Thai, Korean barbecue, Cantonese dim sum, fiery Szechuan, Vietnamese pho, Indo-Pak curries and dosai, and the ingredients to make your own? One of Georgia's most ethnically diverse counties, Gwinnett has scores of restaurants, food markets, and other services catering to large communities from Asia, Mexico, Central and South America, and homegrown Anglos and others looking for some adventure for their palates.

For information contact the Gwinnett Convention and Visitors Bureau, 6500 Sugarloaf Pkwy., Duluth. Phone (770) 623-3600 or (888) 494-6638 or visit www.gcvb.org.

Yellow River Wildlife Game Ranch is a peaceful place in the woods in the midst of south Gwinnett County's suburban explosion. Just off very busy US 78, 3 miles east of Stone Mountain Park, the 24-acre privately owned nature preserve is home for dozens of free-roaming brown deer, huggable bunnies, goats, sheep, coyotes, ducks and geese, pigs and porcupines, foxes, wolves, donkeys, a skunk named William T. Sherman, and a spring-forecasting groundhog named Gen. Beauregard Lee.

Deer are Yellow River's self-appointed reception committee. You're no sooner on the tree-shaded walking trail than whole families of gentle does, bucks, and fawns are ambling up for handouts of bread and crackers and a scratch behind the ears. During summer, fragile newborn fawns are an especially appealing sight. Lambs, piglets, baby ducks, and goat kids are also very much in the spotlight.

Young children get a kick out of the Bunnie Burrows, an enclosed area where rabbits of all sizes and colors seem to enjoy being petted and hand-fed raw carrots and celery.

What's purportedly the largest herd of American buffalo east of the Mississippi roams a back meadow. Black bears, bobcats, mountain lions, foxes, and wolves are secured in open-air enclosures, out of the reach of little fingers. If you spread a picnic lunch in a grove by the Yellow River, expect some "deer" friends to drop by for a treat.

You may reserve Yellow River's *Birthday House* for your youngster's special day or for a family reunion or other group activity. Yellow River Wildlife Game Ranch, at 4525 Hwy. 78, Lilburn, (770) 972-6643, www.yellowrivergame ranch.com, is open daily 10 a.m. to 5 p.m. Admission is $8 for adults; $7 for children 3 to 11; free for children 2 and under.

The *Sugar Hill Municipal Golf Course* (8 miles north of the Suwanee exit off I-85, 770-271-0519), is a sweet layout for those who'd like to play like the pros but have an amateur's budget. Spread over 300 acres at the north Gwinnett County town of Sugar Hill, the well-maintained par-72, 18-hole

I'll Have a Co-coler

For millions of people around the world, Atlanta is synonymous with Coca-Cola. The soft drink was created in a Peachtree Street pharmacy in 1886. Dr. John Stith Pemberton, originally from Columbus, Georgia, was seeking a nonalcoholic cure for the common headache. He blended coca leaves, African kola nuts, and other ingredients into an elixir he called Coca-Cola. It was first sold as a heavy syrup diluted with water. But one day the clerk substituted soda water for tap water, and voilà, Coke was on its way around the world.

Headquartered in Atlanta, the company closely guards its secret formula. If you visit the massive interactive World of Coca-Cola near Centennial Olympic Park and the Georgia Aquarium (121 Baker St., 404-676-5151, www.worldofcoca-cola.com), you'll be treated to animated films and videos on Coke's history, as well as hundreds of exhibits and souvenir items, a bottling room, an art gallery, a gift store, and free samples of Coke and soft drinks the company tailors for specialized tastes around the world. It's open for self-guided tours daily 9 a.m. to 5 p.m.; 8 a.m. to 6 p.m. in June, July, and Aug. Admission is $16 for adults; $14 age 65 and over; $12 ages 3 to 12. Age 2 and under free. Paid parking is in the attraction's deck on Ivan Allen Jr. Boulevard.

course offers plenty of challenges as it swoops up and down hills and around 6 lakes and 45 traps.

The *Southeastern Railway Museum* in Duluth, 25 miles northeast of downtown Atlanta (3395 Peachtree Rd., Duluth), honors the golden age of passenger trains. Owned and operated by the Atlanta Chapter of the National Railway Historical Society, the 30-acre indoor and outdoor museum invites train buffs to sit in red cabooses, hauled around the yards by vintage diesel locomotives. Each Saturday and most Thursdays (except June and July on Wednesday), the cabooses are hooked to huffing, puffing steam locomotives. Before and after the ride, there's time to look at more than 90 pieces of rolling stock, exhibits, and displays. One of the showpieces is "Superb," the 1911 Pullman car that carried President Warren G. Harding across the country in the early 1920s. When Harding died in San Francisco in 1923, "Superb" carried him back to Washington and then to burial in Ohio. Army chefs prepared meals for the troops in a military kitchen car parked nearby. You can walk through locomotives, passenger coaches, dining cars, a railway post office, and Pullman sleeper cars. Kids and grown-up "kids" who enjoy the sport of model railroading can see the miniature train in the exhibit hall. From downtown Atlanta, take I-85 North to exit 104/Pleasant Hill Road and follow the signs. There is no set schedule on park train rides, but the museum is open Thurs through Sat from 10 a.m. to 5 p.m. throughout the year as well as Mon and Wed during summer months. Admission is $8 adults; $6 age 65 and over; $5 ages 2 to 12. Caboose rides are an additional $3 with park train rides $2. The complex is available for birthdays, meetings, and other events. Phone (770) 476-2013 for more info or visit www.srmduluth.org.

Amid the burgeoning suburbs of Rockdale County, a short drive off the busy lanes of I-20, about 25 miles east of downtown Atlanta, the **Monastery of the Holy Ghost** is a place of inordinate peacefulness. Since the late 1940s, Benedictine Trappist monks have dwelt and prayed in this cloistered sanctuary at 2625 Hwy. 212, Conyers, (770) 483-8705. The Spanish Gothic–style buildings, even the stained glass in the main church, are all products of their labors.

Men and women can attend Sunday morning Mass in the church, which is highlighted by the monks' chants and prayers. Men may make retreats at the modern guesthouse nearby. A small shop sells bread, cheese, jam, religious items, and produce and herbs grown in the monastery's fields. You may also bring a picnic lunch to tables that sit by a lake beside the cloister.

The abbey does not observe a strict rule of silence, and most monks can converse with visitors.

Just east of Conyers on I-20 is Covington in Newton County. Fans of TV's *In the Heat of the Night* will recognize many of the show's locations around the **Covington** courthouse square. Many beautiful white-columned homes are on the tree-shaded streets radiating from the square.

You'll also find a trove of antebellum treasures around nearby **Oxford College of Emory University,** which welcomed its first freshman class in 1839.

Twenty miles southeast of downtown Atlanta, via GA 155, **Panola Mountain State Conservation Park** is a peaceful 585-acre day-use park where you may have a walk in the woods, enjoy a picnic, and wonder at a 100-acre granite outcropping that's been part of the Henry County landscape for about a million years. The lichen-covered monadnock is part of a major belt of granite, most dramatically evidenced by Stone Mountain a few miles away.

We Like it Sweet

Georgians, like their fellow Southerners, are addicted to iced tea. We drink gallons of it summer, winter, fall, and spring. And the sweeter, the better. Real Southern iced tea has the sugar brewed in; adding it later doesn't have the same effect. When you order, you'll usually be asked, "Sweet or unsweetened?" If you want it sugarless and aren't asked for a preference, you're liable to get a glassful so syrupy it will make your teeth and gums ache. Half & Half is also a good and accepted option.

Stop first at the park's Nature Center for information on trails leading through the woodlands and around the mountain. Meandering through hardwood and pine forests, the 1.25-mile Watershed Trail is a moderately strenuous course. Several stations along the way have benches and markers describing the park's fauna and flora. At the base of Panola Mountain, a 3-acre pond is alive with turtles, frogs, fish, and small reptiles.

The 0.75-mile Rock Outcrop Trail takes you through the woods to an overlook on one of the mountain's major outcroppings. The truly ambitious could tackle the 12-mile PATH foundation/Panola Mountain Trailhead which connects Panola Mountain with Arabia Mountain and Stonecrest Mall. On Saturday and Sunday afternoon, park naturalists conduct walks and give talks at the small amphitheater close to the Nature Center. Picnic tables are located near restrooms and soft drink machines. Pets on leashes may be walked in the picnic area but aren't allowed on the nature trails.

The park is open daily from 7 a.m. to sundown. There is a $5 parking fee. Contact the superintendent in Stockbridge, (770) 389-7801, (800) 864-PARK, www.gastateparks.org.

If you didn't surmise it while battling the perpetual traffic on **Henry County's** streets and highways, the south suburban metro county is the third-fastest-growing county in Georgia and fourth-fastest in the entire United States. So it's a pleasant surprise to drive into the courthouse square in **McDonough,** the county seat, and wonder if you haven't drifted plum out of Henry into some rural place far from Metro Atlanta.

With a population of about 22,000, tidy, compact McDonough (pronounced "Mcdunnah") is a throwback to calmer, less frantic small-town times. Stop first at the McDonough Hospitality and Tourism Bureau in a regeared 1920s Standard Oil station on the square, pick up a map and helpful pointers, and start poking around the antiques malls, "attics," flea markets, gift, and specialty shops. The **Geranium House** (monogramming and gifts, 770-610-6060), **Bell, Book and Candle** (used books, gifts, and jewelry, 770-957-1880), **Planter's Walk Antique Mall** (thousands of antiques and collectibles, 678-432-5250), and **Secret Garden** (home accessories and unique gifts for the young and old, 678-432-6888) are good places to start.

Dining on the square includes **R. L.'s Off the Square,** a white-tablecloth restaurant in an early 1900s building serving food with an elegant Cajun flare, (770) 385-5045; **Gritz,** serving Southern-style breakfast and lunch, (770) 914-0448; **PJ's Cafe,** American cuisine and a popular bar, (770) 898-5373; and the **Koffee Klutch,** coffee and pastries, (678) 432-4499.

Scarlett's Retreat and Day Spa, in a historic house just off the square, offers the full range of body treatments (678-432-7474).

"The Geranium City" lives up to its nickname during late January's **Geranium Festival.** Blooming with thousands of the colorful plants, the park in the square features music, entertainment, food, and more than 300 craftspeople selling their wares.

For information contact McDonough Hospitality and Tourism Bureau, 5 Griffin St., McDonough, (770) 898-3196, www.tourmcdonough.com.

Bargain lovers should put the Spalding County seat of **Griffin** high on their shopping lists. The textile town of 20,000, on US 19/US 41, 40 miles south of Atlanta, has some especially tempting values in antiques and socks.

Spalding Hosiery Shoppe (770-227-4362) has the answer to virtually all your hosiery needs. Aisles are jammed with colorful argyles, athletic socks, dress socks, and heavy-duty work socks, as well as pantyhose, sweatshirts, and other items made by major manufacturers. Irregulars, with all but impossible to discern blemishes, go for at least half the price you'd normally pay. First-run items are more expensive, but still very much a bargain. It's open Mon through Sat from 8:30 a.m. to 5:30 p.m. No credit cards accepted; find it at 432 E. Broad St., across from the redbrick Spalding Mills, a block from the center of town, www.sockshoppe.com

The **Antique Griffin at Dovedown** (315 W. Solomon St., 770-227-7708), displays the treasures of more than three dozen dealers in a 4,500-square-foot former textile mill in downtown Griffin. Take your pick of china, old coins, Civil War relics, vintage toys, country primitive and Victorian furniture, decorative accessories, jewelry, and folk art. **Aging Gracefully Antiques,** 10 N. Hill St., (770) 233-9000, has eclectic selections of pottery, furniture, quilts, and oil, gas, and kerosene lamps.

Architecture buffs can stroll downtown Griffin and see a range of styles surviving from the late 1800s to the 1930s. Most of the downtown commercial buildings, on Broad, Solomon, and Taylor Streets, are two stories high, constructed of brick, with wood or cast-iron storefronts and plate glass display windows. Many of the old buildings have been adapted for contemporary use.

Lewis Grizzard & Antebellum Newnan

Coweta and Fayette Counties, on Metro Atlanta's southwest periphery, are perfect for a one-day getaway from the big city, and they have more than enough to keep you happily occupied for much longer than that.

Take I-85 exit 47, 40 miles south of Atlanta, and follow Bullsboro Drive/GA 34 into downtown **Newnan.** First stop is the Coweta County Welcome Center, 100 Walt Sanders Memorial Dr., Newnan, 1 mile off I-85 exit 47. Call (770) 254-2627 or (800) 826-9382, or visit www.explorecoweta.com. They'll fill you

Judge Landis

In the wake of the Chicago "Black Sox" betting scandal during the 1919 World Series, Judge Kenesaw Mountain Landis was named Major League Baseball's first commissioner. He is credited with restoring the game's integrity and saving it from self-destruction. He was named for Marietta's Kennesaw Mountain, where his father was wounded during the Civil War. His father spelled the name with only one *n* instead of two.

in on every place to see, do, eat, and sleep in and around the city of 15,000. Open Mon through Sat, 9 a.m. to 5 p.m. Be sure to pick up an ***Antebellum and Victorian Newnan Driving Tour of Homes*** guide, which describes 23 pre–Civil War landmarks. Many of the homes welcome visitors during the annual ***Tour of Homes and Arts and Crafts Show*** the third week of April. Before your driving tour, park around the majestic old courthouse in the center of the square and browse the many antiques, gift, and bookshops that lure locals away from the ubiquitous malls on the outskirts.

If you're a fan of the late syndicated humor columnist Lewis Grizzard—a Coweta native son—you'll find all his books and tapes at ***Scott's Book*** (770-253-2960). Owner Earlene Scott was a close friend of Grizzard's, and she's always happy to share her memories. A Grizzard museum, described below, is in the small community of Moreland, south of Newnan.

Male Academy Museum (30 Temple Ave., Newnan, 770-251-0207, www.nchistoricalsociety.org) is a must for Civil War enthusiasts. The historic school building displays a major collection of uniforms, weapons, artifacts, and soldiers' personal effects. You'll also find clothing, furniture, and photographs from the mid-19th to the early 20th centuries and an 1890s classroom. Open Tues through Thurs from 10 a.m. to 3 p.m. and Sat and Sun from 2 to 5 p.m. Admission is $5, children $2.

Lewis Grizzard wrote fondly about growing up in tiny Moreland (population 450). In appreciation, townsfolk opened ***The Lewis Grizzard Memorial Museum*** (www.lewisgrizzard.com/museum). The collection ultimately outgrew its original home in an old gas station and was relocated in 2011 to the historic Moreland Mill, which also houses artifacts of Moreland's history. The Grizzard collection takes up a large portion of the Mill's exhibit area and displays his many books, photos, battered manual typewriters, his favorite Gucci loafers, high school letter jacket, and other memorabilia. The Mill is open Thurs through Sat 10 a.m. to 3 p.m. If you're a true fan, be here the first Saturday of April when thousands of his friends and fans come for the ***Annual Lewis***

Grizzard Storytelling and Barbecue. A shameless male chauvinist, he even found humor in his three failed marriages. A bumper sticker urges, "Honk, if you've been married to Lewis Grizzard." He died of heart disease in 1994. A section of I-85 in Coweta County is called "Lewis Grizzard Highway."

Although he was vilified by Southerners for his scathing takes on rural morals and manners, Coweta Countians have restored ***"The Little Manse,"*** birthplace of novelist Erskine Caldwell. The author of *God's Little Acre* and *Tobacco Road* was born in The Manse in 1903 when his father was a Presbyterian pastor here. The family left when Caldwell was 5 years old, and he never lived here as an adult. But the simple frame house is very much as he knew it. Biographical exhibits, personal items, copies of his books in several languages, and a video trace the career of the author, who died in 1987. The house is on Moreland's Town Park, off US 29, Moreland; open by appointment. Admission is $2 for adults, $1 for children 6 to 12. Call Winston Skinner at (770) 254-8657 for more information. You can go directly to Moreland from I-85 exit 41 and driving south on US 29.

Dunaway Gardens (3218 Roscoe Rd./GA 70, Newnan, 6 miles north of Newnan, near the small community of ***Roscoe,*** 678-423-4050, www.dunaway gardens.com), was created in the 1920s and 1930s by popular Chatauqua Circuit actress Hettie Jane Dunaway, as a theatrical training center and floral rock gardens. In its prime, the gardens hosted ballet and modern dance troupes, a drama school, indoor and outdoor theater, and celebrities such as Walt and Roy Disney. Sarah Ophelia Colley, later famous as the Grand Ole Opry's Minnie Pearl, headed the drama school. After Dunaway's death in the early 1960s, the 25-acre gardens were abandoned to weeds, vines, kudzu, and poison ivy. Now, thanks to a 3-year-effort by Jennifer and Roger Bigham of Newnan, visitors are once again welcome to explore 5 descending staircases, with rock walls, a natural rock amphitheater, slate patios, waterfalls, goldfish ponds, hanging gardens lush with native plants and flowers, and a 1-acre granite outcropping called "Little Stone Mountain." The gardens are open from Mar through Nov Thurs through Sat 10 a.m. to 5 p.m. and Sun 1 to 5 p.m. Adults $10, children $8. Group tours are available by appointment. It's a popular, picturesque setting for weddings.

Senoia, a drowsy little Coweta County town on GA 85, 40 miles south of Atlanta, is like a delightful trip through Norman Rockwell–land. With over 113 sites on the National Historic Register, it is a perfect movie location so don't be surprised if you run into some sort of production underway during your visit. In fact, the town is so dedicated to maintain its looks, any new building has to be constructed to fit in with the historic motif.

The ***Culpepper House*** in Senoia dates to 1871, when it was built by Dr. John Addy, a returning Civil War veteran. Innkeepers Suzanne and Sam

Helfman have 3 guest rooms with private baths and furnished with Victorian antiques. Public areas shine with gingerbread trim, stained glass, and pocket doors. A full Southern breakfast is included in the inexpensive to moderate rate for a double with private or shared bath. Contact them at 35 Broad St., Senoia, or call (770) 599-8182, www.culpepperhouse.com.

Four miles north of Senoia, at the junction of GA 85 and GA 74, stands *Starr's Mill,* one of Georgia's most photographed landmarks. One look at the 200-year-old red frame mill, by a pond and waterfall, and you'll be rushing for your camera, too. When you go, be sure to bring along a blanket and picnic.

If you are feeling more adventurous you may want to check out **Historic Banning Mills** (770-834-9149; www.historicbanningmills.com) near the little town of Whitesburg off US 27. Now a popular corporate retreat location, ruins of centuries-old mills dot Snake Creek, which meanders through the 1,200-acre forest preserve. In addition to its conference center, Banning Mills is home to 5 levels of zip line canopy tours, including the Screaming Eagle, the highest zip line east of the Mississippi.

Sherman Meets the Suburbs

Since 1968 the picturesque rapids of Sweetwater Creek and the adjacent hardwood and piney woodlands have been the heart of Sweetwater Creek Conservation Park, a peaceful day-use state park. A short drive off I-20, 15 miles west of downtown Atlanta, the park serves the populace of rapidly growing Douglas County and many others who find it a delightful retreat from the hurly-burly of big-city life.

The ghostly ruins of the *New Manchester Manufacturing Company,* a Civil War–era enterprise torched by General William T. Sherman's troops, stands by the churning rapids, which provided the company with power to produce uniforms for the Confederate army. During the summer, kick off your shoes and join others wading in the swift, cool waters. Be careful of the slick patches of moss covering the rocks.

Five miles of nature trails lead you through the woods beside the creek. A 250-acre reservoir is stocked with bass, catfish, and bream, which you can fry in a pan and serve on one of the park's picnic tables. Fishing supplies are available at the park's bait shop, and during warmer months boat rentals are also available. The park is open daily from 8 a.m. to sundown. There is a $2 parking fee. Contact the superintendent at (770) 732-5871, (800) 864-PARK, or www.gastateparks.org.

With more than 690,000 residents, affluent *Cobb* is one of the nation's fastest-growing counties and the northwest flagship of the Atlanta metropolitan area. Off the well-beaten paths of freeways and around the corner from high-rise hotels, glitzy shopping galleries, and trendy eateries, you'll find fascinating historic sites, charming town squares, and outdoor recreation.

Acworth, in northern Cobb County, is one of Metro Atlanta's newest and most successful turnaround stories. An influx of domestic and overseas new-comers has transformed the once-sleepy little town by the train tracks into a buzzing hub of contemporary dining and shopping.

Along 2 blocks of Main Street, just off busy I-75, exit 277, diners choose from an eclectic array of cuisines. At **Red Peppers,** (770) 529-3636, Elias and Marta Endara prepare "down-home" Mexican, Cuban, and South American–style cooking. **Teacup Cottage,** (678) 574-6011, pours international teas with soups, salads, sandwiches, and desserts in a delightful gift shop. Other options include **Henry's Louisiana Grill,** (770) 966-1515; **Fusco's Via Roma,** (770) 974-1110; and **Charlie's Original Oyster King,** (770) 917-1707. Antiques, book, jewelry, clothing, housewares, garden accessory, and wine shops and an ice-cream store are spaced among the restaurants. For information: Acworth Area Visitors Bureau, 4415 Senator Russell Ave., Acworth, (770) 974-8813, www .acworth.org.

After the fall of Chattanooga in late 1863, the Confederates grudgingly fell back to Kennesaw Mountain, 25 miles north of Atlanta and the site of **Kennesaw Mountain National Battlefield Park.** For two weeks in June 1864, 60,000 soldiers dug into the wooded flanks of the 1,808-foot mountain. When a series of assaults failed to dislodge the Southerners, Union commander General William T. Sherman executed a flanking strategy, which forced the Confederates to leave the mountain and retreat to Atlanta.

Stop first at the National Park Service Visitors Center and view the slide presentation and exhibits. Outside are some of the cannons that took part in the battle. From Mon through Fri you may drive your car up a paved road to a parking area 200 yards below the summit. From there take an easy walk through the woods studded with cannons, earthworks, and markers telling the story of the battle. On Sat and Sun the mountain road is open only to a free shuttle bus that makes the trip every half hour. In fair weather many visitors hike at least one way on an easy 1-mile trail. If you've the stamina, you can extend your hike from the Kennesaw summit 4 miles to **Cheatham Hill** and 7 miles to **Kolb's Farm,** other principal battlegrounds in the Kennesaw theater. The two areas are also accessible by car.

Picnic tables, grills, and restrooms are in a grove of trees near the visitor center parking area. The park, about 4.5 miles west of I-75 exit 269 (Barrett Parkway) in Kennesaw, is open Mon through Fri from 8:30 a.m. to 5 p.m., Sat and Sun to 6 p.m. Free admission, but the shuttle is $2 for adults and $1 for

TOP ANNUAL EVENTS

Southeastern Flower Show
mid-March, Cobb Galleria
2 Galleria Pkwy.
(770) 989-5095
www.sehort.org/flower_show

Conyers Cherry Blossom Festival
late March, Georgia International Horse
Park
(770) 918-2169
www.conyerscherryblossomfest.com

Atlanta Dogwood Festival
early April, Piedmont Park
(404) 329-0501
www.dogwood.org

Atlanta Gay Pride Parade and Festival
Mid-October
(404) 929-0071
atlantapride.org

Georgia Renaissance Festival
September and October
7795 Spence Rd., Fairburn
(770) 964-8575
www.garenfest.com

Inman Park Spring Festival and Tour of Homes
late April, Euclid and Edgewood
Avenues
no phone
www.inmanparkfestival.org

Stone Mountain Village Arts Festival
mid-June, Main Street
Stone Mountain
(770) 498-2097

Peachtree Road Race 10K
July 4, Peachtree Road–Peachtree
Street
(404) 231-9064
www.peachtreeroadrace.org

Christmas at Bulloch Hall
Mid-November throughout December
Roswell
(770) 992-1731
www.bullochhall.org

Christmas at Callanwolde
early to mid-December
Callanwolde Fine Arts Center
(404) 872-5338
www.christmascallanwolde.org

children. Contact the superintendent at PO Box 1167, Marietta, (770) 427-4686, www.nps.gov/kemo.

Civil War and old-time train buffs can have a great day exploring the **Southern Museum of Civil War and Locomotive History** in Kennesaw. The celebrated steam locomotive "General" is the centerpiece of the 40,000-square-foot, Smithsonian-affiliated museum. In April 1862, Union raiders hijacked the engine and several cars at the Kennesaw depot and drove it north toward Chattanooga. The train's crew, breakfasting at a trackside hotel during the heist, pursued the hijackers by foot, platform car, and locomotive for 87 miles. When the "General" ran out of fuel, near Ringgold, Georgia, 22 raiders were captured and 8 were hanged as spies. The secretary of war later presented fourteen of the raiders with the Congressional Medal of Honor. In 1956 Walt Disney Pictures dramatized the episode in *The Great Locomotive Chase,* starring Fess Parker. With eight wheels, a barrel-shaped smokestack, and a bright red cowcatcher, the "General" sits on original track in its own spacious exhibit hall. The museum's other displays include a history of Southern railroading, Civil War weapons, uniforms, and soldiers' personal items. A large wing re-creates the Glover Machine Works, a foundry in nearby Marietta where 300 locomotives were built during the early 1900s. Special exhibits from the Smithsonian are held all year. The museum is at 2829 Cherokee St., Kennesaw, off I-75 exit 273, about 25 miles north of downtown Atlanta. Open Mon through Sat 9:30 a.m. to 5 p.m., Sun noon to 5 p.m. Adults, $7.50; age 60 and over, $6.50; children 4 to 12, $6.50; under age 4, free. Phone (770) 427-2117 or visit www.southernmuseum.org.

For more train memorabilia, and big helpings of Southern comfort food, step across the street to the **Whistle Stop Cafe,** open every day. Phone (770) 794-0101 for info.

Londoners rendezvous by Big Ben, New Yorkers under the Grand Central Station clock. Since the early 1960s, motorists navigating the highways of Marietta and Cobb County have set their sights by **The Big Chicken,** a 56-foot red-and-white sheet-metal rooster that preens on the façade of a KFC outlet on busy US 41/Cobb Parkway. The Big Chicken was "hatched" in 1963 by S. R. "Tubby" Davis, who wanted a really big sign to ballyhoo his fast-food restaurant. In the 1970s, KFC bought out Tubby and reluctantly retained the Chicken, which had become a landmark and popular icon. When it was severely damaged by a 1993 tornado, KFC bowed to public demands and spent "buckets" on a makeover.

The Chicken's flapping beak and rolling eyes point travelers a mile west to Marietta's lovely old courthouse square. Something of an anomaly in a city of nearly 60,000, seat of 690,000-strong Cobb County, the square's centerpiece, **Glover Park,** is a peaceful Victorian throwback, with big trees, flowering plants, a gazebo, a bandstand, benches, and kids' play areas.

Low-rise late 19th- and early 20th-century buildings on three sides of the square house a slew of antiques shops and others with clothing, jewelry, gifts, stationery, toys, garden accessories, folk art, and a pet bakery. Restaurants cover the map, with Turkish, Slovakian, Italian, Mexican, Australian, Irish, and American cuisines. Pubs and music clubs feature live music. **Theatre in the Square,** www.theatreinthesquare.com, is one of Metro Atlanta's finest professional companies. Academy Award–winning actress Joanne Woodward credits this theater with introducing her to acting.

Before ducking into any of the above, stop in the Marietta Welcome Center, in the 1898 Western & Atlantic railroad depot (4 Depot St., Marietta, 800-835-0445 and 770-429-1115, www.mariettasquare.com), for maps and information on museums and walking and driving tours of the city's five National Register historic districts.

A few steps from the welcome center, the *Marietta* **Gone With the Wind** *Museum's* Scarlett On the Square exhibit tells you all about Atlanta author Margaret Mitchell's all-time best-selling novel and the 1939 film. Several hundred pieces collected by Dr. Christopher Sullivan of Akron, Ohio, include costumes, conceptual artwork, rare press and publicity books, film posters, editions of the novel in many languages, programs from the 1939 Atlanta movie premiere, contracts, promotional items, and much more. One of the most valuable artifacts is the bengaline silk gown that Vivien Leigh, as Scarlett O'Hara, wore on her New Orleans honeymoon with Rhett Butler/Clark Gable. Other exhibits highlight Mitchell's life and a tribute to Hattie McDaniel, the first African American to receive an Oscar, for her role as "Mammy."

The museum is at 18 Whitlock Ave., Marietta, a block from the Marietta Square, (770) 794-5576, www.gwtwmarietta.com. Open Mon through Sat 10 a.m. to 5 p.m. Adults $7; seniors 60 and over, and children 8 and older, $6; and $5 per person for groups of 15 or more.

The adjacent *Marietta Museum of History* is located in a historic landmark, 1 Depot St., Marietta, (770) 528-0431, www.mariettahistory.org, open Mon through Sat 10 a.m. to 4 p.m., Sat 1 to 4 p.m., adults $7, seniors ages 55 and up and students $5. In its original life as the Kennesaw Hotel, the building housed James Andrews and his Union raiders the night before they train-jacked the locomotive "General" from the depot in nearby Kennesaw, an event immortalized in the Disney film *The Great Locomotive Chase*.

Cinch up your hiking shoes, pump up your bike tires, and head for a blissful day on the *Silver Comet Trail.* The tree-shaded, 61-mile paved path takes you from suburban Smyrna into northwest Georgia's peaceful rural countryside. As you head for the Alabama border, you'll cross a towering 500-foot-long railroad trestle, over streams, around rock formations, through tunnels, pine forests, modest hills, and farmlands. Mavell Road in Smyrna, the trail access closest to Atlanta, is the busiest, but once you're free of the suburbs, it's just you and your fellow travelers, with no hassles from trucks and cars. The Silver Comet extends across the Alabama border, where it connects with the Chief Ladiga Trail, providing a 101-mile trail from Atlanta to Anniston, Alabama. It's part of a metro-wide greenways system being developed by the nonprofit PATH Foundation. In the city of Atlanta, PATH partnered with the Atlanta Development Authority to create a 22-mile BeltLine of trails and parks around the city utilizing a former railway corridor. The Beltline is being developed in stages, but the Eastern Corridor, already completed and located near the Carter Presidential Center, has proven to be very popular. For information on the BeltLine, go to www.beltline.org and for Silver Comet and other pathways, phone (404) 875-7284, www.pathfoundation.org.

Pickett's Mill Battlefield Historic Site, 5 miles northeast of Dallas, should be high on Civil War buffs' "must-do" list. The battlefield is much as it was when blue and gray troops fought here during the Battle of Atlanta campaign. Living-history programs demonstrate cooking, weapons firing, and military drills of the Civil War era. Artifacts and exhibits are in the interpretive center/visitor center. The battlefield is at Mt. Tabor Road, Dallas, (770) 443-7850, (800) 864-PARK, www.gastateparks.org. Admission is $5 for adults, $3 for students. Open Thurs through Sat.

Places to Stay in Metro Atlanta

DOWNTOWN ATLANTA

The Ellis Hotel
176 Peachtree St.
(404) 532-5155
www.ellishotel.com
Expensive
Now one of Atlanta's most popular boutique hotels, the Ellis was originally called the Winecoff and was the scene of a fatal 1947 fire. It's hard to believe such a modern building had such a past. The 127 guest rooms and suites have all the modern comforts and conveniences. Several bars and its innovative Terrace Restaurant cater to both hotel guests and downtown visitors. The 10th floor is reserved for women guests, with special decor and amenities. The Georgia Aquarium and other downtown attractions, shops, and dining are close by.

The Glenn Hotel
110 Marietta St.
(404) 521-2250
(866)-40GLENN
www.glennhotel.com
Expensive
Downtown Atlanta's first boutique hotel is a hip makeover of a 1920s office building. Close to the Georgia Aquarium, CNN Center, and other attractions, the Glenn has 93 guest rooms and 16 suites, with deluxe furnishings and accessories. A rooftop terrace overlooks the downtown skyline and Centennial Olympic Park.

MIDTOWN/VIRGINIA/ HIGHLAND/LITTLE FIVE POINTS AREA

The Saint Charles Inn
1001 Saint Charles Ave.
(404) 875-1001
www.thesaintcharlesinn
.com
Moderate to Expensive, including breakfast
Six rooms with private baths are in this delightful 1913 Craftsman-style bed-and-breakfast within walking distance of the Virginia-Highland action. Guests can relax in the Southern-style walled garden.

Hotel Indigo
683 Peachtree St.
(404) 874-9200
www.midtownatlanta.com
Moderate to Expensive
The flagship of Intercontinental Hotels' luxury boutique brand, the Indigo is

Bed-and-Breakfast Atlanta

If you'd like to stay at a homey bed-and-breakfast inn and meet some engaging Atlantans, contact Bed-and-Breakfast Atlanta: 790 North Ave., #202, Atlanta, (404) 875-0525, (800) 967-3224, www.bedandbreakfastatlanta.com.

Accommodations are in beautiful private homes, and rates usually include a full breakfast and the opportunity to meet Atlantans on an informal basis.

in the heart of Midtown's thriving dining, entertainment, and cultural area. The Fox Theatre, where touring Broadway shows, ballets, concerts, and other events are staged, is across the street. The Woodruff Art Center/High Museum of Art complex is 10 blocks north. The Georgia Aquarium, Georgia Dome, and other downtown attractions are about a mile south. Many popular restaurants and bars are within walking distance of the hotel, which has 140 guest rooms and suites with contemporary furnishings and amenities in a 12-story building. Pets are welcome. Parking is on the premises.

King-Keith House Bed & Breakfast
889 Edgewood Ave.
(404) 688-7330
(800) 728-3879
www.kingkeith.com
Moderate to Expensive, includes full breakfast
The spectacular Queen Anne–style "painted lady" mansion is on a tree-shaded street in Inman Park, a regentrified Victorian neighborhood 2 miles east of downtown. Jan and Windell Keith have 5 guest rooms with antiques and modern amenities. Close to shops, restaurants, live theater, entertainment, and the Inman Park MARTA rapid rail station.

Shellmont Inn
821 Piedmont Ave.
(404) 872-9290
www.shellmont.com
Moderate to Expensive, includes full breakfast
The Shellmont, built in 1891, is a beautiful old inn and Atlanta landmark located in the heart of Midtown. Debbie and Ed McCord have been the innkeepers since 1983 and have helped lead its impeccable restoration. The common space alone is worth the visit with its 2-story foyer complete with Tiffany stained glass. The Shellmont features 5 rooms as well as a carriage house cottage. Each room is decorated in antiques and has plush bathroom features.

GRANTVILLE
Bonnie Castle Bed & Breakfast
2 Post St.
(770) 683-3090
(800) 261-3090
www.bonnie-castle.com/grantville.htm
Inexpensive, includes full Southern breakfast and evening refreshments
This brick Romanesque-Revival Victorian is a startling contrast to Newnan's white columns. Built in 1896 by a wealthy Coweta County family, the turreted mansion, with a slate roof and wraparound porch, has been updated by owners James and Dee Latimone, who invite guests to relax in the romantic ambience of antique furnishings, regional art collections, hardwood floors, gilded ceilings, and stained glass. Off I-85, 15 minutes south of Newnan.

KENNESAW
Hill Manor Bed & Breakfast
2676 Summers St.
(770) 428-5997
www.hillmanor.com

Moderate, includes big Southern breakfast
Two large guest rooms in Paul and Kelly Ewing's 1890 Victorian home have antique furnishings, private bath with Jacuzzi tub, and access to gardens and verandas. Southern Museum of Civil War & Locomotive History, antiques shops, restaurants, and Kennesaw Mountain National Battlefield Park are close by.

MARIETTA

The Stanley House
236 Church St. Northeast
(770) 426-1881
Moderate, includes full breakfast
Just a few blocks off Marietta's historic square, the Stanley House Mansion is an historical treasure. With its Savannah-style courtyard and wraparound porch, the Victorian mansion is probably best known for its elegant ballroom. Lloyd and Cathy Kilday make you feel right at home. There are 5 rooms available in this moderately priced inn.

Whitlock Inn Bed & Breakfast
57 Whitlock Ave.
(770) 428-1495
www.whitlockinn.com
Moderate, includes continental breakfast
Innkeeper Alexis Amaden has 5 guest rooms with private baths in her Victorian mansion a block from the Marietta square. The

spacious public rooms are popular for weddings, corporate gatherings, and other special events.

ROSWELL

Ten-Fifty Canton Street Bed & Breakfast
1050 Canton St.
(770) 998-1050
www.bandbfinder.com
Moderate to Expensive
The Victorian cottage in downtown Roswell's historic district is close to the town square, Bulloch Hall, restaurants, and scores of antiques shops and collectibles malls. There are 3 cozy guest rooms with private baths and continental breakfast.

STONE MOUNTAIN

The Village Inn Bed & Breakfast
992 Ridge Ave.
(770) 469 3459
(800) 214-8385
www.villageinnbb.com
Moderate, includes full breakfast
This is one of the oldest surviving homes in Stone Mountain and has 6 guest rooms with private baths and antiques. Some have 2-person whirlpool baths and fireplaces. Just outside Stone Mountain Park, within walking distance of village shops and restaurants.

Places to Eat in Metro Atlanta

DOWNTOWN

Ted's Montana Grill
133 Luckie St.
(404) 521-9766
www.tedsmontantagrill.com
Moderate to Expensive
Ted, as in Turner, as in founder of CNN and former owner of the Atlanta Braves. Ted is also a rancher and came up with an idea of a restaurant selling beef and bison. Ted's has awesome steaks and burgers and comfort food sides. Be careful not to fill up on the garlic pickles on the table. (There are several Ted's locations around Atlanta.)

Luckie Food Lounge
375 Luckie St.
(404) 525 5825
www.luckiefoodlounge.com
Moderate
Luckie Food Lounge leads a double life. By day, it caters to families and other guests of the neighboring Georgia Aquarium and World of Coca-Cola. Creamy pimiento cheese "stacked" on lavash crackers, burgers, po' boys, and barbecue are kids' favorites, while adults latch onto fresh sushi, seafood, chicken, beef, pork, pasta, thin-crusted pizza, and vegetarian dishes.

The Charm convenience market, with a separate entrance on Luckie Street, serves Italian gelato, coffee, and the day's newspapers. At night, the lights go down low, accentuating the huge saltwater aquariums, teeming with colorful tropical fish. A DJ plays upbeat listening and dance music for the stylish grownup set, creating a hopping bar scene. Complimentary valet parking.

Max Lager's American Grill and Brewpub
320 Peachtree St.
(404) 525-4400
www.maxlagers.com
Inexpensive to Moderate
A variety of house-brewed beers, wood-fired cuisine, and great views of downtown.

Pleasant Peasant
555 Peachtree St.
(404) 874-3223
Moderate to Expensive
An Atlanta favorite for more than three decades. Pressed tin ceilings, black-and-white tile floor, an Atlanta mainstay for innovative beef, chicken, pastas, and great desserts. Dinner daily.

Trader Vic's
Atlanta Hilton Hotel
255 Courtland St.
(404) 659-2000
www.tradervics.com
Moderate to Expensive
Like a fantasy trip to the movie *South Pacific,* Trader Vic's carries out the Polynesian theme with faux palm trees, a tiki bar, and a menu of exotic South Seas dishes and libations. The Mai Tai was reputedly invented by Trader Vic in 1944. Good place to take the kids, and adventurous adults.

The Varsity
61 North Ave., near Georgia Tech
(404) 881-1706
www.thevarsity.com
Inexpensive
An Atlanta landmark, this is where the term "car hop" was invented. The self-proclaimed "World's Largest Drive-In," this mammoth emporium of chili dogs, hamburgers, french fries, onion rings, ice cream, and other short-order treats that might not be so good for the waistline, but are mighty satisfying all the same, is where thousands go every day to get their "grease fix." Enjoy it in your car or in one of the rooms, with TVs tuned to sports events and other popular shows.

ROSWELL

Greenwood's
1087 Green St.
(770) 992-5383
www.greenwoodsongreen
street.com
Inexpensive
Only truly prodigious appetites finish the huge servings of meat loaf, fish, chicken, duck, pork chops, fresh vegetables, and desserts in this former country home. Dinner Wed through Sun.

Mittie's Tea Room Cafe
25 Plum St., Roswell
(770) 594-8822
and 62 N. Main St.,
Alpharetta
(770) 772-0850
www.mitties.com
Inexpensive to Moderate
Mittie Bulloch would feel right at home in these cozy cafes, serving Southern-style breakfast, lunch, and tea. *Southern Living* magazine proclaims, "The chicken salad is wonderful."

Pastis
928 Canton Rd.
(770) 640-3870
Moderate to Expensive
A touch of France in the heart of historic Roswell. Elegant, historical setting, but with affordable prices and live music on the weekends.

The Swallow at the Hollow
1072 Green St.
(678) 352-1975
www.swallowatthehollow
.com
Inexpensive
Sauce-smeared patrons gorge on heaping plates of barbecue and ribs, Brunswick stew, and mac 'n' cheese with the joyful noise of loud, lively music. Lunch and dinner Wed through Sun.

HELPFUL WEBSITES

Georgia Tourist Division
www.georgia.org and
www.gastateparks.org
(Both sites have information on all the
state's regions.)

Atlanta Convention & Visitors Bureau
www.acvb.com

Atlanta Braves Baseball
www.atlantabraves.com

High Museum of Art
www.high.org

**DeKalb County Convention & Visitors
Bureau**
www.dcvb.org

Marietta Welcome Center
www.mariettasquare.com

**Historic Roswell Convention &
Visitors Bureau**
www.visitroswellga.com

Georgia State Parks
www.gastateparks.org

MIDTOWN/VIRGINIA/ HIGHLAND/LITTLE FIVE POINTS AREAS

American Roadhouse
892 N. Highland Ave.
(404) 872-2822
Inexpensive
Busy family-friendly neighborhood eatery. Terrific breakfasts, also great for lunch and dinner sandwiches, salads, fresh vegetables, chicken, fish, meat loaf, and pasta plates. Breakfast, lunch, and dinner daily.

Blind Willie's
828 N. Highland Ave.
(404) 873-2583
www.blindwilliesblues.com
Inexpensive
Some of the country's best-known blues rockers come close to blowing the roof off this popular storefront club, which packs in the crowds every night of the week.

Doc Chey's Noodle House
1424 N. Highland Ave.
(404) 888-0777
www.doccheys.com
Inexpensive
This Pan-Asian noodle house is a beehive-busy place to enjoy huge, cheap helpings of Vietnamese soup and other noodle- and rice-based dishes. Lunch, dinner daily.

Eats
600 Ponce de Leon Ave.
(404) 888-9149
www.eatsonponce.net
Inexpensive
Another perpetually packed "filling station." Students, families, and business types stand in usually long cafeteria lines for pasta, jerk chicken, and fresh veggies at rock-bottom prices. Lunch and dinner daily.

George's Restaurant
1041-A N. Highland Ave.
(404) 892-3648
Inexpensive
Longtime neighborhood tavern hasn't changed in more than 40 years. Some of the best hamburgers in town. Open daily.

Limerick Junction
824 N. Highland Ave.
(404) 874-7147
www.limerickjunction.com
Inexpensive
Rollicking Irish pub has Guinness and Harp on tap, musicians from Dublin and Belfast (and Limerick), and plenty of hearty pub-style eats. Dinner and entertainment nightly.

Manuel's Tavern

602 N. Highland Ave.
(404) 525-3447
www.manuelstavern.com
Inexpensive
Atlanta's all-time favorite neighborhood saloon. Generations of journalists, politicians, and just-plain folks have whiled away their days and nights at the worn wooden booths and long bar festooned with photos of JFK, Hubert Humphrey, and other Democratic icons. Put away chili dogs, burgers, BLTs, onion rings, and steak fries while you sip beer and spirits and watch sports on big-screen TVs. Like *Cheers,* after a couple of visits, they'll know your name and your poison. Open daily.

Mary Mac's Tea Room

224 Ponce de Leon Ave.
(404) 876-1800
Inexpensive
Two blocks east of Peachtree Street, this maze of a cheerful dining room has served celestial fried chicken, turnip greens, squash soufflé, biscuits, and cornbread to several generations of Atlantans and out-of-towners seeking the truth in Southern home cooking. Lunch and dinner Mon through Sat.

Surin of Thailand

810 N. Highland Ave.
(404) 892-7789
www.surinofthailand.com
Inexpensive to Moderate
Spicy Thai curry, noodle, rice, seafood, meat, and chicken dishes make this spacious restaurant one of Virginia-Highland's mainstays. Lunch and dinner daily.

Trattoria Il Localino

467 N. Highland Ave.
(404) 222-0650
www.localino.info
Moderate to Expensive
Chef Giovanni has made a name for himself with some of the freshest and most creative pasta dishes you'll find in Atlanta. Tucked in a century old store front, this elegant Italian restaurant has great ambience to match the food and will make you want to come back time and time again.

The Vortex Bar & Grill

438 Moreland Ave.
(404) 688-1828
and 878 Peachtree St.
(404) 875-1667
www.thevortexbarandgrill
.com
Inexpensive
Don't let the laughing-skull front door scare you away from some of the best burgers and zaniest surroundings in town. Top your whopper with blue cheese, pimiento cheese, bacon, or jerk sauce, and sit back and enjoy the experience and big-time attitude. Lunch and dinner daily.

DEKALB COUNTY'S LITTLE ASIA

Havana Restaurant

3979 Buford Hwy., #108
(404) 633-7549
www.havanarestaurant
atlanta.com
Inexpensive
Havana is known for its incredible Cuban sandwiches, which are huge, but do yourself a favor and try some of the meals. Their milkshakes have an unusual variety of flavors. Huge portions and great prices.

Machu Picchu

Northeast Plaza Shopping Center
3375 Buford Hwy.
(404) 320-3326
Inexpensive to Moderate
A delightful little Peruvian entry into Buford Highway's ethnic stewpot. Decorated with colorful woven tapestries, with weekend music by an Andean flute and guitar combo, the restaurant's specialties include several varieties of ceviche (slices of raw fish "cooked" in lime juice acid, with cilantro) and large plates of seafood, chicken, and pork mixed with rice and potatoes. Lunch and dinner daily.

Seoul Garden

5938 Buford Hwy.
(770) 452-0123
Inexpensive to Moderate
A large, friendly restaurant in a former chain steak house is one of the best of numerous Korean eateries. Kimchee, seafood

pancake, barbecued meats, and rice and noodle dishes are excellent. There's also a sushi bar. Lunch and dinner daily.

DECATUR

The Brick Store Pub
125 E. Court Sq.
(404) 687-0990
www.brickstorepub.com
Inexpensive
A cleverly revamped brick-walled former mercantile store that now dispenses a global variety of bottled and draft beers and ales, over a dozen single-malt scotches, and other spirits. The pub fare menu includes fish and chips, burgers, sandwiches, and salads. You can toss darts in the upstairs den and make believe you're in Brussels in the wood-paneled Belgian Bar, which features high-octane beers and ales. Families are welcome. Lunch and dinner daily.

Cafe Alsace
121 E. Ponce de Leon Ave.
(404) 373-5622
www.cafealsace.net
Moderate
A cozy, charming French Alsatian bistro with quiches, seafood, salads, sandwiches, soups, and chicken, beef, and duck dishes. Lunch Mon through Fri, dinner daily.

Taqueria del Sol
359 W. Ponce de Leon Ave.
(404) 377-7668
www.taqueriadelsol.com
Inexpensive
Soft tacos and enchiladas with spicy fillings, daily seafood and chef's blue plate specials, chowders, revved-up collard greens, and potent margaritas in a retuned service station 3 blocks east of the Decatur Square. Have a frosty 'rita while you wait in line to order. Lunch Mon through Sat, dinner Tues through Sat. It's a companion to locations at 1200 Howell Mill Rd., in northwest Atlanta, (404) 352-5811, and 2165 Cheshire Bridge Rd., northeast Atlanta, (404) 321-1118.

Wahoo! A Decatur Grill
1042 W. College Ave.
(404) 373-3331
www.wahoogrilldecatur.com
Inexpensive to Moderate
The quintessential neighborhood bistro, with comfortable ambience, feel-good food, and moderate prices. Located in a brick storefront near downtown Decatur, Wahoo's menu focuses on seafood with a Southern flair—shrimp and creamy grits, Georgia rainbow trout, and namesake wahoo, a meaty, warm-water ocean fish—as well as chicken, beef, pasta, and duck. The European-aura main dining

room features an open kitchen and a long bar. Many diners prefer the outdoor garden patio. Dinner Mon through Sat, Sunday brunch.

Watershed
1820 Peachtree Ave.
(404) 378-4900
www.watershedrestaurant.com
Moderate to Expensive
Emily Saliers, half of the folk-rock duo Indigo Girls, is the guiding light and part-time bartender at this handsomely retuned service station, which prepares sophisticated New Southern and American cuisine, deluxe sandwiches, and salads, and carries an extensive wine selection for patrons who come to downtown Decatur from all over Metro Atlanta. Lunch and dinner daily and Sunday brunch.

NEWNAN

The Redneck Gourmet
11 N. Court Sq.
(770) 251-0092
www.redneckgourmet.com
Inexpensive
Downtown Newnan's *Cheers* kind of place for breakfast, lunch, dinner, and small-town hospitality since 1991, Redneck Gourmet's menu features traditional Southern breakfast and a full array of sandwiches, salads, soups, and light meals. Local favorites include the Redneck Club, with ham, turkey,

American cheese, lettuce, tomato, bacon, and mayo on 3 slices of honey wheat bread; the Redneck Dawg, a beef hot dog with chili, cheese, onions, and slaw; and the Scrambled Dawg, the "Redneck" without the bun. Breakfast, lunch, and dinner, Mon through Sat.

10 East Washington
10 E. Washington St.
(770) 502-9100
www.teneastwashington
.com
Moderate to Expensive
Czech native George Ravosky and his wife, Carmela, oversee Newnan's most stylish restaurant. Their urbane dining room delights lunch and dinner guests with everything from hamburgers and Reubens to pastas, crab cakes, steaks, lamb tenderloin, seafood, and European-style desserts. Excellent wine list. Dinner Tues through Sat.

NORCROSS

Dominick's Little Italy
95 S. Peachtree St.
(770) 449-1611
www.dominicksitalian.com
Moderate
Proclaims, "Little Italy, Lotta Food," and they're not kidding. The handsomely redone 19th-century mercantile building, with brick walls, wooden floors, and original tin ceilings, serves platters of every kind of pasta, seafood, chicken, and veal dishes ample enough for two or three major appetites. It's fun to come with a large group and pass the platters Italian-family style. You can also get half-portions, which are still big enough to share. Open for lunch Mon through Sat, dinner daily.

Norcross Station Cafe
In the refashioned depot
40 S. Peachtree St.
(770) 409-9889
www.norcrossstation.com
Moderate
The eclectic menu includes shrimp, steak, baby-back ribs, pastas and other Italian dishes, quesadillas, quiches, sandwiches, soups, salads, and kids' plates. Open for lunch and dinner Mon through Sat.

SOUTHWEST GEORGIA →

Chattahoochee Trace

LaGrange, a pretty town of 30,000 near the Georgia–Alabama border, was named in honor of the Marquis de Lafayette's French estate, which accounts for the bronze likeness of the marquis in the center of downtown Lafayette Square. Away from the square, regal white-columned mansions preside over well-tended lawns, gardens, and tree-shaded streets.

Bellevue Mansion (204 Ben Hill St., LaGrange, 706-884-1832, www.lagrangechamber.com) was the stately Greek Revival home of US senator and acclaimed orator Benjamin Harvey Hill. Built in the early 1850s, the home is an architectural treasure inside and out, filled with magnificent furnishings and artwork. It's the LaGrange area's favorite wedding venue. Open Tues through Sat from 10 a.m. to noon and 2 to 5 p.m. Admission is $5 adults, $3 children.

Lamar Dodd Art Center (706-880-8211, www.lagrange.edu), on the neighboring LaGrange College campus, 302 Forrest Ave., LaGrange, is a strikingly modern museum displaying changing regional and national exhibitions and a permanent collection of Native American art. Named for late LaGrange

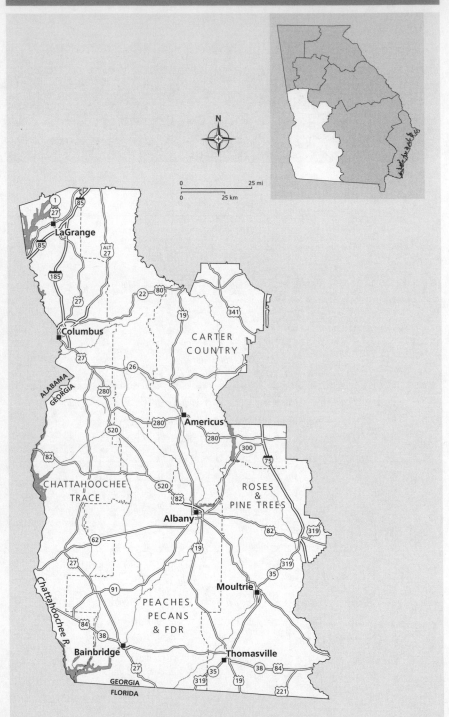

artist Lamar Dodd, whose work is featured, the museum is open Mon through Fri from 8:30 a.m. to 4 p.m. Free admission.

The **LaGrange Art Museum,** formerly the Chattahoochee Valley Art Museum (112 LaFayette Pkwy., LaGrange, 706-882-3267, www.lagrangeart museum.org), near Lafayette Square, displays paintings, sculpture, and decorative arts in a restored 1890s jail building. It's open Tues through Fri from 9 a.m. to 5 p.m., Sat 11 a.m. to 5 p.m. Free admission.

In 1841, Sarah Ferrell created a formal boxwood garden in west Georgia wilderness that only a few years earlier had been part of Creek and Cherokee lands. Nearly 170 years later, Sarah Ferrell's garden is the centerpiece of Hills & Dales Estate. The home of two generations of the Callaway family, the estate, opened to the public in 2004, is one of west Georgia's most beautiful attractions.

Sarah Ferrell's garden was actually begun in 1832 by her mother. When she inherited it nine years later, Sarah expanded it into one of the Southeast's most acclaimed gardens. Deeply religious, she planted an area called "The Sanctuary," with religious symbols sculpted in boxwoods. A harp, a circular boxwood bed planted with yellow flowers, symbolized an offering plate full of coins. A nearby boxwood topiary is shaped like a church organ.

The "God" topiary, planted at the formal entrance to the garden, was a reference to the Genesis passage, "In the beginning, God created the heavens and earth." On the upper terrace near the house, she planted "God Is Love," and for her husband, a judge and Mason, she created the Masonic emblem and *Fiat justitia* ("Let Justice Be Done").

Sarah continued working her garden until her death in 1903. In 1908, the property was purchased by Fuller E. Callaway and his wife, Ida Cason Callaway, who renamed the estate Hills & Dales.

A wealthy west Georgia textile manufacturer, Callaway commissioned renowned Atlanta architect Neel Reid to design an opulent Georgian-Italianate villa. Completed in 1916, the 30-room house was furnished with American and European antiques and family keepsakes.

The Callaways restored Sarah Ferrell's gardens and installed classical statuary, sunken gardens, terraces, and fountains to complement the Italian character of their house. They added greenhouses and herb gardens, and thousands of trees, flowers, and shrubs.

When Fuller Callaway died in 1928, followed by Ida in 1936, the estate was inherited by Fuller Callaway Jr. and his wife, Alice Hand Callaway. They enhanced the beauty of the house and gardens until their deaths in 1992 and 1998, respectively, after which the estate was granted to the Fuller E. Callaway Foundation and opened to the public. Cason Callaway, who created nearby Callaway Gardens, was Fuller Jr.'s older brother.

SOUTHWEST GEORGIA'S TOP HITS

Bellevue Mansion

Hills & Dales Estate

LaGrange Art Museum

West Point Lake

Day Butterfly Center

Callaway Gardens

Chattahoochee Riverwalk

National Infantry Museum

Port Columbus National Civil War Naval Museum

Providence Canyon State Park

Florence Marina State Park

Westville

George T. Bagby State Park

Kolomoki Mounds State Historic Park

Lake Seminole

Little White House

Franklin D. Roosevelt State Park

Pasaquan Folk Art Compound

Parks at Chehaw

"Swamp Gravy"

Climax Swine Time

Rattlesnake Roundup

American Camellia Society

Albany's Flint RiverQuarium

Andersonville National Cemetery and Historic Site

Windsor Hotel

Jimmy Carter National Historic Site

Georgia Rural Telephone Museum

Georgia Veterans Memorial State Park

Georgia Agrirama

Downtown Tifton

Lapham-Patterson House

Pebble Hill Plantation

Thomasville Rose Garden

Tours of the estate begin at the Hills & Dales Visitor Center. Designed in classical style and inspired by Neel Reid's Italianate villa, the center includes an exhibit gallery, an orientation film, and a gift shop.

A motorized tram takes visitors to the villa on a hill overlooking the gardens. Guests enter the home under 4 Doric columns, which support a covered 2-story porte cochere and red tile roof.

Guided tours begin in the library, the Callaways' favorite room. Reminiscent of an English drawing room, the room is paneled in Circassian walnut, with American and English furnishings and family portraits. Although additions to the library and adjoining living room and dining room were made over the years, the house has retained the comfortable ambience of a fine country estate, in accordance with Fuller Callaway Sr.'s wishes for "a home in the real sense, to express, inside and outside, grace, naturalness and cheery friendliness."

Hills & Dales Estate is on the edge of the LaGrange College campus, a few blocks west of Lafayette Square, in downtown LaGrange. Open Mar to June Tues to Sat from 10 a.m. to 6 p.m., Sun 1 to 5 p.m.; July to Feb Tues to Sat from 10 a.m. to 5 p.m. For House and Garden, adults and seniors $15; age 7 to college students with ID $7. Garden only tickets $8. For information: Hills & Dales Estate, 1916 Hill and Dales Dr., LaGrange, (706) 882-3242, www.hills anddalesestate.org.

West Point Lake, a mammoth 26,000-acre inland sea a few minutes from downtown LaGrange, offers plenty of opportunities for fishing, boating, swimming, waterskiing, and sunbathing. Contact the West Point Lake Resource Manager, 500 Resource Management Dr., West Point, (706) 645-2937. The lake's commercial outlets include Highland Marina Resort (1000 Seminole Rd., LaGrange, 706-882-3437) where you can rent fishing boats and go after the lake's channel catfish and white and largemouth bass. Also at the marina, you can rent a houseboat or stay in a campground or furnished cottage. The lake is a US Army Corps of Engineers impoundment of the Chattahoochee River, which forms most of the Georgia–Alabama border.

In the mood for a hot dog? **Charlie Joseph's** has been serving them up, and Troup Countians have been gobbling them up, since 1920 when Charlie's opened as a fruit stand in downtown LaGrange. It's been at 128 Bull St. (706-884-5416, www.charliejosephs.com) since 1946. You can have your dog with just plain mustard and onions, or dressed up with slaw, chili, cheese, relish, and other fixin's. Or try the hamburgers and breakfast-time egg-and-cheese sandwiches. Charlie's second location, 2238 West Point Rd., (706) 884-0379, serves breakfast, lunch, and early dinner. Both are open Mon through Sat.

Butterflies—over 1,000 of them, of more than 50 species, in all sizes and colors, from exotic places around the world—are free and on the wing at the **Day Butterfly Center at Callaway Gardens** in Pine Mountain. Opened to visitors in September 1988, America's first such natural attraction was inspired by similar preserves in Europe and Asia, with some distinctive Georgia touches. Named in honor of Cecil Day, late founder of the Days Inns of America motel corporation, it's a year-round, indoor-outdoor experience.

As you walk into an 8,000-square-foot, glass-enclosed "rain forest," you're suddenly caught in clouds of feathery giant swallowtails *(Papilio cresphontes)*, Paris peacock swallowtails *(P. paris)*, green-banded swallowtails *(P. palinurus)*, owl butterflies *(Caligo sp.)*, passion flower butterflies *(Helinconius sp.)*, and a rainbow of other iridescent beauties from Asia, the Andes, and the South Pacific. Butterflies and tropical birds perch side by side on exotic plants. A waterfall gently spatters. Bleeding-heart doves hide in the thick tropical foliage. Indoors, you'll find educational displays and a theater with a film all about the remarkable lives of butterflies.

Outside, the native butterfly garden is cunningly designed to lure home-grown butterflies to **Callaway Gardens** (Pine Mountain, 800-225-5292, www .callawaygardens.com). If you'd like to have your own butterfly center, Callaway's horticulturists will show you how to plant a "tender trap" in your backyard.

While you're at Callaway Gardens, you can also take a driving tour of the 2,500 acres of gardens planted with 700 varieties of azaleas and more than 450 types of holly, mums, mountain laurel, rhododendron, dogwood, and wildflowers. These may be viewed in their natural habitat along 13 miles of roads and walking trails, and inside the *John A. Sibley Horticultural Center,* a stunning indoor-outdoor conservatory with pools, cascades, and scores of floral displays that change with the season.

Callaway's 14,300 rolling, wooded acres also embrace 13 lakes for swimming, fishing, boating, and waterskiing. Golfers may play 63 picturesque holes and sample from a recreational smorgasbord that includes tennis, skeet shooting, biking, and a summertime big-top circus. A half-dozen restaurants range from candlelight to casual.

Another unforgettable attraction is *The Virginia Hand Callaway Discovery Center.* Overlooking Mountain Creek Lake, at the end of a scenic 2.5-mile drive through woodlands and meadows, guests reach the Discovery Center from the gardens' new main entrance at GA 18 and GA 354. (The former main entrance on US 27 is closed.) Named for founder Cason Callaway's late wife, the 35,000-square-foot, $14 million center includes an information desk, a 100-seat orientation theater, interpretive exhibits, a gift shop, a lakeside restaurant, and interactive kiosks about the gardens' flora and fauna. A 3,000-square-foot museum displays late Italian artist Athos Menaboni's collection of bird paintings. From the Discovery Center, visitors can explore the gardens' many other attractions by foot, bike, tram, or water taxi.

The 40-acre *Callaway Brothers Azalea Bowl,* purportedly the world's largest azalea garden, contains more than 3,400 of the colorful shrubs in numerous domestic and exotic varieties. Set among streams, arched bridges, and wide, curving trails, the azaleas burst into banks of radiant, multicolored blooms in March and April. All-inclusive admission to most attractions is $18 for adults, $15 for seniors, $9 for children 6 to 12, 6 and under free.

Lodgings range from rooms at the Mountain Creek Inn to deluxe villas and cottages. The Marriott-operated *The Lodge's* 150 deluxe guest rooms have a wide range of decorative styles, contemporary comforts and conveniences, and balcony views of surrounding forests. The Lodge is associated with *Spa Pruni-folia,* named for an azalea native to this area, which offers the full range of massages, wraps, facials, and other treatments. Callaway Gardens lies 12 scenic miles from Warm Springs and Franklin D. Roosevelt's *Little White House.*

At *Pine Mountain Wild Animal Safari* (1300 Oak Grove Rd., Pine Moun-tain, 2 miles north of the town of Pine Mountain, 706-663-8744, 800-367-2751, www.animalsafari.com), you can drive your own car or take the Safari Bus through a 500-acre preserve populated by zebras, giraffes, camels, axis deer, gnus, antelopes, water buffalo, and other wild, nonpredatory creatures. Also visit the petting zoo, monkey house, and serpentarium. Open daily from 10 a.m. to 5:30 p.m. Admission is $19.95 for adults; $16.95 for age 60 and over and ages 3 to 12. Free for age 3 and under. If you'd rather not drive your vehicle through the park, you can rent a "Zebra Van," which holds 15 passengers, for $15. The 7-passenger "Zebra Mini-Van" is $11.

Blanton Creek Park, I-185 exit 11, is a nicely kept Georgia Power Com-pany recreation area on 5,800-acre Lake Harding. The park features 51 RV and tent camping sites ($10 a night), which have electrical and water hookups. The park also has boat ramps, picnic pavilions, and playgrounds. Call (706) 643-7737.

If shopping's your favorite sport, indulge to your heart's content on *Pine Mountain's Main Street* (US 27). More than a dozen shops on both sides of the street have antiques and fine art, collectibles, handcrafted pottery, paint-ings, designer jewelry, books, toys, glass, and furniture. Nearly a century old, *Kimbrough Brothers General Store* (706-663-2528) knew the area when Callaway Gardens was still a gleam in Cason Callaway's eye. Before you begin, stop by the Pine Mountain Tourism and Welcome Center (800-441-3502, www .pinemountain.org) in the center of town.

A number of moderately priced motels, bed-and-breakfasts, cottages, and chalets are around Pine Mountain, Hamilton, and Warm Springs. Contact the Pine Mountain Tourism Association at 101 E. Broad St., Pine Mountain, (706) 663-4000, (800) 441-3502, www.pinemountain.org.

Columbus is Georgia's third largest city. To get your bearings in the city of 300,000, stop by the *Columbus Convention and Visitors Bureau* (706-322-1613 and 800-999-1613, www.visitcolumbusga.org) at 900 Front Ave., Colum-bus, facing the Chattahoochee Riverwalk.

The *Chattahoochee Riverwalk,* a wide brick pathway with trees, benches, and attractive lighting, meanders 14 miles along the Chattahoochee and in the downtown historic district. It's adorned with lots of ornamental brick and ironwork, flowers and landscaping, and steps that lead right to the river's edge.

TOP ANNUAL EVENTS

Rattlesnake Roundup
last weekend of January, Whigham
(229) 377-3663

Thomasville Antiques Show and Sale
late February, Exchange Club
Fairgrounds
(912) 225-3919
www.thomasvilleantiquesshow.com

Thomasville Rose Festival
late April
(800) 704-2350
www.thomasvillega.com

Callaway Gardens Spring Celebration
mid-April
(800) 282-8181
www.callawaygardens.com

Riverfest Weekend
late April, Columbus Riverwalk
(706) 322-0756
www.historiccolumbus.com

National Mayhaw Festival
third weekend of April, Colquitt

National Grits Festival
mid-April, Warwick
(229) 395-4737
www.gritsfest.com

Cotton Pickin' Country Fair
early May, Gay
(706) 538-6814
www.cpfair.com

Andersonville Antiques, Crafts and Civil War Artifacts Fair
late May
(912) 924-2558

Watermelon Festival
Late July, Cordele
(912) 273-1668

Christmas in Thomasville
mid-December
(912) 226-2344
www.thomasvillega.com

Swine Time
weekend after Thanksgiving, Climax
www.swinetimefestival.com

Mule Day
first Saturday of November, Calvary
(229) 872-3612
www.calvarylionsmuleday.com

Christmas Festival of Lights
Callaway Gardens
(800) 282-8181
www.callawaygardens.com

Close to the Riverwalk, *Heritage Corner Tours,* sponsored by the Historic Columbus Foundation, takes you through 4 homes at the corner of Broadway and 7th Street. They include an early-1800s pioneer log cabin; an 1828 Federal-style cottage; the Victorian cottage of Dr. John Stith Pemberton, a Columbus pharmacist who left here for Atlanta, where he invented Coca-Cola in 1886; a mid-19th-century farmhouse that now houses the Period Pieces Gift Shop; and the Victorian townhouse at 700 Broadway that serves as the Historic Foundation's headquarters. Tours are by appointment only and begin at the headquarters for an all-inclusive $5. Phone (706) 323-7979 or visit www.historiccolumbus.com.

If it's open—or holding one of its many regular stage productions—don't miss a chance to see the restored *Springer Opera House* (706-327-3688,

888-332-5200, www.springeroperahouse.org), built in 1871, which has hosted such illuminati as Oscar Wilde, Will Rogers, and Edwin Booth.

You can also take a walking/driving tour of numerous historic homes, churches, and public buildings with an illustrated brochure called *"Original City Tours,"* available at the Historic Columbus Foundation.

The *Coca-Cola Space Science Center* (701 Front Ave., Columbus, 706-649-1470; www.ccssc.org) is one of Riverwalk's most exciting attractions. Developed in conjunction with Columbus State University, its components include the Mead Observatory, which captures high-detail images of far-flung celestial bodies (you can take a space flight and land on the moon); the Challenger Learning Center, an interactive, hands-on experience that helps sharpen science, math, team-building, and communications skills for schoolchildren and other groups; and the Omnisphere Theater, which projects laser shows, science and science fiction movies, concerts, and theatrical performances onto a giant domed ceiling. An accurate replica of the Apollo space capsule is one of the many permanent exhibits. Special events include "Night Out Under the Stars," an overnight campout at the Space Center that includes a Challenger Center Mission, the Omnisphere Theater, construction and launch of a model rocket, a laser concert, and a science fiction movie. Open Mon through Thurs from 10 a.m. to 4 p.m., Sat from 10:30 a.m. to 8 p.m. Closed Sun. Adults $6; military and seniors $5; ages 4 to 12 $4.

The *Columbus Black Heritage Tour* is a self-guided tour of more than two dozen sites that played vital parts in the city's rich African-American culture. The tour begins with the last home of legendary blues singer Gertrude "Ma" Rainey (1886–1939) and includes churches, schools, theaters, businesses, and landmarks that showcase achievements of the city's black community. Pick up the free brochure at the Convention and Visitors Bureau.

Oxbow Meadows Environmental Learning Center (South Lumpkin Road, north of the Fort Benning Military Reservation, Columbus, 706-687-4090, www.oxbow.columbusstate.edu) is a fun and fascinating place to get out in the countryside and learn something about the world around you. Start your visit to the 1,600-acre site in the Chattahoochee River floodplain in a 2,000-square-foot building where you can observe live, mounted, and re-created plant and animal life. Two nature trails will let you stretch your legs in the wetlands and woodlands and come face to face with the creatures that live there. Open Tues through Fri from 9 a.m. to 4 p.m., Sat 10 a.m. to 3 p.m., and Sun from noon to 5 p.m. Free admission.

Even if you're staunchly antiwar, don't miss the *National Infantry Museum* (101 4th Ave., Columbus, 706-685-5800, www.nationalinfantry museum.org) on the mammoth Fort Benning Army compound, 1775 Legacy

Trade Ya My Apple for That Baloney Sandwich

If you're old enough to remember when you took your sandwiches and cookies to school in a metal lunch box, take a trip down memory lane at Allen Woodall's collection of thousands of metal, plastic, and vinyl boxes with images from the *A-Team* to *Zorro,* and scenes from popular radio and TV shows like *Hopalong Cassidy, Howdy Doody, The Green Hornet, Lost in Space, Little Lulu,* and *The Jetsons.* Originating in the 1890s, metal boxes were replaced with plastic and vinyl in the 1980s, when parents argued that the metal type were potential weapons. Woodall's 2,000 lunch boxes, and collections of furniture, glassware, military items, and other collectibles, are displayed at River Market Antiques and Art Center, 3226 Hamilton Rd., Columbus. Phone (706) 653-6240.

Way, Fort Benning. The museum's 3 floors and 12 spacious galleries exhibit more than 6,000 items from the French and Indian War and the American Revolution, through the world wars, to Vietnam and the Persian Gulf conflict and Iraq. You'll see a porthole from the battleship *Maine,* 16th-century English armor, the wing of a World War II Japanese Zero, ancient Korean and Chinese weapons and armor, gas masks worn by World War I horses, and wartime documents signed by 20 US presidents. A 5-story-high IMAX theater will put you right into the action. Open Tues through Sat from 9 a.m. to 5 p.m. (except for major national holidays), Sun from 11 a.m. to 5 p.m. Free admission except IMAX. IMAX is $9 for adults; military, seniors, and students $9; and children ages 4 to 13 $8.

The ***Port Columbus National Civil War Naval Museum*** (1002 Victory Dr., Columbus, 706-327-9798, www.portcolumbus.org), covers the war on the high seas, from blockade runners to conventional wooden gunboats, the new age of ironclads, and Union and Confederate amphibious operations. Visitors to the 40,000-square-foot museum witness simulated battles from inside an ironclad and view naval artillery pieces, weapons, uniforms, personal effects, flags, interpretive exhibits, and artwork. The Confederate iron ram CSS *Jackson* is the museum's star attraction. Built at the Columbus Shipyards, less than a mile from the museum, the *Jackson* was within a few of weeks of completion when Union raiders crossed the Chattahoochee River from Alabama in December 1864, and burned it to the waterline. The hull drifted 30 miles downriver and sank to the bottom, where it was salvaged in the 1960s. Visitors view the *Jackson's* 225-foot hull from a platform above the bow and at floor level. A steel "ghost" superstructure over the hull helps viewers appreciate the ship's enormous size. Fully operational, it would have been sheathed in two layers of iron plate, been armed with six big cannons weighing about 700,000 pounds, and would have sat only 7 feet deep in the water. Other exhibits include a partial replica of the USS *Hartford,* the flagship that Union Admiral David Farragut rode into Mobile Bay, shouting, "Damn the torpedoes, full speed ahead!" Inside the *Hartford,* mannequins of enlisted sailors lie in hammocks and pass the time playing harmonicas and banjos, writing letters, and embroidering. In the officer's ward room, the ship's only table did double duty. When the medical officer wasn't suturing and sawing, it was wiped down and set for dinner. An 87-foot reconstruction of the ironclad CSS *Albermarle* gives visitors an "inside" audiovisual look at a Union surprise attack. A little-known fact: During the Civil War, a young man named Isidor Strauss was the overseas agent for a Columbus group, which financed construction of Confederate blockade runners in England. After the war, Strauss went to New York, where he built Macy's Department Stores; he died on the *Titanic* in 1912. Open Tues through Sat 10 a.m. to 4:30 p.m. and Sun and Mon 12:30 to 4:30 p.m. Admission is $7.50 for adults; $6.50 for military and seniors age 65 and older; $6 for students; age 6 and under free.

The *RiverCenter for the Performing Arts* (900 Broadway, Columbus, 706-256-3612, www.rivercenter.org) is a spectacular downtown Columbus cultural complex, with 5 interconnected buildings joined by a dramatic 4-story atrium lobby and glass curtain exterior wall. The 245,000-square-foot center's components include the 150-seat Studio Theater; 430-seat Legacy Hall, with a 4,000-pipe organ; and 2,000-seat Bill Heard Theater. Performances range from classical and country music to touring Broadway musicals, ballet, and contemporary dance. It also houses Columbus State University's Schwob School of Music.

The *Columbus Museum* is a peaceful place to spend a few hours browsing. Permanent exhibits include a hands-on discovery gallery for youngsters and adults, a fine arts decorative gallery, a regional history gallery, and changing exhibits of regional art. Located at 1251 Wynnton Rd., Columbus (706-748-2562, www.columbusmuseum.com), the museum is open daily except Mon. Admission is free, but donations are invited.

Providence Canyon State Park, near the small town of Lumpkin, south of Columbus, preserves the scenic beauty of an area often referred to as "Georgia's Little Grand Canyon." More than a dozen canyons in the 1,108-acre park have been chiseled out over the past 150 years by the slow, relentless process of soil erosion due to poor farming practices during the 1800s. As deep as 150 feet, the canyons offer a geological primer and a stunning visual display of stratified soil layers. Many fascinating formations stand alone in the midst of the canyons.

AUTHOR'S FAVORITES

Lamar Dodd Art Center and LaGrange Art Museum	FDR's Little White House Parks at Chehaw
Hills and Dales Museum	National Prisoner of War Museum, Andersonville National Cemetery and Historic Site
Flint RiverQuarium	
Day Butterfly Center, Callaway Gardens, Pine Mountain	Jimmy Carter National Historic Site
Chattahoochee Riverwalk	Windsor Hotel
River Market Antiques' Lunch Box Museum	Pebble Hill Plantation
	Climax Swine Time
Providence Canyon State Park and Westville Village of the 1850s	Rattlesnake Roundup

During spring and fall, those making the easy hike to the canyon floor are rewarded by multicolored wildflowers, which complement the pinks, purples, and whites of the Providence soils. From July to Sept, the rare plumleaf azalea blooms in shades from light orange to salmon and various tones of red and scarlet.

Stop first at the park's interpretive center (229-838-6202, 800-864-PARK, www.gastateparks.org) for an overview. A day-use park, Providence has picnic tables, shelters, and restrooms. It's on GA 39C, Lumpkin, 7 miles west of Lumpkin, and is open daily from 7 a.m. to dark. There is a $5 per visit parking fee. Backcountry and pioneer campsites are available in the park by reservation at a cost of $9 a night. You can also stay overnight and fish and boat in the Chattahoochee River at *Florence Marina State Park,* Route 1, Omaha (229-838-6870, 800-864-PARK, www.gastateparks.org). Campgrounds have electricity, water, restrooms, and showers. Furnished efficiency apartments, sleeping up to 5, with kitchenettes are available. Six 2-bedroom cabins are completely furnished and have fully equipped kitchens. Call (800) 864-PARK or visit www.gastateparks.org for rates and reservations. The park also has a swimming pool, tennis courts, a playground, and a small grocery store. It is on GA 39C, 10 miles west of Providence Canyon. There is a $5 per visit parking fee.

If *Westville* were near an interstate highway, more than a million visitors a year would enjoy it. As it is, far from major thoroughfares at the tiny Stewart County seat of Lumpkin, Georgia's "Village of the 1850s" is appreciated by only a fortunate 50,000 or so annually. Forty miles southeast of Columbus, 25 miles west of Jimmy Carter's Plains, this Williamsburg-style living history re-creation includes more than two dozen authentic 19th-century homes, public buildings, and craftspeople's shops lining the hard-packed clay streets.

As you walk about the town, you'll be treated to a symphony of workaday sounds: the blacksmith hammering nails, horseshoes, farm implements, and household utensils; the cobbler tapping together a pair of fine riding boots; the schoolmarm calling her charges to class. Elsewhere, townsfolk make their own soap, furniture, and candles; hand-stitch quilts; and cook corn breads, stews, and gingerbread over an open hearth. A mule plods in stoic circles, turning an enormous round stone that grinds sugarcane into thick, amber syrup.

Lifestyles range from the rich and famous at the Greek Revival McDonald House to the cottages of the working folk. Every season has its special events: the Spring Festival in early April; May Pole Dances, May 1; Early American Festival, July 4; the Fair of the 1850s, late October–early November; and, at Christmas, strolling carolers and Yule log lighting.

Westville (9294 Singer Pond Rd., Lumpkin, 229-838-6310, 888-733-1850, www.westville.org) is open Tues through Sat from 10 a.m. to 5 p.m., Sun from 1 to 5 p.m. Admission is $10 for adults; $8 for senior citizens 65 and over, college students, and military personnel; and $4 for other students.

With its redbrick courthouse, granite Confederate soldier, and 1-story buildings flanking the quiet square, *Lumpkin* could be moved, intact, into a museum as an exhibit of 19th-century Americana. The *Bedingfield Inn on the Square* (229-838-6419) was built in 1836 as a doctor's residence and stagecoach inn. This museum is open Tues through Sat from 10 a.m. to 5 p.m.

George T. Bagby State Park, fronting the Chattahoochee River's 48,000-acre Lake Walter F. George (also known as Lake Eufaula), is a resort-style getaway. The 60-room Walter F. George Lodge and Conference Center has all the modern comforts and a full-service restaurant. Call (800) 864-PARK for lodge and cottage rates and reservations. Around it you'll find boat ramps and marinas, swimming pools, tennis courts, an 18-hole championship golf course, and hiking and picnic areas. You can also stay in furnished cottages. There's a $5 per visit parking fee. Contact 330 Bagby Pkwy., Fort Gaines, (229) 768-2571. Phone (800) 864-7275 or visit www.georgetbagby.com for lodge, cottage, and campsite reservations. For tee times at the golf course, call (800) 434-0982.

At *Frontier Village* in neighboring Fort Gaines, a one-third-scale replica of the original fort, built in 1814, has Civil War cannons and authentic log cabins that reflect the area's frontier heritage. Phone (229) 768-2248 or visit www.fortgaines.com.

Kolomoki Mounds State Historic Park (Route 1, Blakely, 229-724-2150, 800-864-PARK, www.gastateparks.org) is an important archaeological site, as well as a recreation area. Within the 1,294-acre park you can climb some of the 7 burial mounds and temple mounds built by Creek Indians in the 12th and 13th centuries. Dating back to between 350 and 750 AD, the largest mound is 57 feet high. The small museum has artifacts unearthed from the mounds and the excavated burial mound of a tribal chief. Also in the park, you're invited to swim in 2 pools, fish and boat in a pair of lakes, have a picnic, and play miniature golf. The park's 35 camping sites have group shelters, water and electricity, hot showers, and restrooms.

Driving around the **Early County Courthouse** in Blakely, look for the stone monument to the peanut.

If ever a body of water were created with anglers in mind, it's got to be **Lake Seminole.** Formed by an impoundment of the Chattahoochee and Flint Rivers, the 37,500-acre lake, with a 250-mile shoreline, is especially bountiful grounds for bass fishing. Largemouth routinely weigh in at upward of 15 pounds. Anglers also snare a wealth of bodacious black bass, white bass, hybrid bass, and stripers, as well as bream, chain pickerel, catfish, yellow perch, and many other varieties.

Yet the marshy, reedy lake—afloat with thousands of acres of grass beds and lily pads and spiked with the ghostly trunks of cypress and live oak trees— is so far off the beaten path, down where Georgia's southwestern corner bumps against Alabama and Florida, that when more than 50 boats appear on a single day, old-timers grumble that "Ol' Sem" is turning into a waterbound I-75.

The lake's largest public recreational area is **Seminole State Park,** off GA 39, 16 miles south of Donalsonville (229-861-3137, www.gastateparks.org). Activities include fishing, boating, swimming, waterskiing, picnicking, and camping; furnished cottages are available. Call (800) 864-PARK for camping and cottage rates and reservations. There is a $5 per visit parking fee.

Peaches, Pecans & FDR

President Franklin Delano Roosevelt left his everlasting imprint on the hills and piney woodlands of Meriwether County. The future president first came to this isolated rural county, 85 miles southwest of Atlanta, in 1924 to immerse his polio-afflicted limbs in the mineral waters of Warm Springs. His **Little White House,** secluded in a wooded grove, became his sanctuary from the monumental pressures of World War II. Now maintained by the Georgia Department of Natural Resources, the comfortable little house remains as he left it when he died there on April 12, 1945.

In the kitchen, simple dishes, pots and pans, a hand-cranked ice-cream maker, and other utensils are neatly stacked. In the woodwork, FDR's cook penciled this touching message: "Daisy Bonner cooked the first meal and the last one in this cottage for President Roosevelt."

Dedicated in 2004, the **FDR Memorial Museum** emphasizes Roosevelt's life at Warm Springs and his impact on Georgia, the South, and the rest of Depression-ravaged rural America. Connected to the entrance plaza and visitor center, the 12,000-square-foot museum's hundreds of exhibits include his 1938 Ford convertible equipped with hand controls; his wheelchair, leg braces, and canes; photos of his life at Warm Springs; a 1930s kitchen with his "Fireside Chats" playing on a radio; and displays featuring the Rural Electrification Administration, the Tennessee Valley Authority, and other New Deal programs, which brought modern conveniences into millions of homes for the first time.

A film narrated by Walter Cronkite includes historic footage of FDR swimming in the Warm Springs pools, visiting with neighbors, having picnics, playing with his Scottie dog, Fala; and his funeral procession, when he left his Little White House for the last time. While posing in the living room for a portrait by Madame Elizabeth Shoumatoff on April 12, 1945, he suffered a stroke and died. The famous *Unfinished Portrait* is in the museum, with a *Finished Portrait* Madame Shoumatoff painted after World War II. FDR's Little White House State Historic Site (US 27-A, Warm Springs, 706-655-5870, www .fdr-littlewhitehouse.org) is open daily. Adults $10, seniors and ages 6 to 18 $6, 5 and under free. Special observances on April 12 commemorate FDR's extraordinary presidency.

The adjacent village of **Warm Springs** (population 480) has been revived with visitors in mind. More than 60 stores along the main street are stocked with antiques, collectibles, and Georgia-made arts and crafts.

The **Warm Springs Welcome Center** (800-FDR-1927, 706-655-3322, www .warmspringsga.com), on the village's main street, is open every day for information and brochures.

The **Hotel Warm Springs Bed & Breakfast Inn** (47 Broad St., Warm Springs, 800-366-7616, www.hotelwarmspringsbb.org) once housed the press, Secret Service, and visitors to FDR's Little White House. Now the 3-story 1907 hotel receives bed-and-breakfast guests who come here to see the FDR shrines and shop at Warm Springs' dozens of handicraft stores. Fourteen guest rooms with 2 full beds are furnished with original oak Val-Kill Furniture. The Presidential Suite has 2 separate rooms with a connecting bath. The lobby has original ceramic tile floors, a vintage Stromberg-Carlson cord switchboard, stenciled walls, and 16-foot ceilings. The hotel has a restaurant and an old-fashioned soda shop with ice cream (homemade Georgia peach is innkeeper Lee Thompson's special treat). A bountiful Southern "Breakfast Feast" is included in the inexpensive to moderate rates.

Franklin D. Roosevelt State Park, about 5 miles west of Warm Springs, on GA 190, is ideal for a mini-vacation. On the wooded crest of Pine Mountain, the 9,480-acre park has a lake for swimming, fishing, and boating; hiking trails; horseback riding; and picturesque picnic spots. Many of the fieldstone buildings in the park were the product of the Depression-era Civilian Conservation Corps. Campsites ($10 a night) have water, electricity, hot showers, and restrooms. Cottages have fireplaces and fully equipped kitchens for standard state fees. Call (800) 864-PARK or log on to www.gastateparks.org for rates and reservations. There is a $5 per visit parking fee. The park office, Box 749, Pine Mountain, (706) 663-4858, is open daily from 8 a.m. to 5 p.m.

A seated statue of FDR overlooks the Pine Mountain Valley, at Dowdell's Knob, a rocky 1,395-foot spur of the Pine Mountain ridge. One of FDR's favorite picnic and contemplation sites, it's off GA 190, inside FDR State Park. Hikers in your crowd can lace up their boots and hit the scenic 23-mile *Pine Mountain Trail.* Starting at the Callaway Gardens Country Store on US 27, the trail winds past rock formations, waterfalls, big stands of trees, and lush vegetation on its way to its terminus at the TV tower on GA 85W near Warm Springs. One of the country's southernmost mountain trails, it has 12 access points, so you can get on and off with ease. Pick up a trail map at the FDR Park office.

If you'd like to spend some time canoeing on a scenic, unspoiled river, get in touch with *Flint River Outdoor Center* (4429 Woodland Rd., Thomaston, 706-647-2633, www.flintriveroutdoorcenter.com). Guided and self-guided trips on the river begin at GA 36, 15 miles south of Warm Springs. You pass through mostly mild rapids, waterfalls, hills and valleys, wildflowers, ferns, and animal habitats. Canoe, kayak, and equipment rentals are available. The center features campsites and 5 RV hookups for those who would like to overnight.

The *Pasaquan Folk Art Compound* would probably seem extraordinary even in the Land of Oz. In rural Marion County, near the tiny county seat of Buena Vista, this outdoor ensemble of toothy totem faces, smiling snakes, whirling pinwheels, suns, moons, and stars—all painted in brilliant primary colors—is positively otherworldly. It was the product of the late Eddie Owens Martin, who was born here in 1908, traveled to New York and abroad, and returned in 1950 to create this fabulous legacy. To finance his creativity, Martin came to town in a turban and robes and told fortunes and sold jewelry around the courthouse.

Since Martin's death in 1986, his "Land of Pasaquan" has been meticulously restored and opened to the public by appointment. Open Apr through Nov on the first Saturday of each month. Call (229) 649-9444 to verify. The compound is at 238 Eddie Martin Rd., Buena Vista, www.pasaquan.com

The *Sign of the Dove Bed & Breakfast and Restaurant* (108 N. Church St., Buena Vista, 888-690-3663, 229-649-3663, www.sign-of-the-dove.com) has 3 large guest rooms in a 1905 neoclassical home and a 4-bedroom cottage. The restaurant serves Southern food, steaks, and seafood. Inexpensive to moderate.

Approaching **Albany** from any direction, you'll pass symmetrical groves of papershell pecan trees. Pecans are available year-round, still in the paper-thin shell or roasted and boxed. Some groves invite you to come in and pick your own. The attractive city of 77,000 has other pleasant surprises as well.

While Atlanta boasts the world's largest aquarium with the world's largest fish, Albany is just as proud of its *Flint RiverQuarium.* Although the 175,000-gallon RiverQuarium would be a drop in the fish tank compared to the 8-million-gallon Georgia Aquarium in downtown Atlanta, it's a symbol of rebirth in the city Albanians call "All-benny" that has had its share of watery woes.

In 1994, a month of torrential rains overwhelmed the Flint River and kept much of the city under water for several weeks. In the disaster's wake, the Downtown Riverfront Plan was conceived and a new nonprofit organization, Albany Tomorrow, was created to implement a revival of the neglected riverfront.

The Flint RiverQuarium was the linchpin in the redevelopment plan, which also includes an IMAX-style theater, the first new downtown hotel in a half century, and parklands, play areas, and plazas.

As visitors enter the lobby, they go up a ramp to a room called Skywater, the Creek Indian name for Blue Hole Springs. A re-creation of a natural river spring, the 22-foot-deep hole is open to the outside. Viewed through a 25-foot window, the Blue Hole teems with life. Snapping turtles, sliders, cooters, and other turtles swim through the clear water and sun themselves on logs that jut above the spring. Largemouth bass, 5-foot-long gar, 50-pound catfish, and dozens of other species drift through underwater caves and partially submerged cypresses and live oak trees, whose above-water branches house native birds, herons, and egrets. Juvenile and 6-foot-long gators have their own portioned-off habitat. Divers go into the Hole every day to feed the fish and amphibians.

A large tank in the gallery area showcases the sometimes ornery Flint River, which is born in a spring near Atlanta's Hartsfield-Jackson International Airport and twists more than 300 miles across middle and southwest Georgia, through Albany down to Lake Seminole. There it joins the Chattahoochee to form the Apalachicola, which flows through the Florida Panhandle into the Gulf of Mexico.

Albany's Ray Charles

The Ray Charles statue and plaza honors the entertainment icon born in Albany on September 23, 1930. He went with his family to Florida when he was a small child, became blind at age 6, and overcame his disability to become one of the world's most beloved musicians. He died in California in 2004. Dedicated in 2007, his illuminated bronze statue, slowly revolving around Ray Charles Plaza on the downtown Albany riverfront, depicts him with his signature dark sunglasses, seated at a piano, perhaps playing "Georgia On My Mind," "I Can't Stop Loving You," "What'd I Say," or another of his many classic gold and platinum hits. Along with the main statue, surrounded by a fountain, the plaza also features a "maquette," a miniature version that visitors can touch. In 1979, Charles performed "Georgia On My Mind" for the state legislature, which named it Georgia's official state song.

The aquarium's star and mascot is Big Al, a 90-pound, 90-year-old alligator snapping turtle. His lovably homely image graces mugs, T-shirts, and other souvenir items. If you have never seen an albino alligator, the pink-eyed "Moonshine" is easy to spot in the dark waters of Cypress Creek. Cypress is also home to the only native bird aviary in Georgia. There, you will find over 40 native birds flying around the 35-foot-tall enclosure.

Fish, reptiles, and other creatures from the Amazon, Ganges, and other world rivers populate the "World of Water" exhibit.

In Discovery Caverns, kids can play interactive games that focus on stewardship of natural resources. They make their own weather, change a river's flow, and crawl through a cave to find creatures that live underground.

Playgrounds, benches, and picnic tables are in Riverfront Park outside the aquarium. Festively decorated fiberglass turtles are goodwill ambassadors. Visitors can stay at the neighboring *Hilton Garden Inn.*

The Flint RiverQuarium is at 117 Pine Ave., Albany. Open Tues through Sat from 10 a.m. to 5 p.m., Sun 1 to 5 p.m. Adult RiverQuarium admission $9, seniors 62 and over $8, ages 4 to 12 $6.50. Call (877) 463-5468 or visit www .flintriverquarium.com.

At *Parks at Chebaw,* on GA 91, Albany, 2.5 miles northeast of the city, (229) 430-5277, www.parksatchehaw.org, African black rhinoceros and zebra, Andean llamas, North American black bears, bobcats, elk, bison, and deer roam in natural habitats designed by Jim Fowler, former naturalist with TV's *Wild Kingdom.* You view the animals from protected, elevated walkways. Admission to the zoo and a companion recreational park with play areas, jogging, hiking, and biking trails, a re-created Creek Indian village, miniature train rides, a boat dock, and picnic areas for adults is $8.75, age 62 and over $7.75, military $5.75, and ages 4 to 12 $5.75. The *Chehaw National Indian Festival,* held in the park the second weekend in April, is one of the Southeast Tourism Society's top 20 yearly events. The park is open from 9 a.m. to 5:30 p.m. daily. The zoo is open 9 a.m. to 5 p.m.

Thronateeska Heritage Foundation (100 Roosevelt Ave., Albany, 229-432-6955, www.heritagecenter.org) is a delightful, hands-on science experience for young and old alike. The science complex is adjacent to an early 1900s "prairie style" train depot, a 1910 steam locomotive, and an 1840s house, and includes a planetarium where you can witness a variety of live astronomy presentations. It's open Thurs through Sat 10 a.m. to 4 p.m. Admission is free during normal operating hours.

The **Albany Museum of Art** (311 Meadowlark Dr., Albany, 229-439-8400, www.albanymuseum.com) has both permanent and changing displays of regional and national artists. The African Art Center collection is one of the nation's most outstanding. Open Tues through Sat from 10 a.m. to 5 p.m. Admission is free but contributions are appreciated.

Albany Civil Rights Institute (326 Whitney Ave., Albany, 229-432-1698, www.albanycivilrightsinstiture.org) is the restored Mount Zion Baptist Church, where Dr. Martin Luther King Jr. preached during the 1961 civil rights demonstrations. Photos and exhibits illustrate Dr. King's pivotal part in the "Albany movement." He was arrested and jailed for his civil disobedience activities, and freed through the intervention of US Attorney General Robert Kennedy. Open Tues through Sat, 10 a.m. to 4 p.m., Sun 2 to 5 p.m. Adults $6, seniors and students $5, first- through fourth-graders $3, and preschoolers $2.

Contact the Albany CVB & Welcome Center at 225 W. Broad Ave., Albany, (800) 475-8700, www.albanyga.com.

Every spring in the swamps and bogs of southwestern Georgia, a thorny, scrubby, rather homely tree called the mayhaw produces an applelike fruit prized by gourmets and homemakers. The small, coral-hued fruit is gathered in fishing nets and by hand, then turned into a delectable sweet-tart jelly that's sold in stores around the small Miller County seat of Colquitt. The fruit is the star of **Colquitt's Mayhaw Festival,** the third weekend of April. Phone (229) 758-2400.

While you're in the Colquitt area, try to catch a performance of *"Swamp Gravy,"* an entertaining folklife play about the comedies and tragedies, tall tales, music, dance, and songs of Miller County and rural Georgia. Sponsored by the Colquitt/Miller Arts Council, it's performed in Jan, Mar, Apr, Oct, and Nov at the Cotton Hall Theater, 166 E. Main St. Call (229) 758-5450 for more information, or visit www.swampgravy.com.

"If walls could talk" isn't wishful thinking in Colquitt. Walk around the town square and 5 bigger-than-life murals, created by the Colquitt/Miller County Arts

Council's Millennium Mural Project, "speak" about events that shaped the lives of the peanut farming community of 2,500. The 4 panels of *Saturday On the Square,* by Alabama artist Wes Hardin, capture the excitement when "The Circus Comes to Town"; when a runaway "Bull Comes to Colquitt"; "When a Young Soldier Leaves Colquitt"; and "Hanging Out on the Square." Other murals depict neighbors helping neighbors; Saturday morning in Colquitt's black community; and the story of the South's three dominant cultures: Native American, black, and white. Contact Colquitt/Miller County Chamber of Commerce at 166 S. 1st St., Colquitt, (229) 758-2400, www.colquitt-georgia.com.

The Tarrer Inn (155 S. Cuthbert St., Colquitt, 229-758-2888 and 888-282-7737, www.tarrerinn.com) is another welcome newcomer to downtown Colquitt. Built in 1861 as a boardinghouse, the inn has been refurbished as a comfortable small hotel. Twelve guest rooms are decorated with antiques and modern amenities. Lunch is served Tues, Wed, Thurs, Fri, and Sun, dinner on Fri and Sat. Inexpensive to moderate rates include full Southern country breakfast.

If you're a fan of country fairs and enjoy good, old-fashioned fun, put **Climax Swine Time** (229-246-0910) on your post-Thanksgiving calendar. Held the Friday and Saturday after Thanksgiving in the Decatur County community of Climax, many of the activities are pig-related: a hog-calling contest, best-dressed pig competition, a greased-pig chase, and a "chitlin" (chitterling) eating contest. Also on the agenda are a parade, country and gospel music, a 10K race, cane grinding and syrup making, and barbecue and fried chicken for those who care not for "chitlins." Contact Bainbridge/Decatur County Chamber of Commerce at 100 Boat Basin Rd., Bainbridge, (229) 246-4774, (800) 243-4774, www.swinetimefestival.com.

The Rattlesnake Roundup, the last weekend of January, is the social event of the year at the small Grady County town of **Whigham,** 6 miles east of

Grits Is Groceries

The National Grits Festival, held in mid-April at the little Worth County town of Warwick, 17 miles north of Albany, celebrates "The Official Processed Food of Georgia." Imaginative cooks gussy up the humble cornmeal porridge with everything from apples to zucchini, pizza, pineapple, peach pie, and chocolate. The 1-day event includes a corn-shucking contest, arts festival, antique tractor show, a beauty contest, and the tour de force—a group wallow in the Grits Pit, a cattle trough filled with cold cooked grits. First prize goes to the contestant who comes out with the greatest quantity of the white stuff stuck to himself or herself. If you'd like to take the plunge, phone (229) 869-5550 or visit www.gritsfest.com.

Climax. The event began a couple of decades ago when Whigham residents, tired of being accosted by the hissing reptiles every time they walked through their fields and farms, decided to do something about it and have some sport at the same time. On the big day, visitors pack tiny downtown Whigham as snakes by the hundreds are brought in and displayed. Contact Bainbridge/ Decatur County Chamber of Commerce, (229) 246-4774, (800) 243-4774, www .bainbridgega.com/chamber.

Mule Day, in Calvary, the first Saturday of November, salutes the stalwart workhorses of the fields. Hundreds of jacks and jennies parade through Calvary, on US 11 in Grady County, just north of the Florida border. Contestants are judged on beauty, poise, congeniality, and mulish cussedness. They go haunch to haunch in a plowing contest and other events. Humans exhibit their skills at cane grinding, corn shucking, quilting, and syrup making. For information phone (229) 872-3612 or visit www.calvarylionsmuleday.com.

Carter Country

Peach County leaves little doubt that it's the heart of Georgia's most luscious industry. Traveling on I-75 at night, you can't miss "The Big Peach," an enormous illuminated rendition of the fruit on a 100-foot-pole at the Byron/ Fort Valley exit. During the summer, visitors have plenty of opportunities to go into the orchards and pick their own or to buy fresh peaches at packing houses and roadside stands. The Byron/Fort Valley exit 49 is the northern end of the Andersonville Trail, which leads through Fort Valley to Plains on GA 49 and US 280.

In early June you're invited to the *Georgia Peach Festival* in Byron and Fort Valley (www.worldslargestpeachcobbler.com). This weeklong event includes parades, street dances, peach pie cookoffs, peach-eating contests, and a king-and-queen coronation.

At *Lane Packing Company* (50 Lane Rd. at GA 96, 478-825-3592, www .lanepacking.com) you can tour the orchards and take home bushels or bagsful of the succulent fresh fruit, peach jam, and other peachy products. Open daily. Free tours.

Six miles south of Fort Valley, at the Peach/Macon County line, look for a left turn off GA 49 into Massee Lane Gardens, home of the *American Camellia Society.* Between Nov and Mar, pink and white blossoms in every known variety bloom in the society's more than 100-acre botanical gardens. Year-round, you're invited to the society's Williamsburg-style headquarters to admire the 170 porcelain birds and flowers created in the studios of the late American artist Edward Marshall Boehm. The pieces are so lifelike they appear to be on the verge of flight. Some were created as gifts of state for presidents and kings.

Contact the American Camellia Society at 100 Massee Ln., Fort Valley, (478) 967-2358, www.camellias-acs.com. Open year-round, the gardens have other blooming plants but camellia season is from Jan through Mar. Tues through Sat from 10 a.m. to 4:30 p.m.; Sun from 1 to 4:30 p.m. Free to the public.

Part of the Andersonville Trail, **Macon County** is the home of Georgia's largest Mennonite community. You can admire antebellum white columns in the small towns of Marshallville and Montezuma.

The Macon County seat and a thriving Mennonite community, **Mont-ezuma** was named by returning Mexican War veterans. The area has made a remarkable recovery from the devastating Flint River floods that occurred in 1994. Nearly 100 Mennonite families give the little town some of the appearance of the Pennsylvania Dutch country. Drive east of Montezuma on GA 26 past the neat barns and silos and the contented herds of the Mennonite dairy farms.

Three miles from Montezuma—and 14 miles west of I-75 exit 127—look for a black buggy parked in front of **Yoder's Deitsch Haus,** (478) 472-2024, a sparkling clean cafeteria where Mennonites in traditional dress prepare truly admirable Southern cooking, spiced with such Pennsylvania Dutch specialties as shoofly pie and pot roast. Before leaving, stop by the bakery for a sackful of cakes, cookies, breads, and strudel. It's open for breakfast, lunch, and dinner Tues through Sat. Handmade Mennonite dolls, afghans, coverlets, garden ornaments, and other items are on sale in the adjacent gift shop.

Pick up a driving tour map from the Macon County Chamber of Commerce, 109 N. Dooly St., Montezuma, (478) 472-2391, www.maconcountyga.org.

Sumter County, the epicenter of Georgia's peanut industry, is home of the world's most famous peanut farmer, our 39th president, Jimmy Carter. The southern anchor of the Andersonville Trail, Sumter is also the site of the Civil War's most notorious prisoner-of-war camp, Camp Sumter military prison.

These days, all is green and peaceful at the **Andersonville National Cemetery and Historic Site,** GA 49, Andersonville, (229-924-0343, www.nps.gov/ande). Stop first at the National Park Service Visitors Center to view the film and exhibits, then take the self-guided driving tour.

Built in 1864 as confinement for 10,000 Union prisoners of war, the 26.5-acre stockade soon became a charnel house for upwards of 33,000 captives. With the Confederacy barely able to feed and clothe its own forces, about 12,000 of the Andersonville inmates perished of disease and starvation. As park rangers point out, however, Southern prisoners in the more well-off North often fared no better than the Union prisoners at Andersonville.

After the war, the camp commander, Swiss-born Captain Henry Wirz, was found guilty of war crimes and hanged. The self-guided tour leads you past thousands of graves and impressive memorials erected by states whose sons died here. Tunnels testify to the prisoners' usually failed attempts to escape the horrors.

The *National Prisoner of War Museum,* www.nps.gov/ande, on the Andersonville grounds, honors the 800,000 American soldiers, sailors, and airmen who've endured the horrors of capture and imprisonment from the American Revolution to the Persian Gulf conflict and the Iraq War. The 10,000-square-foot museum was built in partnership by the American Ex-Prisoners of War (AXPW), a national organization of 20,000 former POWs, and Friends of the Park, local citizens who support the National Park Service at Andersonville. Funds were raised by the sale of 270,000 commemorative coins created by the US Mint. More than 10,000 donors and corporations gave about $700,000, and the Georgia Department of Transportation built a new entrance road and parking areas. Andersonville was chosen for the museum in recognition of the site's tragic history as the nation's most infamous POW camp. During the tour, you "experience" the terror of being captured by enemy troops and taken to prison. One room highlights the horrors of World War II's Bataan Death March and the forced marches to North Korean POW camps. Another room displays drawings, poetry, carvings, and clandestine radios POWs created to help them keep their sanity. The tour ends with a full-scale replica of POWs digging an escape tunnel under a Nazi prison camp. The museum's courtyard opens onto the remains of the Civil War Andersonville stockade. A fountain gushing water into a stream symbolizes the lack of fresh water prevalent in most POW camps.

A granite springhouse marks the site of *Providence Spring,* which legend says flowed from barren ground in answer to prisoners' prayers.

Across Highway 49, the Civil War village of *Andersonville* (population 255, 229-924-2558, www.andersonvillegeorgia.com) has been returned to its 1860s appearance. The quaint little town welcomes visitors with antique and craft stores, picnic groves, and antebellum churches and homes. Stop by the Welcome Center, which is located in the lobby of the Drummer Boy Museum right on Main Street. The museum houses an extensive collection of guns, swords, battle flags, and documents signed by Jefferson Davis and Abraham Lincoln. The village's major yearly happenings are the *Great Southern Carriage and Wagon Auction* in early April, the *Andersonville Antiques and Civil War Artifacts Fair* Memorial Day weekend, and the *Andersonville Historic Fair* in early October, which features battle reenactments and scores of craftspeople and musicians.

A charming bed-and-breakfast called *A Place Away* has 2 bedrooms in a comfortable, rustic-looking cottage with private baths, refrigerators, and

Peanuts! Fresh Roasted Peanuts!

Jimmy Carter, Georgia's peanut farmer–president, drew the world's attention to the state's most bountiful crop. His native southwest Georgia is the heart of this tasty industry, and it produces most of the more than 2 billion pounds of goobers grown in the state every year.

Breaking it down, there are about 200 peanut pods to a pound, and usually 2 peanuts per pod. They would make a mountain of about 800 billion peanuts. Laid end to end, they'd extend for more than 6 million miles, about 25 times the distance from the Earth to the Moon. "Goober" is believed to come from an African word, *nguba,* which, of course, means "peanut."

coffeemakers. Guest rooms and a sitting room are decorated in kick-off-your-shoes casual country style. The inexpensive rate comes with a bountiful Southern breakfast. Contact Andersonville Welcome Center at (229) 924-2558.

At nearby *Americus,* stop at the Americus/Sumter County Tourism Council Welcome Center, 123 W. Lamar St., Americus, (229) 928-6059, (888) 278-6837, www.therealgeorgia.com, for a driving guide to the historic showplaces around the pleasant city of 20,000. Memorabilia of our 39th president are displayed at the *James Earl Carter Library* of Georgia Southwestern University.

After leaving the presidency in 1980, Jimmy Carter received worldwide acclaim for his efforts on behalf of Habitat for Humanity International. Since 1976, when it was founded in Americus as a nonprofit housing ministry, Habitat for Humanity has partnered with more than 500,000 families to build simple, affordable houses in every state and more than 80 countries. *The Global Village and Discovery Center* in downtown Americus has model homes and exhibits about the organization's history. It's open Mon through Sat. Adults are $4, students/seniors $3. Habitat for Humanity International is at 721 W. Church St., Americus, (229) 924-6935, (800) HABITAT, www.habitat.org/gvdc.

If you love old movie palaces, try to be in Americus for a performance at the gorgeously restored *Rylander Theater.* Opened in 1921, the ornate theater was the setting for 30 years of vaudeville, silent movies, stellar attractions like bandmaster John Philip Sousa, the Ziegfeld Follies, political speeches, graduations, dance recitals and concerts, and films from Hollywood's golden era. The theater closed in 1950 and was forgotten until 1992, when a restoration movement began. Reopened in 1999, the venerable house, with 630 seats on 3 levels and a 1928 "Mighty Mo" Möller pipe organ, hosts touring musicals, plays, concerts, and festive events of all sorts. It's at 310 W. Lamar St., next to Habitat for Humanity Headquarters. Phone (229) 931-0001 or visit www.rylander.org.

In 1923, four years before he captured the world's imagination with his historic trans-Atlantic solo flight, an unheralded barnstormer named Charles A. Lindbergh made his first-ever solo flight at Souther Field, a US Army aviation training camp at Americus. "The Lone Eagle" made his flight in the first plane he ever owned, a single-engine WWI surplus, *Jenny*. It was obviously love at first flight. His feat is remembered on a plaque at what's now Americus Airport: "I had not soloed up to the time I bought my *Jenny* at Americus, Georgia [signed] Charles A. Lindbergh." Contact the Americus Welcome Center at 123 W. Lamar St., Americus, (229) 928-6059, (888) 278-6837, www.the realgeorgia.com.

For contemporary comforts wrapped in a splendid turn-of-the-century package, check into the **Windsor Hotel** in downtown Americus. This is no doubt the fanciest Best Western Hotel you will ever see. Built in 1896, the redbrick, turreted-and-towered Italianate landmark reopened in 1991 to rave reviews. The 53 large guest rooms are beautifully furnished and decorated. The Grand Dining Room serves high-Southern and continental cuisine, and there's a full bar and an open veranda with wicker rockers. The private Lindbergh Dining Room was named for "Lucky Lindy," who purchased his first plane and made his first solo flight from nearby Souther Field. Lindbergh used to stay in the Windsor and would play pool across the street from the hotel. The Windsor is at 125 W. Lamar St., Americus. Call (229) 924-1555 or (888) 297-9567 or visit www.windsor-americus.com. Inexpensive to moderate.

Nearly three decades after Jimmy Carter left the White House, the 39th president's sleepy little Sumter County hometown of Plains treasures the legacy of the quiet-spoken peanut farmer who made it world-famous. Visitors still come to town to visit the simple, unassuming places included in the *Jimmy Carter National Historic Site.* The National Park Service Visitor Center in the former Plains school is the best place to start. In the late 1930s and early 1940s, when Carter sat in the classrooms and walked its corridors, the brick school housed grades 1 through 11. There was no 12th grade in those days. Today the school is a museum, showcasing life in the rural South during the Great Depression. Stiff-backed wood and metal school desks are lined up like rows of peanuts in a red clay field. On an audiotape, today's Carter talks fondly of Julia Coleman, his teacher and school principal, who advised him and fellow students to "accommodate changing times, but cling to unchanging principles." When students got out of hand, a wooden paddle, legal in those days, was there to get them back in line. Wouldn't Julia Coleman be proud to know her former pupil became president and won the 2002 Nobel Peace Prize? The Visitor Center (300 N. Bond St., Plains, www.plainsgeorgia.com) is open daily from 9 a.m. to 5 p.m. Admission is free.

Elsewhere in town, the old railroad depot, made famous by the 1976 presidential campaign, is now the **Depot Museum,** dedicated to that historic campaign.

Also part of the National Historic Site, the **Jimmy Carter Boyhood Home,** in the Archery community, 2 miles from Plains, includes the farmhouse, barns, outbuildings, and the farm store where Carter grew up in the 1930s. In push-button audios around the site, Carter describes the no-frills life on his father's farm. The house had no electricity until the early 1940s, and the family's day usually began before dawn and ended not long after dark. A battery-operated radio with newscasts and popular shows like *Amos 'n Andy* and *Fibber Magee and Molly* was one of the family's few sources of entertainment.

The **Plains Inn and Antique Shop,** a 2-story building on Main Street, has a 24-booth antiques mall on the street floor and 7 luxury suites on the second floor, each decorated in the style of a decade from the 1920s to the 1980s. Inexpensive to moderate. Phone (229) 824-4517 or visit www.plainsinn.net.

A peanut with a famous toothy grin welcomes visitors to Plains. Made of wooden hoops, chicken wire, aluminum foil, and polyurethane, the 13-foot-tall goober was a gift to the town from Carter's friends. When termites took a liking to "Mr. Peanut" a few years back, townsfolk came to the rescue with patches of cement.

The Carters' current home, a modest ranch-style house, will eventually be included in the National Historic Site. Carter and his wife, Rosalynn, can often be seen around town when they're taking time out from their services with Habitat for Humanity International and their peacemaking efforts around the world. Visitors are welcome when the former president teaches Sunday school at Maranatha Baptist Church. For information about the National Historic Site, write National Park Service, Plains 31780 (229-824-4104, www.nps.gov/jica). All sites are open daily, and admission is free. Plains is on US 280 about 40 miles west of I-75 exit 101. Shops on Plains's main street are stocked with Carter memorabilia and peanuts in many different guises.

Hello, Central! The **Georgia Rural Telephone Museum** in the small Sumter County town of Leslie recalls the bygone era when the telephone was a friend, not an impersonal convenience and telemarketing nuisance. Tommy Smith, who owns the local Citizen's Telephone Company, opened the museum in 1995 in a 1911 cotton warehouse he saved from destruction. His 2,000 pieces of telephonia include hand-cranked wooden voice boxes, early telephones of every size and description, and life-size dioramas of switchboard operators in period dress. You'll also see a re-creation of Alexander Graham Bell's workshop, phone booths, and an early 1900s Model A Ford service truck. The museum is located on US 280 west, 135 Bailey Ave.,

Leslie, 22 miles off I-75 exit 101 (Cordele). Open Mon through Fri from 9 a.m. to 3:30 p.m. Adults $5, seniors $4, children $3. Phone (229) 874-4786 or visit www.grtm.org.

Georgia Veterans Memorial State Park is a tranquil haven 9 miles west of Cordele and the racetrack lanes of I-75. A museum and vintage aircraft honor the state's military veterans. The park sits on Lake Blackshear, an 18-mile-long waterway renowned for catfish, black bass, bream, pickerel, and other delicious catches. Visitors can also enjoy boating, an 18-hole golf course, swimming in a freshwater pool, and a nature interpretive center and playground. The 100 camping and trailer sites have electricity, water, restrooms, and hot showers. Ten 2- and 3-bedroom cottages, with fireplaces and fully equipped kitchens, are available. There is a $5 per visit parking fee. The park office, on US 280, Cordele, (229) 276-2371, (800) 864-PARK, www.gastateparks.org, is open daily from 8 a.m. to 5 p.m. The *Lake Blackshear Resort & Golf Club* is a deluxe resort inside Georgia Veterans Park. Looking more like a modern art museum than a state park lodge, the retreat's 88 smartly furnished guest rooms and villas are moderately priced. Amenities include an upscale restaurant overlooking the water, full bar, indoor and outdoor pools, fitness center, conference center, golf, fishing, and water sports. Moderate to expensive. Call (800) 459-1230, (229) 276-2004, or visit www.lakeblackshearresort.com.

Daphne Lodge, on US 280 near the Veterans park entrance, (229) 273-2596, www.daphnelodge.com, is a pleasantly rustic, family-owned restaurant famous for its fried catfish and hush puppies. They also serve shrimp, steaks, quail, country ham, and fried chicken at dinner Tues through Sat, 5 to 9:30 p.m..

If you're down this way in late June, join in the fun of Cordele's annual *Watermelon Festival.*

Calling all train nuts! The *Savannah-Americus-Montgomery Shortline* is now accepting passengers for its 36-mile daily run between Cordele and Plains. Opened in late 2002, the state-operated excursion train, dubbed "The Rolling State Park," glides through pecan groves, peanut fields, and small towns and makes a scenic crossing of Lake Blackshear. It stops at the Jimmy Carter National Historic Site and the Georgia Rural Telephone Museum and also gives riders time to tour Habitat for Humanity's Tour Center and Museum in Americus. The SAM Shortline gets its name from a historic route that dates back to 1888 and these days goes nowhere near Savannah. Passenger car fares are adults $27.99; ages 62 and over and military, $25.99; ages 3 to 12, $17.99. Premium car with chairs and tables, adults $35.99, children $25.99. Phone (229) 276-0755 or (877) GA-RAILS or visit www.samshortline.com.

Roses & Pine Trees

The Georgia Museum of Agriculture and Historic Village (or Agrirama for short) is an off-the-beaten-path experience less than 0.25-mile off the well-beaten path of I-75 exit 63B. About three dozen vintage farm buildings make up the state's 95-acre agricultural heritage center. Inside the gates of this 19th-century time warp, youngsters may go nose to nose with friendly farmyard animals and take a trip on a steam-powered logging train. Cotton is planted in the old-fashioned way by a farmer in bib overalls commanding a mule and a plow. The village blacksmith hammers out nails and utensils over a white-hot forge. Sugarcane is harvested by hand and ground into syrup and corn into grits and meal at a picture-postcard gristmill. A country store sells handmade quilts, preserves, cookbooks, toys, and corn shuck dolls.

The *Agrirama* (1392 Whiddon Mill Rd., Tifton, 229-391-5200, 800-767-1875, www.agrirama.com) is open year-round Tues through Sat, 9 a.m. to 4:30 p.m. All-inclusive admission Tues through Fri is $7 for adults, $6 for senior citizens 55 and over, $4 children 5 to 16; free for children under 4. On Saturday is when the train runs so admission is $10 for adults, $8 for seniors and $5 for children.

Downtown Tifton has been revitalized thanks to the Georgia Main Street Program. About 30 shops and eateries are now attracting visitors to a complex of restored 19th- and early 20th-century buildings. The 1906 Myon Hotel now houses City Hall, a permanent collection of regional art, shops, offices, and a restaurant. Contact the Tifton/Tift County Tourism Association, 100 S. Central Ave., Tifton, (229) 382-8700, (800) 550-8438, www.tiftontourism.com.

From 1870 to the turn of the new century, Thomasville was a Southern Newport, the forefather of Palm Beach and Miami. Encouraged by reports of the area's healthy climate, wealthy Northerners came by private train to spend the winter at grand hotels, which brought chefs and orchestras all the way from New York and Europe. Many regular visitors built their own lavish homes and purchased surrounding plantations for grouse and quail hunting. In the early 1900s, the rich and famous discovered Florida, and Thomasville's "Golden Age" was over. Left behind was a remarkable heritage. Presidents, aristocrats, and "commoners" still flock to the city of 20,000 to hunt game birds and antiques, tour homes and plantations, and participate in late April's Thomasville Rose Festival.

Stop first at the Thomasville/Thomas County Convention and Visitors Bureau (144 E. Broad St., Thomasville, 229-228-7977, 866-577-3600, www .thomasvillega.com) where you can load up on maps, brochures, and self-guided walking and driving tour information. Guides can be arranged for tour groups. The Welcome Center is open Mon through Fri from 9 a.m. to 5 p.m. and Sat from 10 a.m. to 3 p.m.

On your own, stop at the ***Thomas County Historical Museum*** (725 N. Dawson St., Thomasville, 229-226-7664) where you'll see hundreds of photos and souvenirs of the "Golden Age." It's open Mon through Sat from 10 a.m. to 5 p.m. Admission for adults is $5, for students $1.

Nearby, the ***Lapham-Patterson House State Historic Site*** (626 N. Dawson St., Thomasville, 229-225-4004, 800-864-PARK, www.gastateparks.org) is an outlandish Victorian mansion built for Chicago shoe manufacturer C. W. Lapham. Maintained as a state historical museum, the tri-winged, mustard-yellow mansion is highlighted by cantilevered interior balconies, double-flue chimneys, and fish-scale shingles. It's open Fri 1 to 5 p.m., Sat from 10 a.m. to 5 p.m., Sun from 2 to 5 p.m. Admission is $5 for adults, $2.50 for children 6 to 18; free for children 5 and under.

Pebble Hill Plantation (229-226-2344, www.pebblehill.com) is a "must-see." The 28-room Georgian and Greek Revival main house and the gardens, stables, and kennels were left as a museum by the late Pansy Ireland Poe. Inside the house are 33 original John James Audubon bird prints and extensive collections of silver, crystal, and antique furnishings. Five miles southwest of Thomasville, on US 319, Thomasville, it's open Tues through Sat from 10 a.m. to 5 p.m. and Sun from 12 to 5 p.m. Adult admission fee is $5 and $2 for children for the self-guided tour of the grounds, $15 for the guided main house tour; ages 6 to 12, $6; children under 6 not permitted in main house.

The ***Thomasville Black Heritage Trail*** was created by retired Air Force officer James "Jack" Hadley to give visitors an opportunity to learn about the city's rich African-American history. The 2.5-hour "step-on, step-off" tour includes churches, historic sites, schools, cemeteries, businesses, parks, and a black-owned bed-and-breakfast. More than a half-dozen sites focus on the life of Lt. Henry Ossian Flipper, who was born a slave on a Thomasville area

Lieutenant's Scrambled Dogs

Lieutenant Stevens, who prepared them for many years, has retired from active duty. Fortunately for those who can't get through a day without a Scrambled Dog, he passed on his recipe to the staff at Columbus's Dinglewood Pharmacy. They still prepare it by splitting and splaying 2 hot dogs on a bun in a banana split dish and dressing them with cheese, mustard, pickles, and a rich coating of Lieutenant's secret-recipe chili, topped with a shower of oyster crackers. Betcha can't eat more than one! Incidentally, Lieutenant is Stevens's real name. He was born on Armistice Day, 1931, and his parents wanted their son to honor America's armed forces. Dinglewood Pharmacy is at 1939 Wynnton Rd., near downtown Columbus. Call (706) 322-0616.

plantation in 1856 and 21 years later became the first black graduate of the United States Military Academy at West Point. For information: Thomasville Black Heritage Trail, (229) 228-6983, www.jackhadleyblackhistorymuseum.com/trailTour.html. The *Jack Hadley Black History Museum*'s 2,000 artifacts and pictorial exhibits highlight Thomasville's black achievers and also commemorate state and national black leaders. At 214 Alexander St., (229) 226-5029, www.jackhadleyblackhistorymuseum.com, it's open Tues through Sat from 10 a.m. to 5 p.m. Adults $5; students $3.

Several of Thomasville's most beautiful old homes welcome bed-and-breakfast guests. All take pride in their antique furnishings and traditional south Georgia hospitality. They include the AAA Four Diamond 1884 Paxton House (445 Remington Ave., 800-278-0138, 229-226-5797, www.1884paxtonhouseinn.com), Dawson Street Inn (324 W. Dawson St., 229-226-7515, http://dawsonstinn.com/index.htm), the Magnolia Leaf (501 E. Washington St., 229-226-4499, www.themagnolialeaf.com), Mitchell-Young-Anderson House (319 Oak St., 229-226-3463), and Southwoods Bobwhite Bed & Breakfast (8025 US 19 South, 229-226-0170). All have private baths, antiques, and personable hosts. Rates range from inexpensive to expensive.

You can't leave town without stopping by the corner of Crawford and Monroe Streets to see "The Big Oak." It's estimated this giant Southern live oak was planted around 1685. Its limb span is over 165 feet. President Dwight Eisenhower was so impressed that he took photos of it himself during a visit to Thomasville. For a bit of fun, go to the Big Oak Cam sign, stand in front of the tree, and dial (229) 236-0053. You'll get instructions what to do, but basically you'll strike a pose while looking at the camera on the pole across the street. Your photo will show up on bigoak.rose.net.

If you'd like to enjoy a bit of Thomasville's sporting life, shoot some skeet, and hunt birds and game, contact *Myrtlewood Plantation,* PO Box 32, Thomasville 31799, (229) 228-6232, www.myrtlewoodplantation.com.

Thomasville's really big annual event is the late-April Rose Festival, a week of parades, pageantry, home tours, and rose judgings that attracts visitors from many countries. In the good-news-bad-news category, the renowned Thomasville Rose Test Garden has closed, but it's been replaced by the Thomasville Rose Garden, which displays scores of varieties of blooming plants around the shores of Cherokee Lake, at the corner of Covington and Smith Avenues. Admission is free.

Places to Stay in Southwest Georgia

ALBANY

Hilton Garden Inn
101 S. Front St.
(229) 888-1590
www.hiltongardeninn.com
Moderate to Expensive
The 125-room hotel, on the downtown riverfront near the Flint RiverQuarium, has a fitness center, pool, full-service restaurant and bar, business center, and in-room high-speed Internet connections.

BUENA VISTA

Sign of the Dove Bed & Breakfast and Restaurant
Church Street and 4th Avenue
(229) 649-3663
(888) 690-3663
www.sign-of-the-dove.com
Inexpensive to Moderate
Donna and Ray Armer's 1905 neoclassical home has 3 guest bedrooms and a guest cottage, near the Pasaquan attraction and Buena Vista's ("Bew-na Vista") courthouse square. The restaurant serves steaks and seafood on Friday nights and a Sunday Southern buffet, with fried chicken, salad bar, veggies, and desserts.

COLQUITT

Tarrer Inn
155 S. Cuthbert St.
(888) 282-7737
(229) 758-2888
www.tarrerinn.com
Inexpensive to Moderate, includes full country breakfast
See p. 60 for details.

CORDELE

Lake Blackshear Resort & Golf Club
(229) 276-2004
(800) 459-1230
www.lakeblackshearresort.com
Moderate to Expensive
See p. 67 for details.

LAGRANGE AREA

Fair Oaks Inn
703 E. Main St.
(706) 637-8828
Inexpensive to Moderate
This Queen Anne Victorian B&B has 6 guest rooms with private bath and full breakfast.

The House on Seventh
311 E. 7th St.
West Point
(706) 645-2064
www.bbonline.com/ga/seventh
Inexpensive
The Queen Anne–style cottage was built in the early 20th century in the small textile town of West Point, on the Georgia-Alabama border. Ira and Emily Culpepper have 3 guest rooms with private baths and period antiques, and serve a generous country breakfast.

Thyme Away Bed and Breakfast
508 Greenville St.
LaGrange
(706) 885-9625
Inexpensive, includes full breakfast
The imposing Greek Revival house in downtown LaGrange has been returned to its 1840s elegance. Guest rooms are furnished with antiques, TV, phone, refrigerator, and private baths with whirlpool tubs and gas fireplaces. You can relax in the parlor, play the piano, and use the fax and modem services.

COLUMBUS

Gates House
802 Broadway
(800) 891-3187
Moderate to Expensive
A short walk from Riverwalk, Carolyn and Tom Gates's 1880 Colonial Revival house is a time-trip to the elegance of Victorian America. Guest rooms have family antiques, private baths, and queen or twin beds. You can have breakfast in the dining room, Victorian garden, or front porch.

Marriott Columbus
800 Front Ave., at the
Riverwalk
(888) 228-6290
(706) 324-1800
www.marriott.com/
columbus
Moderate
Built partially in a 19th-
century ironworks, the
177-room hotel has an outdoor pool, restaurant and
bar, and meeting rooms.
Located across from
the Columbus Conven-
tion Center, a short walk
from the Rivercenter for
Performing Arts and down-
town restaurants.

Rothschild-Pound House
201 7th St.
(706) 322-4075
www.thepoundhouseinn
.com
Moderate to Expensive
Built in the 1870s, the Second Empire–style show-
place has 10 guest suites
and cottages with private
baths, some with Jacuzzi.
Original art and antiques
are throughout the house.
Innkeepers Kristen Jocums
and Mark Stracks offer
full breakfast and evening
cocktails.

PINE MOUNTAIN

**Chipley Murrah Bed and
Breakfast**
207 W. Harris St.
(888) 782-0797
(706) 663-9801
www.chipleymurrah.com
Moderate
This beautiful Victorian
home was built in 1895
and is impeccably fur-
nished with antiques. In
addition to the 4 large
rooms, each with a private
bath, of the main house,
there are 3 cottages as
well. Hosts Paul and Donna
Haynes will make you feel
right at home.

AMERICUS

Americus Garden Inn
504 Rees Park
(229) 931-0122
(888) 758-4749
www.americusgardeninn
.com
Inexpensive to Moderate
Built between 1847 and
1848, Kim and Susan Egel-
seer's 5,000-square-foot
home is set in an acre of
walkways and gardens.
Eight guest rooms have
plush antique furnishings,
large private baths, phone,
TV, and ceiling fan. Three
have tubs large enough for
two, 12-foot ceilings, and
original fireplace mantels.
"Scarlett's Room" has an
optional adjoining room
that makes a 2-bedroom
suite. Well-mannered pets
are welcome.

Windsor Hotel
125 W. Lamar St.
(888) 297-9567
(229) 924-1555
www.windsoramericus.com
Inexpensive to Moderate
See p. 65 for details.

CHULA

**Hummingbird's Perch
Bed & Breakfast**
I-75 exit 23, 5 miles north
of Tifton, Route 1
Box 1870
(229) 382-5431
Inexpensive
Gracious country living,
with bird-watching and
fishing around a small lake.
Three guest rooms, with
private or shared bath.

THOMASVILLE

1884 Paxton House Inn
445 Remington Ave.
(229) 226-5167
www.1884paxtonhouseinn
.com
Moderate to Expensive
This beautiful Queen
Anne–style home has 3
suites and a room in the
main house, as well as
a carriage house, a pool
house, and a cottage on
its grounds. Relax on the
beautiful porches and enjoy
a full spread of Southern
goodies for breakfast.

PLAINS

Plains Inn
(229) 824-4517
www.plainsgeorgia.com
Inexpensive to Moderate
See p. 66 for details.

Places to Eat in Southwest Georgia

COLUMBUS

The Cannon Brewpub
1041 Broadway
(706) 653-2337
www.cannonbrewpub.com
Inexpensive
Pizza, pasta, burgers, steaks, and house brews in a lively pair of vintage downtown storefronts. Look for the Civil War cannon parked on the sidewalk. Open daily.

Country's BBQ
1329 Broadway
(706) 596-8910
www.countrysbarbecue.com
Inexpensive
Chattahoochee Valley–style 'cue—ribs, chopped pork, chicken, and beef grilled over green saplings—is served by the big, saucy plateful in a former Trailways bus depot in downtown Columbus. Eat in the station or an adjoining old road warrior. Open daily.

Minnie's Uptown Restaurant
104 8th St.
(706) 322-2766
Inexpensive
If you can't find Minnie's, just follow your nose and look for the crowds lining up out the doors of the green cinder-block building near downtown Columbus.

Fried chicken, fried fish, meat loaf, turnip greens, stewed corn, black-eyed peas, corn bread, and cobblers, with big glasses of sweet tea, keep the place packed every day but Sunday.

Meritage Cafe and Gallery
1350 13th St.
(706) 327-0707
www.meritageonline.com
Moderate
Enjoy fine American and continental cuisine in a cozy cafe brightened by work of local artists. Specialties include seafood, filet mignon, pastas, and chicken dishes. Lunch Fri only, dinner Fri and Sat, Sunday brunch. For lunch, try the Deli Cafe for homemade soups and unique salads and paninis.

Ruth Ann's
941 Veteran's Pkwy.
(706) 221-2154
www.ruthannsrestaurant.net
Inexpensive
A local staple since 1959, Ruth Ann's is a must for those who want true down-home-style Southern cooking. Serving breakfast and lunch daily, Ruth Ann's serves up a variety of fresh vegetables and lots of wonderfully fried things like chicken and chicken-fried steak. The tomato gravy biscuits will make you wanna slap yo' mamma.

GEORGETOWN

Michelle's of Georgetown
US 82
(229) 334-5912
Inexpensive
Southern home cooking in all its glory is on the daily all-you-can-eat breakfast, lunch, and dinner buffets at this popular dining room on the Chattahoochee River, across from Eufaula, Alabama. Fresh vegetables, fried chicken, chicken and dumplings, barbecue, corn bread, biscuits, sweet potato soufflé, squash casserole, homemade pies, and cakes don't get any better than this. On Sunday morning, churchgoers on both sides of the Chattahoochee pray for a short sermon so they can beat their neighbors to the serving line. Open daily.

PINE MOUNTAIN

Carriage and Horses Restaurant
607 Butts Mill Rd.
(706) 663-4777
www.cometodagher.com
Moderate to Expensive
They call their fare "International country cuisine." The menu ranges from seafood linguini to Mediterranean platters and steaks. Great food in a beautiful Victorian setting.

Chipley's Family Restaurant
324 Main Ave. North
(706) 663-2640
Moderate to Expensive
Grits, biscuits, sausage, and eggs for breakfast,

HELPFUL WEBSITES

Americus-Sumter County Tourism Council
www.therealgeorgia.com

Pebble Hill Plantation
www.pebblehill.com

Columbus Convention & Visitors Bureau
www.visitcolumbusga.com

Massee Lane Camellia Society Gardens
www.camellias-acs.com

and buffet lunch and dinner with fried chicken, fish, meat loaf, pork chops, vegetables, and desserts make this friendly, family-owned place a popular stop for Pine Mountain locals and Callaway Gardens visitors.

Cricket's Restaurant
GA 18
(706) 663-8136
www.cricketsrestaurant.com
Moderate
Features jambalaya, crawfish, blackened fish, oysters, shrimp, gumbo, and other Louisiana Cajun and Creole favorites. Open daily 5 to 9 p.m.

Rose Cottage
111 E. Broad St.
(706) 663-7877
www.rosecottagega.com
Inexpensive to Moderate
English tea, sandwiches, soup, salads, desserts, wine. Lunch Tues through Sun and dinners Fri and Sat.

WARM SPRINGS

The Bulloch House
US 27 just off Warm Springs's main street
(706) 655-9057
www.bullochhouse.com
Inexpensive
Bulloch House offers a full menu with sandwiches and salads, but really big appetites should check out the buffet line. It features a host of Southern goodness from fried green tomatoes to black-eyed peas. Save room for the peach cobbler.

The Victorian Tea Room
Broad Street
US 27, downtown
(706) 655-3508
Inexpensive
A 1906 mercantile store has been turned into a cozy dining room specializing in soups, salads, sandwiches, and Southern home cooking. It's open for lunch Tues through Sun and for dinner Fri only.

THOMASVILLE

The Billiard Academy
S. Broad Street
(912) 226-9981
Inexpensive
Thomasvillians can't seem to get through a day without chowing on Joe Kirkland's hot dogs, dressed in his special chili sauce. Out-of-towners drive miles for their daily fix. Folks in a hurry get 'em to go at the sidewalk window. If you've a little more time, step inside for a friendly game at the billiard tables and have a cool brew and a chat with the boys at the lunch counter/bar. Dogs and billiards are available from early morning to late at night, Mon through Sat.

George & Louie's
217 Remington Ave.
(912) 226-1218
www.georgeadlouies.com
Moderate
Fresh seafood plates, channel catfish, snapper, broiled and fried shrimp

and oysters, scallops, burgers, shish kebab, steaks, and sandwiches draw big crowds for dinner Mon through Sat.

The Homecoming
1164 Myrick Rd.
(912) 226-1143
Inexpensive to Moderate
A short drive out of town, this former country cabin with a big front porch is a nostalgic old-timey place for all-you-can-eat catfish and quail, and fried, boiled, and grilled shrimp, oysters, scallops, fried chicken, and Delmonico steak. A kids-under-12 menu has smaller portions of catfish, shrimp, and chicken, as well as hot dogs, hamburgers, and PB&J sandwiches. Dinner Mon through Sat.

Jonah's Fish and Grits
100 E. Jackson St.
(229) 226-0508
www.jonahsfish.com
Inexpensive to Moderate
Open for lunch and dinner, Jonah's finds inventive ways to serve up seafood from Baja wraps to the signature shrimp and grits.

Market Diner
503 Smith Ave.
(229) 225-1777
Inexpensive
Strap on the feed bag for this Southern-style all-you-can-eat buffet. Consistently good with fresh vegetable daily and everything from fried oysters to chicken and pork chops.

Mom & Dad's Italian Restaurant
1800 Smith Ave.
(912) 226-6265
www.momanddadsitalian
.com
Moderate
Traditional Italian pastas, seafood, chicken, veal, steak, and other American fare. Dinner Tues through Sat.

The Plaza
217 S. Broad St.
(912) 226-5153
www.thomasvilleplaza.com
Moderate
An old, old favorite, the Plaza has served steaks, seafood, prime rib, and Greek dishes for nearly 80 years. Breakfast, lunch, and dinner Mon through Sat.

BBQ & Harness Horses

The pleasant little city of Perry, population 10,000, on I-75 exit 136, 25 miles south of Macon, is home to Georgia's largest fairgrounds, a former US Senator, a revitalized downtown, and a landmark hotel that has catered to travelers since the Roaring '20s. It's the seat of **Houston County** (pronounced "Howston"), population 140,000, home of Robins Air Force Base.

The 628-acre **Georgia National Fairgrounds & Agricenter** hosts livestock and horse shows, fairs, concerts, rodeos, and sporting events year-round. The three biggest events are the **Georgia National Fair** in October; the **Georgia National Junior Livestock Show and Rodeo** in February; and the **"Big, Bang, Boom"** July Fourth celebration. A giant Ferris wheel, cotton candy, and other fun stuff to ride and gorge on give the fairgrounds the festive feeling of an old-time carnival. Phone (478) 987-3247 and visit www.gnfa.com.

The **Sen. Sam Nunn Library** in the 1925 former Perry High School building, now the Houston County Board of Education, 1100 Main St., Perry, (478) 988-6200, exhibits

memorabilia, photos, documents, and videos about the life and political career of the Perry native and lifelong resident, who served as a Democratic US senator from 1972 to 1997. A classroom is like it was when Nunn pondered the "three Rs" here. Open Mon through Fri from 9 a.m. to 5 p.m. Free admission.

You can have a fun time shopping for antiques, gifts, and home decor, or dine at a tearoom and Southern comfort food restaurant on Carroll Street, 3 tree-shaded downtown blocks. At *Priester's Pecans, Candy Kitchen, and Restaurant* (I-75 exit 134, 478-987-6080, www.priester.com) you can take home Middle Georgia's famous nuts made into pralines, divinity, or fudge, or sugar-glazed, plain-roasted, raw, and candied. Open daily.

The *New Perry Hotel* has been a beacon for Middle Georgia travelers since the 1920s. Even now, with most of the traffic a mile away on I-75, motorists still find their way to this surviving vestige of small-town hospitality.

Set among trees and gardens, across from the Houston County Courthouse, the New Perry has 26 rooms in its main building and 17 more in a motel-type addition by the swimming pool. New owners in 2011 have turned the hotel into a family-run operation and have worked to renovate it and restore its

SOUTHEAST GEORGIA'S TOP HITS

Museum of Aviation	Laura S. Walker State Park
Big Pig Jig	Suwannee Canal Recreation Area
Georgia Cotton Museum	Stephen C. Foster State Park
Harness Racing Festival	Wild Adventures Theme Park, Valdosta
George L. Smith State Park	The Crescent, Valdosta
Magnolia Springs State Park	Hahira Honeybee Festival
Georgia Southern University Museum	Reed Bingham State Park
Center for Wildlife Education and Lamar Q. Ball Jr. Raptor Center	Jefferson Davis Memorial State Historic Site
Vidalia sweet onion	General Coffee State Park
Rattlesnake Roundup	Douglas's public golf courses
Lake Grace	Blue and Gray Museum
Edwin L. Hatch Nuclear Plant Visitors Center	Statue of Liberty
Okefenokee Swamp Park	Little Ocmulgee State Park

Southern charm. The hotel dining room serves inexpensive to moderate lunch and dinner.

The Tavery Pub has a full bar and a casual menu. Contact the New Perry Hotel at 800 Main St., Perry, (478) 224-1000, www.newperryhotel.com.

Henderson Village, a luxurious country inn and restaurant 10 miles south of Perry, is an Old South dream come true for German electronics manufacturer Bernard Schneider. As a youngster in postwar Munich, Schneider was fascinated by *Gone With the Wind* and other movies depicting the romanticized antebellum South. In the 1980s Schneider bought 8,000 acres of farmland, began restoring vintage Southern country houses and cottages, and created Middle Georgia's nicest resort.

Guests stay in 28 designer-decorated rooms and suites with deluxe private baths, feather beds, fireplaces, stereos, TVs, and CD players. In the dining room, in the early 1900s Langston House, the European chef prepares upscale American and continental cuisine, with a full bar. Things to do include horseback riding, swimming in the outdoor pool, skeet shooting, fishing, and quail hunting. The formal gardens have become a favorite place for weddings and outdoor events. Take I-75 exit 127 and go 1 mile south to GA 26 in the unincorporated community of Henderson. Moderate to expensive double occupancy rates include full breakfast. Phone (478) 988-8696 or (888) 615-9722 or visit www.hendersonvillage.com.

The *Museum of Aviation and Georgia Aviation Hall of Fame* (GA 247 and Russell Parkway, Warner Robins, 478-926-6870, 888-807-3359, www .museumofaviation.org), 2 miles south of Warner Robins Air Force Base, Warner Robins, is the second largest US Air Force museum and a tribute to our winged military might. In 4 huge buildings you can admire more than 100 military aircraft and missiles. You can also see a film on the history of the Air Force and numerous exhibits and displays. The Aviation Hall of Fame honors men and women who have made significant contributions to aviation in Georgia. Take I-75 exit 146 (Centerville/Warner Robins) and follow the signs through the city of Warner Robins. Open daily from 9 a.m. to 5 p.m. Free admission.

Barbecue is dear to Georgians' hearts, celebrated in song and story, and exalted at annual festivals such as the Big Pig Jig the first weekend of November at the little middle-Georgia town of Vienna (pronounced "VIGH-enna"). Dubbed the "Cadillac of Barbecue Contests" and proclaimed the state of Georgia's official barbecue cooking contest by the state legislature, this is serious business indeed. The winning team takes home prize money, trophies, bragging rights, and the honor of representing Georgia at the annual World Championship Barbeque Cooking Contest in Memphis, Tennessee—and just maybe coming back as world champion of the barbecuing arts.

Of course, there's a fun side to all this serious business. Judges sample the secret sauces, which, according to the rules, may include "any nonpoisonous substances," and the flavors and textures of ribs, shoulders, and other succulent portions of the porkers. Famished festivalgoers also get their chance to savor the entries in a "People's Choice" competition and take part in a host of other activities. There's always plenty of bluegrass and country music, square dancing and clog dancing, arts and crafts, a 5-kilometer "Hog Jog," and a "Whole Hog Parade," featuring handsome porkers, still not ready for the grill, decked out in all manner of zany costumes.

For information, contact Dooly County Chamber of Commerce, 117 E. Union St., Vienna, (229) 268-8275, www.doolychamber.com and www.bigpig jig.com.

Cotton may no longer be king, but it's still important to the economy of Dooly and other southeastern Georgia counties. At harvest time in September and October, the white bolls cover the ground like fresh-fallen snow. The **Georgia Cotton Museum** (I-75 exit 109, Vienna, 229-268-2045, www.historic vienna.com/museum), created by farmers and other Dooly Countians, looks at "white gold's" past, present, and future with artifacts, displays, and tools that planted, plowed, and harvested the cotton in the days before mechanized farming. It also looks at the dark side, the slave labor that was vital to its production. It's at 1321 E. Union St., Vienna. Open Mon through Sat from 9 a.m. to 4:30 p.m. Admission is free.

Hawkinsville, the Pulaski County seat, is Georgia's harness racing capital. The **Harness Racing Festival** (www.hawkinsvilleharnessfestival.com), the last weekend of April, celebrates this sport, which has been a part of Pulaski County's life since the late 1800s, when the county's mild climate made it a popular winter training grounds for harness horses from the Midwest, the Northeast, and Canada.

Nowadays, more than 350 of the sleek, high-stepping trotters and pacers come to the town of 4,000 between October and April. On the 2-day festival weekend, more than 10,000 spectators crowd the grandstand at the festival grounds to watch the races and enjoy the country fair atmosphere that surrounds the red clay track. For those not familiar with the sport, the horses have two decidedly different gaits. Pacers wear plastic leg hoops (called hobbles) that cause the legs on each side of their body to move in tandem: left front and left rear, right front and right rear. Trotters navigate with a diagonal gait: left front and right rear legs move together, likewise right front and left rear. They seem to effortlessly pull the colorfully silked jockeys riding behind them in light two-wheeled sulkies.

After the festival the horses pack up and head for the big-money tracks up north. One thing missing from the event is parimutuel betting. Georgia law prohibits it, but that doesn't mean you can't find some friendly unofficial wagers around the track. For information, call the Lawrence Bennett harness training facility at (478) 892-3240. It's on US 129, Hawkinsville.

Away from the track, Hawkinsville's main attraction is its restored early-20th-century opera house. Built in early 1907 as a stop on the vaudeville circuit between New York and New Orleans, the **Old Opera House** was abandoned in the 1950s and was about to fall totally into ruins when a group of Pulaski County businesspeople came to its rescue a few years ago. Now it hosts touring concerts and local productions. If you're here when an event is scheduled, come and spend a nostalgic evening in the restored horseshoe-shaped auditorium at 100 N. Lumpkin St., Hawkinsville (478-783-1884, www.hawkinsville operahouse.com).

Several antiques shops are on Broad Street, Hawkinsville's main street. For other information contact **Hawkinsville-Pulaski County Chamber of Commerce** at 108 N. Lumpkin St., Hawkinsville, (478) 783-1717, www.hawkinsville chamber.org.

Lovers of finely crafted cemetery art should have a "Kodak moment" at **Orphans Cemetery** in Eastman. It's the legacy of the late Albert G. "A. G." Williamson. Born in North Carolina in the mid-1800s, Williamson and his five brothers were orphaned by the Civil War and moved to Dodge County, where they were collectively known as "The Orphans." A. G., the oldest, became a wealthy landowner. In 1887 he learned of the untimely death of a neighbor's 3-year-old son and deeded land for Orphans Cemetery, across from Orphans Christian Church. He planted a magnolia tree by the boy's grave that still blooms every summer. Before his own death, Williamson commissioned a sculptor in Carrara, Italy (where Michelangelo found the right stuff for *David*), to carve the cemetery's masterpiece, a marble-columned canopy with life-size statues of himself, his wife, and nephew for the family mausoleum. The sculptor created the realistic images with only photos to work from. Eastman is on US 341, between McRae and Hawkinsville. Contact the Eastman/Dodge County Chamber of Commerce Welcome Center: 116 9th Ave., Eastman, (478) 374-4723, www.eastman-georgia.com.

Jay Bird Springs Ministries, a recreation area in the small community of Chauncey, 4 miles south of Eastman, owes its beginnings to an accident that became a legend. In the 1800s a logger who injured his leg allegedly followed a blue jay to a natural spring bubbling from the ground. He bathed his leg in the spring's mineral waters and was healed. When word got around, people came to test the waters for themselves. Sensing an opportunity, the landowner built a 60-foot-by-100-foot spring-fed swimming pool, the oldest pool in the state of Georgia. Over the years, owners added a water slide and roller-skating rink, ball fields, picnic grounds, putt-putt golf, and campgrounds. In 2011, the church that owns Jay Bird opted to make the facility private. It is open now to groups and for reunions, catering to those wanting to heal their spirits as well as their bodies. The park is off US 341, at 1221 Jay Bird Springs Rd., Chauncey (229-868-2728).

The Lauren County city of Dublin's 19th-century Irish heritage is reflected in its annual **St. Patrick's Day Festival**, a lively round of parades, beauty pageants, arts and crafts, square dancing, softball, and golf tournaments. Along the emerald-green lawns of the city's **Bellevue Avenue**, many photogenic Greek Revival and Victorian showplaces parade year-round. Less genteel, but a lot of good-natured fun, **East Dublin's Redneck Games**, in late May, pits competitors in such feats as armpit serenade, bobbing for pigs' feet in plastic buckets, the hubcap hurl, watermelon seed spitting, and pond diving—judged on your form as you belly flop into a gooey pit of wet Georgia red clay. Dublin radio station WQZY-FM came up with the games to spoof Atlanta's 1996 Summer Olympics. They expected 500 people to show. Instead, there were 5,000. Today the games are their own entity. For information call (478) 696-3202 or visit www.summerredneckgames.com.

George L. Smith State Park, off US 23, 4 miles southeast of Twin City, is a quiet retreat with 21 fully equipped camping sites, furnished cottages, picnic areas, and a fishing lake with rental boats. An 1880s covered bridge with a working gristmill is the park's scenic landmark. Cornmeal from the mill is sold in the park office. Call (478) 763-2759 or (800) 864-PARK for camping reservations or visit www.gastateparks.org/georgelsmith. Two very nice bed-and-breakfasts are in the Emanuel County seat of Swainsboro: **Coleman House** (323 N. Main St., 478-237-9100, www.facebook.com/colemanhouseinn) and **Edenfield House Inn** (426 W. Church St., 478-237-3007). Both are inexpensive.

Michael Guido Gardens is a lush little oasis 2 miles from I-16 exit 104 at Metter and one of the reasons the town's motto is "It's better in Metter."

AUTHOR'S FAVORITES

Vidalia Onion Festival	Stephen C. Foster State Park
Big Pig Jig	Lamar Q. Ball Jr. Raptor Center
Harness Racing Festival	Folkston Funnel
Okefenokee Swamp Park	East Dublin's Redneck Games
Suwannee Canal Recreation Area	Fitzgerald's Wild Chicken Festival

Adjoining Sower Studios, where TV evangelist Michael Guido, D.D., produces his national *Seed from the Sower* broadcasts, "God's Three Acres" is planted with shade trees, flowers, Biblical topiaries, and a topiary of Guido himself. Fountains and waterfalls splash, birds sing, and a brook winds past gazebos, benches, and a 24/7 chapel. In December the gardens are illuminated with Christmas lights and Nativity scenes. Visitors can tour the broadcast studios Mon through Fri and meet the Sower in person. The gardens are open daily, free of charge, at 600 Lewis St., Metter (912-685-2222, www.sowerministries.org). As you exit I-16, stop at the Metter Welcome Center, in a former lumber company commissary, for information on Guido Gardens and other area attractions. Phone (912) 685-6988, (888) 704-3431, or visit www.metter-candler.com.

Magnolia Springs State Park, US 25, 5 miles north of Millen, is one of the prettiest and quietest in the whole park system. Huge old trees bend their limbs over crystal clear springs flowing at an estimated 9 million gallons a day. With more than 1,000 acres to explore, it's a lovely spot to spread a picnic. You can also swim, dabble your bait for fish, and walk along nature trails. You may even want to camp out overnight or stay in a furnished cottage. There is a $5 per visit parking fee. For camping and cottage reservations contact Magnolia Springs State Park: Route 5, Box 488, Millen, (478) 982-1660 or (800) 864-PARK, www.gastateparks.org.

Tree shaded *Statesboro* (population 21,000) is the Bulloch County seat and home of 14,000 Georgia Southern University students. The *University Museum* (912-681-5444, www.ceps.georgiasouthern.edu/museum) has a fascinating collection of dinosaur fossils, do-touch exhibits, and revolving scientific and technological displays. The "star" attraction is the Plant Vogtle Whale, a 45-million-year-old leviathan that scientists believe walked on sturdy legs. It was discovered at Georgia Power Company's Plant Vogtle in neighboring Burke County. The museum is open 9 a.m. to 5 p.m. Mon through Fri and 2 to 5 p.m. on Sat and Sun. Admission is $2 per person.

The *Center for Wildlife Education and Lamar Q. Ball Jr. Raptor Center* (Georgia Southern University, Statesboro, 800-568-3301 and 912-681-0831, www.welcomegeorgiasouthern.edu/wildlife) is Georgia Southern's most popular attraction. Visitors follow a self-guided nature walk through 6 natural habitats that house 14 birds of prey native to Georgia. They include bald eagles, falcons, ospreys, hawks, and several types of owls. They were rescued after being injured and can't return to the wild. Look up and you'll see a bald eagle camped in a hot tub–size aerie in the forks of a live oak tree, an osprey perched on a limb overlooking a cypress swamp, and a barred owl roosting in the rafters of an old barn strung with sheaves of drying tobacco. The center was designed by naturalist Jim

Fowler, former host of *Mutual of Omaha's Wild Kingdom* TV series. Fowler also designed Albany's Chehaw Wild Animal Park. The center is open Mon through Fri from 9 a.m. to 5 p.m. and Sat and Sun from 1 to 5 p.m. It is closed during summer months (June, July, and Aug). Admission is $2 for adults and $1 for children. A special program is held daily at 3:30 p.m. and is free with admission.

Near the campus, the 10-acre **Botanical Gardens** grow around a restored 19th-century farmhouse and outbuildings. The gardens are open dawn to dusk daily; free admission, ceps.georgiasouthern.edu/garden. After trekking around the gardens, bring your best boardinghouse reach to the **Beaver House Inn & Restaurant,** 121 S. Main St., Statesboro, (912) 764-2821, www.beaverhouseinn .com. The dining room table groans under a delicious family-style buffet that includes fried chicken, fish, baked ham, roast beef, and numerous vegetables, relishes, and desserts. It's open for lunch daily, dinner daily except Sun. Vandy's Barbecue, downtown at 22 Vine St., Statesboro, (912) 764-2444, www .vandysbbqstatesboro.com, is another culinary landmark.

The Victorian/Federal-style **Statesboro Inn and Restaurant,** built in 1872, is a lovely bed-and-breakfast near downtown Statesboro and the Georgia Southern campus. It's located at 106 S. Main St., Statesboro (912-489-8628 or 800-846-9466, www.statesboroinn.com). Architectural features include a spacious veranda, Palladian windows, and numerous brass and wood treatments. Guests stay in the main house or the adjacent Craftsman-style Brannen House. All 19 rooms have private baths, antiques, phones, and cable TV. The dining room's upscale fare features duck, chicken, seafood, beef, and elegant desserts. Dinner Mon through Sat. Moderate.

Statesboro is a short drive north of I-16 exit 116, 60 miles west of Savannah. Contact the Convention and Visitors Bureau: 332 S. Main St., Statesboro, (800) 568-3301, or log on to www.visitstatesboro.com.

Vidalia Sweet Onions, Fruitcakes & Rattlesnakes

The sandy soil of Toombs, Treutlen, and neighboring southeastern Georgia counties yields a favorite gourmet delicacy. The well-known **Vidalia sweet onion** takes its name from the Toombs County town of Vidalia. During the summer, you can buy 'em by the sackful or carload at roadside stands in and around the town of 10,000. For information on farm tours, phone (912) 538-8687 or visit www.vidaliaga.com. The Sweet Onion Festival (www.vidaliaonionfestival.com), the third weekend of April, is the chance to sample the "fruit" in many tasty ways.

Claxton, seat of Evans County, a short drive south of I-16 exit 116, is famous for fruitcakes and rattlesnakes. As you drive into the small town, you're very nearly intoxicated by the sweet aroma of baking fruitcakes. More than 6 million pounds of the holiday treats are produced annually in Claxton's modern bakeries making the town the self-proclaimed "Fruitcake Capital of the World." You can get information on *fruitcake plant tours* and other area attractions at the Claxton Welcome Center, 4 N. Duval St., Claxton, (912) 739-1391, www .claxtonevanschamber.com.

If you're here in mid-March, you can take part in the festivities surrounding the annual *Rattlesnake Roundup.* Begun simply in 1968 as an effort to reduce the venomous reptile's threat to man and beast, the roundup has grown into a major happening, with a parade, hundreds of arts and crafts booths, home cooking, and such rattler-related events as awards for the most snakes brought in, the longest, the fattest, and so on. A reptile expert "milks" the snakes of their deadly venom, which is used in antivenom serums and other medicines.

Ever wonder what 25 million crickets sound like? The answer is at *Armstrong's Cricket Farm* (306 Gordon St., Glennville, 15 miles south of I-16 exit 116/GA 301/US 25, 912-654-3408, www.armstrongcrickets.com) in Glennville. Purportedly the world's largest cricket farm, Armstrong's sells and ships buckets full of the chirping insects to anglers and reptile farms, where they're fed to snakes, frogs, and lizards. Owner Jeff Armstrong says, "One cricket in a room will drive you crazy, but 25 million sound like a big humming engine." Find out for yourself at the cricket farm, which is open Mon through Sat.

In neighboring Tattnall County, *Gordonia-Altamaha State Park,* 322 Park Ln., US 280 West, Reidsville, (912) 557-7744, has 5 cottages, 29 tent and trailer sites with water and electricity, hot showers, and restrooms, as well as a swimming pool, a boat dock, and plenty of good fishing places on its 12-acre lake. There's also an 18-hole golf course. Call (800) 864-PARK or log on to www.gastateparks.org for camping reservations.

If you're a fishing family, you may come close to nirvana in Wayne County. One county removed from the Atlantic Coast, Wayne includes 60 miles of the *Altamaha River,* a waterway rich with several varieties of bass, bream, perch, and catfish. *Altamaha River Campground* (249 Joe Naia Rd., Jesup, 912-586-6300) has 3 big fishing lakes, a spring-fed swimming lake, campsites, and nature trails. It also has some of the best bird-watching around.

Lake Grace, on US 301 near the Wayne County seat of Jesup, is a local favorite. The 250 acres include plenty of secluded fishing spots, as well as opportunities for boating, swimming, waterskiing, picnics, and camping. Contact the park superintendent at (912) 579-6475.

Pine Lake Campground (555 Gardi Rd., Jesup, 912-427-3664), US 341 near the small community of Gardi, features a stocked 20-acre lake tailored for bank fishing. You can also enjoy a swimming pool, shaded picnic areas, and 40 campsites with electricity, water, and restrooms.

Jaycee Landing Bait and Tackle and Campground (912-588-9222), on US 301 north, Jesup, has a number of boat ramps in the Altamaha River, as well as a general store with food and all your favorite kinds of fishing bait. Campsites have water, electricity, restrooms, and showers.

For more information on recreational lakes and rivers, working farm tours, golf courses, fairs, and festivals, contact the Jesup-Wayne County Chamber of Commerce, 124 N.W. Broad St., Jesup, (912) 427-2028, (888) 224-5983, www .waynetourism.com.

When you've bagged your limit, enjoy a large sample of Southeast Georgia cooking at *Jones' Kitchen,* 526 N. Cherry St., in Jesup, (912) 427-4100. The all-you-can-eat daily luncheon spread includes fresh local fish, chicken, meat loaf, vegetables, several kinds of salads, and a peach or apple cobbler for less than you'd pay for lunch at a fast-food outlet.

Jesup, population 10,400, has a number of beautifully maintained Victorian homes, which you can drive past with a brochure provided by the chamber of commerce.

The *Edwin L. Hatch Nuclear Plant Visitors Center,* on US 1 (11036 Hatch Pkwy., Baxley), 14 miles north of the center of Baxley, will tell you all you ever wanted to know about this controversial source of energy. The story is told with films, hands-on exhibits, and animated displays. Open Mon through Fri from 8:30 a.m. to 5 p.m. Phone (912) 367-3668 or (800) 722-7774, or log on to www.baxley.org. Admission is free.

A one-of-a-kind treasure is the *Moody Forest Natural Area* on East River Road. Moody is one of the nation's last remaining old growth forests and its 4,426 acres contains long leaf pines upwards of 300 years old and massive Tupelo cypress trees estimated to be about 600 years old. It is also home to many rare birds, plants, and animals. Open dawn to dusk (912-366-9549).

You can unwind at 170-acre *Lake Mayers,* a locally popular resort with fishing, boating, swimming, waterskiing, and picnic areas. Lake Mayers is off US 341, 8 miles west of Baxley, (912) 367-8190, www.baxley.org.

Nonmembers may play the *Appling Country Club's* 9-hole golf course, 4628 Hatch Pkwy., Baxley, (912) 367-3582. Contact Baxley-Appling County Tourism Board, 305 W. Parker St., Baxley, (912) 367-7731, www.baxley.org.

Land of Trembling Earth

Okefenokee Swamp Park, off US 1, 8 miles south of Waycross, is the most popular of three entrances to the vast, mysterious "Land of Trembling Earth."

Although most of the park is actually outside the boundaries of the 700 square mile, 412,000-acre Okefenokee Swamp National Wildlife Refuge, guided boat tours and cypress boardwalks lead you well into this fascinating world.

The Swamp Park is the most casual, visitor-oriented of the three entrances—the others are in neighboring Charlton County—with numerous exhibits, interpretive centers, wildlife shows, and other visual displays.

Stop first at the cedar-roofed welcome center adjacent to the paved parking areas. Mounted wildlife exhibits and the real thing viewed through one-way windows, along with a 20-minute film, are an excellent orientation. From there, climb the 90-foot observation tower, peer into the dark tannic waters from the boardwalk, and see some of the Okefenokee's three dozen varieties of reptiles at the Serpentarium.

Gate admission—$12 for adults, $11 for seniors and children 3 to 11, free for children under age 2—includes all exhibits and shows. The Low Water boat tour ($20) takes you through some of the original Seminole Indian waterways and includes an even more extensive look at the hundreds of species of birds, otter, armadillo, black bear, deer, and other critters that inhabit the swamp. You'll also see some of the 15,000 gators as they cruise among the reeds and cypresses like ironclad gunboats.

Or hop aboard the "Lady Suwannee" steam engine and the Okefenokee Railroad. The 1.5 mile ride takes you through key parts of the swamp that make up the headwaters of the Suwannee River immortalized by songwriter Stephen Foster.

Okefenokee Swamp Park (US 1 South, Waycross, 912-283-0583, www .okeswamp.com) is open daily in spring and summer from 9 a.m. to 5:30 p.m., fall and winter from 9 a.m. to 5:30 p.m.

Mummified Dog

Pity poor "Stuckie," the hound that chased a rabbit up a hollow tree and ended up as mummified and as immortalized as Old King Tut. Displayed at the Southern Forest World Museum, 1440 N. Augusta Ave., Waycross, (912) 285-4056, the unfortunate 4-year-old brown-and-white doggie was discovered, years after his demise, by loggers who were cutting his "tomb" into pulpwood. A chimney effect in the hollow tree created upward drafts of air that kept his scent from insects and predators. The tree also provided a relatively dry environment, and its tannic acid leatherized Stuckie's skin and even preserved his last, terrified howl for help. While you're here, you can walk through a giant loblolly pine, listen to a talking tree, and view exhibits on forest management by the timber companies that support the museum. Open Tues through Sat 9 a.m. to 4:30 p.m. Adults $3; children under 5 are free.

Two other attractions also mirror the swamp's colorful heritage. *Obediah's Okefenok* (5115 Swamp Rd., Waycross, 912-287-0090, www.okefenokee swamp.com), on a small island at the swamp's southwestern edge, was the early 1800s home of the Obediah Barber family. Their restored cabin and outbuildings are filled with authentic tools and household necessities. With boardwalks snaking through the wetlands, Obediah's is open daily. Admission is $6.50 for adults, $5.50 for seniors 55 and older, and $5 for children 3 to 17.

The *Okefenokee Heritage Center,* 1460 N. Augusta Ave. near downtown Waycross, is an indoor/outdoor museum with historical displays, artwork, a 1912 locomotive and depot, an 1840s farmhouse, a print shop, and antique vehicles. Open Tues through Sat 10 a.m. to 4:30 p.m. Admission is $3, children under 3 are free. Call (912) 285-4260 or visit www.okefenokeeheritagecenter.org.

Nearby *Laura S. Walker State Park and Golf Course* (5653 Laura Walker Rd., Waycross, 912-287-4900, has RV sites and campsites with water, electricity, showers, and restrooms ($27 to $24 per night); a swimming pool; a playground; a golf course; fishing; and picnic tables. There is a $5 parking fee. For reservations call (800) 864-PARK or visit www.gastateparks.org, or contact Waycross and Okefenokee Tourism Bureau, 315-A Plant Ave., Waycross, (912) 283-3744, www.okefenokeetourism.com.

Three gateways lead you into the primeval mysteries of the 412,000-acre *Okefenokee Swamp National Wildlife Refuge* (www.okefenokee.com). Suwannee Canal Recreation Area and Stephen C. Foster State Park are in Charlton County, while the Okefenokee Swamp Park is near Waycross, in Ware County.

Administered by the US Fish and Wildlife Service, *Suwannee Canal Recreation Area* is what remains of one man's frustrated efforts to drain the Okefenokee back in the 1880s. He left behind an 11-mile-long waterway that now provides an easy avenue for boaters, anglers, and sightseers. *Okefenokee Adventures* (4150 Suwannee Canal Rd., Folkston, 912-496-7156, 866-THE-SWAMP, www.okefenokeeadventures.com) is the US Fish and Wildlife Service's concessionaire. It offers 1- and 2-hour daytime, nighttime, and overnight guided boat tours through the swamp, where you'll see many of the swamp's thousands of gators, turtles, fish, egrets, heron, and other bird species, and learn a great deal about this primordial environment. The tour boats are covered with a canopy, but be sure to bring sunscreen, insect repellent, and bottled water. You can also rent motorboats, canoes, kayaks, and bicycles. But be aware that getting lost in the swamp's many tributaries is very easy. The Concession Building stocks groceries, cold drinks, fishing gear, bug spray, and other necessities. The Camp Cornelia Cafe prepares sandwiches and salads. Open daily.

The nearby Richard S. Bolt Visitors Center is the refuge's official welcome center and has a 15-minute orientation film and interpretive exhibits on the swamp's plant and animal life, some of which you can see from nature trails, a boardwalk, and an observation tower.

A short drive from the concession building and museum, *Chesser Island Homestead* is the pine and cypress cabin once home to several generations of the Chesser family.

Suwannee Canal Recreation Area (Route 2, Box 336, Folkston, 912-496-7836), is open daily sunrise to sunset. A $5 gate fee is charged at the Folkston entrance by the Okefenokee Swamp National Wildlife Refuge. Drive on GA121/US 23 for 8 miles south of Folkston, then turn right (west) at the Okefenokee Refuge sign and continue 3 miles.

Stephen C. Foster State Park, (912) 637-5274, is so far off Georgia's beaten path that the shortest way to get there from Suwannee Canal is a loop detour through northeastern Florida. From Suwannee Canal, drive 15 miles south on US 23 to St. George, 37 miles west on GA 94 and GA 2 in Florida, and back into Georgia at Fargo. From Fargo, go right on GA 177 and for 18 miles cross a domain of sentinel pines and palmetto thickets, swampy canals, egrets, great blue heron, deer, gators, armadillos, opossum, raccoons, reptiles, and amphibians. Beyond a sign warning that the gates close between sundown and sunup, you arrive at Stephen Foster's compound.

The state park is an 80-acre island entirely within the Okefenokee Swamp National Wildlife Refuge. Rangers conduct boat tours, replete with swamp legends and lore, practical lessons in fauna and flora, and lots of hilarious tall tales. You're bound to see plenty of gators, exotic birds and plants, turtles, and trees. You may also rent boats and canoes and venture forth on your own. There are also a 0.25-mile hiking trail, picnic shelters, a playground, and a small museum.

Staying overnight, serenaded by the symphony of the swamp, is an unforgettable experience. Campsites with electricity, water, hot showers, and restrooms are available, as are 2-bedroom cottages completely furnished with full kitchens and fireplaces, heat, and air-conditioning. There is a $5 per visit parking fee. The park's small grocery has minimal supplies, so be sure to stock up before leaving Fargo.

The park is open from 7 a.m. to 7 p.m. from mid-Sept to the end of Feb and from 6:30 a.m. to 8:30 p.m. from Mar 1 to mid-Sept. For cottage and camping reservations call (800) 864-PARK or log on to www.gastateparks.org. When the gates are locked at night, only a dire emergency will open them before sunrise. This is done to protect you from roaming critters and the critters from roaming poachers. Also, bear in mind that a swamp is full of mosquitoes, other biting pests, and uncomfortable summer heat and humidity. Bring insect repellent and dress comfortably. In addition to the Folkston route, you may get to the park on US 441 to Fargo.

If you're wondering where everybody in *Folkston* is most any time of day, check out the covered platform that overlooks the *"Folkston Funnel,"* twin sets of tracks that carry more than 70 trains a day through the town of 2,300. Day and night, hundreds of Folkston folks and out-of-towners gather on the 32-foot-long, 15-foot-wide platform 2 blocks west of US 301. Train-spotting passion was sparked by Marvin "Cookie" Williams, an avid model-train collector whose enthusiasm for the real thing attracted others to the sport and led to a tourism development grant that funded the platform. While they're spotting passenger trains, coal trains, refrigerator cars, orange juice trains from Florida, military transports, and trains carrying chemicals and timber, the "spotters" enjoy the platform's camaraderie, picnic tables, grill, ceiling fans, and floodlights that illuminate trains that pass in the night. For information contact Folkston City Hall, (912) 496-2536, www.folkston.com.

Valdosta & the Great Southeast

Depending on your perspective, *Lowndes County* is either the jumping-off place for Florida or your reentry point to Georgia. With 109,000 residents, Lowndes is Georgia's 16th most populous county. Valdosta, the county seat, with close to 55,500 residents, is the state's 10th largest city. With so much traffic flowing back and forth from Florida on I-75, much of the city is devoted to chain motels, fast-food strips, and factory outlet malls. Behind these contemporary distractions, under canopies of live oaks and palm trees and banks of azaleas and camellias, the city has many historic homes, churches, and public buildings.

Stop for free information and the Historic Tours self-guided map at the Valdosta-Lowndes County Convention and Visitors Bureau's Tourism Information Center off I-75 exit 16, One Meeting Place, Valdosta, (229) 245-0513 and (800) 569-8687, www.valdostatourism.com. Among the 26 landmarks, the most outstanding is *The Crescent.* Built in 1898 at a cost of $12,000 by Valdosta educator Colonel William S. West, the grand 23-room neoclassical mansion is graced by 13 Doric columns supporting a crescent-shaped portico. In 1913 President Woodrow Wilson attended a gala dinner in the ballroom. Now maintained by the Valdosta Garden Center, the mansion has been restored to its original grandeur and appointed with many original furnishings and period antiques. Guided tours Mon through Fri, 2 to 5 p.m. Donations accepted. The gardens are always in bloom. It's at 904 N. Patterson St., Valdosta, (229) 244-6747, www.valdostagardencenter.com.

You're driving through south Georgia on a hot summer day. The kids are cranky, and you can't wait to see Orlando. Outside of Valdosta, a billboard advertises **Wild Adventures Theme Park,** "Over 100 Rides & Attractions." Stop for the day or a couple of days—you might forget all about Florida. True to its billing, Wild Adventures (I-75 exit 13, 3766 Old Clyattville Rd., Valdosta, 229-559-1330, 800-808-0872, www.wildadventures.com) has 100 things to see and do, without the crowds and lines at the Florida theme parks. Nine roller coasters and 11 water rides range from wild to mild. A tram puts you up close and personal with elephants, antelopes, zebra, lions, tigers, kangaroos, wallabies, birds, monkeys, and reptiles. You can pet small animals and hand-feed giraffe. A yearly concert calendar, included in gate admission, features top-name celebrities like Sugarland, Trisha Yearwood, Alabama, Wynonna, and Lynyrd Skynyrd. Daily admission is $45.99 for adults, and $40.99 for ages 3 to 9 and those age 55 and over. Season passes start at $69.99.

Before heading on, relax awhile at Valdosta's parks, boating and fishing lakes, and public golf courses and tennis courts.

The small Lowndes County town of **Hahira,** north of Valdosta at I-75 exit 84, is a center of Georgia's tobacco industry. From July to Oct you can witness the age-old ritual of tobacco auctioning at the town's warehouses. If you're here the first week of October, drop by the **Hahira Honeybee Festival.** To get the buzz on what's happening in town, and enjoy good home cooking, take a seat for breakfast or lunch at **The City Cafe** on Main Street. The Hahira Chamber of Commerce, 102 S. Church St., Hahira, (229) 794-2567, www.hahira .ga.us, offers tobacco and honey tours.

At **Reed Bingham State Park,** off GA 37, Adel, 6 miles west of Adel, the Cook County seat, you can go boating, fishing, waterskiing, and swimming on a 375-acre lake. The park also has a nature trail, campsites, and picnic grounds—and one rather unusual event. **Buzzard Day,** the first Sat of Dec, hails the thousands of buzzards that roost in the park each winter. Enjoy arts and crafts and musical entertainment while you watch the skies, or choose to take part in the 10K "Road Kill Run." Phone (229) 896-3551. For campsite reservations call (800) 864-PARK or log on to www.gastateparks.org.

The **Jefferson Davis Memorial State Historic Site,** GA 32, in the small community of Irwinville, commemorates the site where the Confederate president was captured by Union troops on May 10, 1865. The museum has Civil War artifacts and part of the tree where Davis was standing when captured. A 13-acre park around the museum has nature trails and picnic areas. Open Wed through Sun from 9 a.m. to 5 p.m. Admission is $4 for adults, $2.75 for children. Phone (229) 831-2335.

In *Douglas,* stop first at the Douglas Area Welcome Center in the historic *Ashley-Slater House* (211 S. Gaskin St., 912-384-1873 and 888-426-3334, www.douglasga.org). The neoclassical 1912 mansion is furnished with original antiques, a 70-foot pastoral mural in the dining room, and (some say) ghosts of the original owners, who can't bear to depart from their lovely home.

Railroad buffs will enjoy the *Heritage Station Museum's* exhibits in the old Georgia & Florida train depot in downtown Douglas (912-389-3461). Other exhibits highlight Coffee County's abundant agriculture. Open Thurs through Sat 10 a.m. to 4 p.m. Admission $1. Several antiques shops and gift shops are in the Main Street City's vibrant downtown.

Broxton Rocks Preserve, 778 pristine acres north of Douglas, contains some of the most dramatic outcrops of ancient sandstone in the southeastern United States. Formations sculpted by rivers millions of years ago, and dense woodlands and swampy bogs, are home to more than 500 species of plants, birds, and animals, many of them threatened and endangered. Entrance to the Rocks is by appointment with the Nature Conservancy of Georgia, which owns the property (404-253-7216) or the City of Douglas Tourism Office (912-384-4555).

General Coffee State Park, 46 John Coffee Rd., Nicholl, 6 miles east of the center of Douglas, offers a wealth of recreational opportunities. You can fish the lake and streams for catfish, gar, and bream, and swim in the outdoor pool. A nature trail winding through the wooded 1,490-acre park puts you in photo range of many species of birds, reptiles, deer, and other critters. There are also playgrounds and picnic shelters. Heritage Farm has nature trails, wildlife habitats, antique farm equipment, a cane mill, and barnyard animals. There are also almost 13.5 miles of equestrian trails for horse lovers. You can stay overnight in full-service campsites and in a group cabin sleeping 36. Phone (912) 384-7082. For camping and cabin reservations call (800) 864-PARK or log on to www.gastateparks.org.

In Douglas, home to South Georgia College and a pretty college town of 15,000 folks, you can play the 18-hole *Beaver Kreek Golf Club* course (485 Beaver Creek Rd., Douglas, 912-384-8230, www.breaverkreekgolf.com), or you might want to try your swing at the 9-hole *Douglas Community Golf Course* (440 Elton D. Brooks Blvd. South, Douglas, 912-384-7353). Rental clubs are available at both. After your round, drive into Douglas's revived downtown area—it's one of Georgia's Main Street Program cities—and enjoy dinner Tues through Sat at *Fern Bank Bar & Grill* (235 Peterson Ave. South, Douglas, 912-384-4385), a historic brick-walled building with good steaks, seafood, and Southern dishes and many relics from the city's past.

The small town of *Fitzgerald* (population 9,000) is a living memorial to the nation's post–Civil War reunification. In the 1890s Indiana newspaper

TOP ANNUAL EVENTS

St. Patrick's Day Festival
March 17, Dublin
(912) 272-5546
www.dublinstpatricks.com

Old South Farm Days
mid-March, Tea Grove Plantation,
Walthourville
(912) 368-7412

Harness Racing Festival
third weekend in April, Hawkinsville
(912) 783-1717
www.hawkinsvilleharnessfestival.com

Baxley Tree Festival
early April, Tri-County Fairgrounds,
Baxley
(912) 367-7731
www.baxley.org

Mossy Creek Barnyard Festival
mid-April and Mid-October, I-75 near
Perry
(912) 922-8265
www.mossycreekfestival.com

**Okefenokee Art Festival & Earth Day
Celebration**
mid-April, Okefenokee National Wildlife
Refuge, Folkston
(912) 897-1184
www.okefenokeeadventures.com

Vidalia Onion Festival
late April–early May
(912) 538-8687
www.vidaliaonionfestival.com

Redneck Games
early July, East Dublin
(478) 272-4422
www.summerredneckgames.com

Fitzgerald's Wild Chicken Festival
mid-March
(800) 386-4642
www.wildchickenfestival.com

Georgia National Fair
early October, Georgia National
Fairgrounds & Agricenter, Perry
(912) 988-6483
www.georgianationalfair.com

Big Pig Jig
second weekend in October, Vienna
(912) 268-4500
www.bigpigjig.com

Buzzard Day
first Saturday of December, Reed
Bingham State Park, Adel
(912) 896-3551

**Celebration of Lights and Winter
Wonderland**
early December, Baxley
(912) 367-7731

publisher P. H. Fitzgerald envisioned a place where he and other Union veterans could live in peace with their former Southern foes. When Ben Hill County farmers sent trainloads of food in response to a Midwestern drought, it became the chosen place. The town was laid out on a grid, with streets on the west side named for Confederate generals, those on the east side for Union generals. Other streets were named for Northern and Southern trees and flowers.

The ***Blue and Gray Museum*** in the former train depot at 116 N. Johnston St., Fitzgerald, displays thousands of Civil War artifacts, including uniforms, weapons, newspaper articles about Lincoln's assassination, and the history of this unique town. *Marching As One,* a professionally produced documentary film, tells the story of Fitzgerald's founding with rare archival photographs of the city's early years. The Colony Days Gallery exhibits clothing, china, glassware, cooking utensils, and other items that tell the story of women in the city's first struggling years. The museum is open Tues through Sat from 10 a.m. to 4 p.m. and Sun from 1 to 5 p.m. Adults $3, students $1. Phone (229) 426-5069, (800) 386-4642, or visit www.fitzgeraldga.org.

All those chickens crossing the roads in Fitzgerald are the result of an experiment gone "afowl." In the 1960s, the Georgia Department of Natural Resources released flocks of Burmese junglefowl, with brilliant orange, yellow, and black plumage, on the Ocmulgee River, a few miles from the city. They were supposed to be a new kind of game bird, but many of them migrated into town and liked it so well they stayed and raised families. They now number about 2,500 to 5,000. Although the chickens' messy manners rile some home-owners and businesses, the city bows to a no-win situation and makes them the honored guests at the **Wild Chicken Festival** in late March (www .wildchickenfestival.com).

You usually need to commit a crime to merit "time." Seventeen miles west of Fitzgerald is Ashburn's **Crime and Punishment Museum,** where you just pay your "dime." The museum is located in a former jail that housed inmates upstairs and the jailers and their families downstairs. The fortress was built in 1906 at a cost of $10,000, and was known to inmates and Turner Countians as "Castle Turner" for its ornate Romanesque architecture. Jailers and their families kept the grounds so attractively landscaped, travelers sometimes mistook it for a hotel.

Today visitors can experience the original draconian cells, the death cell, the hanging hook, and the trapdoor, where, in the interest of time and economy, two felons could be dispatched at a time.

After the grim tour, visitors are ushered into the cheerful Last Meal Cafe, where Southern-style comfort meals "to die for" are served in the jailers' former living quarters.

The Crime and Punishment Museum (241 E. College Ave., Ashburn, 800-471-9696, 229-567-9696, www.jailmuseum.com) is open Tues through Sat from 10 a.m. to 4:15 p.m. Adults $6, seniors $4, students $2. The Last Meal Cafe serves Tues through Sat from 11 a.m. to 1 p.m.

Before leaving Ashburn, take a gander at "The World's Largest Peanut," standing a majestic 20 feet tall, along I-75. Take exit 82/GA 107 into Ashburn and follow the signs to the Peanut and a gazebo, where you can have a tree-shaded picnic.

If you're around here the fourth weekend of March, join the fun of the annual Fire Ant Festival (www.fireantfestival.com). One of the highlights is the

Fire Ant Calling Contest. "You can call 'em any way you want," festival sponsors say, "but if they answer, you're in a whole heap o' trouble."

Until July 4, 1986, most motorists passed through the little Telfair County seat of **McRae,** 25 miles north of Fitzgerald, without a second thought. Nowadays, they have a reason to stop, get out of their cars, and take a picture. Right in the middle of town, where US 341, US 441, US 280, US 23, and US 319 come together, there's a replica of the Statue of Liberty, a Liberty Bell, and copies of the Declaration of Independence, the Constitution, and other documents. "Miss Liberty" stands 35 feet tall—a 1/12-scale reproduction of the original in New York Harbor. And she's entirely homemade: Her head is carved from a black gum tree stump from a nearby swamp, her torch is actually an insulated electrician's glove, and her fiberglass coating was created by a McRae boat manufacturer. Contact the Telfair County Chamber of Commerce at 120 E. Oak St., McRae, (229) 868-6365, www.telfairco.org.

Little Ocmulgee State Park, with *Pete Phillips Lodge and Convention Center,* off US 441, 2 miles north of McRae, is a resort park with lots of things to keep you happily occupied. The well-maintained 18-hole, par-72 Wallace Adams Golf Course has both carts and clubs available to rent at the pro shop. You can also swim, play tennis, and hike nature trails. Pete Phillips Lodge and Conference Center has 60 modern motel-type guest rooms, an outdoor pool, a full-service restaurant, and meeting rooms. You can also pitch your tent or park your RV in full service campsites and stay in furnished cottages. For camping, cottage, and lodge reservations, phone (800) 864-PARK or log on to www .gastateparks.org. For general information, contact the Park Superintendent: 80 Live Oak Trail, Helena, (229) 868-7474.

Places to Stay in Southeast Georgia

EASTMAN

Dodge Hill Inn
5021 9th Ave.
(478) 374-2644
www.dodgehillinn.com
Inexpensive

Ann and Don Dobbs are gracious hosts at this 1912 home, filled with antiques and original art. Five guest rooms have private baths, TV, refrigerators, and phones. Make yourselves at home in the parlor, read, and play the grand piano. Breakfast, included in the rate, is one of the best reasons for staying here. The huge spread includes fresh fruit, hot baked breads, ham, biscuits, pancakes, cheese grits, and eggs.

FOLKSTON

The Inn at Folkston
509 W. Main St.
(888) 509-6246
www.innatfolkston.com
Inexpensive
After a big day exploring the Okefenokee Swamp National Wildlife Refuge

or the Cumberland Island National Seashore, Janice Richtmyer and Bill Whitaker's restored 1920s heart-pine bungalow is only a few minutes away. Four spacious guest rooms have feather beds, private baths, and plenty of AC. You can recount your day's adventures in wicker chairs and rockers on the front veranda. Rates include full breakfast.

VIDALIA

The Inn at Still Pond
120 Sutton Way, Axson
(912) 816-0254
www.innatstillpond.com
Expensive
The Inn at Still Pond is located on a 6-acre lake in 150 acres of forest and provides a secluded and romantic getaway. Also on the grounds is a working certified organic farm. You can be assured the breakfast is hearty and healthy. The inn has 2 suites and 3 rooms available.

HOMERVILLE

The Helmstead
1 Fargo Rd.
(912) 487-2222
(888) 224-3567
(800) 502-6303
www.helmsteadbedand breakfast.com
Inexpensive, includes continental breakfast
Jane Helms's 4 guest rooms welcome business travelers and visitors to the neighboring Okefenokee

Swamp National Wildlife Refuge. Rooms have private baths.

UNADILLA

Sugar Hill Bed & Breakfast
2450 Sugar Hill Rd.
(478) 627-3557
www.sugarhillbedand breakfast.com
Inexpensive, includes full breakfast
Four guest rooms with private baths in a mid-1800s farmhouse 4 miles from I-75 exit 122. Also has a swimming pool.

STATESBORO

Statesboro Inn and Restaurant
106 S. Main St.
(912) 489-8628
(800) 846-9466
www.statesboroinn.com
Moderate
See p. 84 for details.

PERRY

Henderson Village
(888) 615-9722
(478) 988-8696
www.hendersonvillage.com
Moderate to Expensive, includes full breakfast
See p. 79 for details.

New Perry Hotel
800 Main St.
(478) 987-1000
(800) 877-3779
www.newperryhotel.com
Inexpensive
See p. 78 for details.

Places to Eat in Southeast Georgia

DOUGLAS

Fern Bank Bar & Grill
235 Peterson Ave. South
(912) 384-4385
Dinner Tues through Sat.
Moderate
See p. 92 for details.

DUBLIN

Jo Jo's Biscuits and Burgers
1010 Telfair St.
(478) 272-6478
Inexpensive
Jo Jo's is much more than the name suggests, although it's hard to pass up their biscuits. Daily specials include pork chops, hamburger steak and gravy, chicken tenders, fried chopped steak, turkey, and a host of vegetables from which to choose.

FOLKSTON

Okefenokee Restaurant
1507 3rd St.
(912 496-3236
Inexpensive to Moderate
Bring your appetite to this down-home cooking buffet. The wide assortment of food ranges from Southern fried chicken to grilled shrimp or rib eyes and of course lots of vegetables. The catfish is a must and Friday night is seafood night.

HELPFUL WEBSITES

Baxley-Appling County Tourism Board
www.baxley.org

Dublin-Laurens County Welcome Center
www.dublin-georgia.com

Folkston/Okefenokee Chamber of Commerce
www.folkston.com

Statesboro Tourism Office
www.visitstatesboro.com

Waycross/Ware County Tourism Bureau
www.waycrossga.com

Valdosta-Lowndes Convention & Visitors Bureau
www.valdostatourism.com

METTER

Jomax Barbecue
GA 121
(912) 685-3636
Inexpensive
After traveling the long, lonely stretches of I-16 between Macon and Savannah, with only a few scattered fast-food outlets to sate your hunger, Jomax is a pleasant and tasty surprise. Tuck into the chopped barbecued pork or ribs, draped with a piquant house-secret sauce (available in bottles to take home), with slabs of starchy white bread and coleslaw and you'll be ready to hit the highway high on the hog. Lunch and dinner Mon through Sat.

PERRY

Rusty's Downtown Grill and Bar
807 Carroll St.
(478) 224-7878
www.rustysgrillandbar.com
Moderate

Part sports bar, part locals hangout, Rusty's has a wide menu ranging from burgers to grilled salmon and steaks to a host of Italian dishes. You can never go wrong with the daily blue plate special.

The Swanson
933 Carroll St.
(478) 987-1938
Inexpensive to Moderate
Located in the historic Cox-Swanson home in downtown, this 1880 home welcomes you with Southern charm and Southern style cooking. Desserts are a specialty. Lunch daily with dinner Mon through Sat.

STATESBORO

Beaver House Inn & Restaurant
121 S. Main St.
(912) 764-2821
www.beaverhouseinn.com
Moderate to Expensive
See p. 84 for details.

Vandy's Barbecue
22 W. Vine St.
(912) 764-2444
www.vandysbbqstatesboro.com
Inexpensive
A barbecue landmark for eons of townsfolk and Georgia Southern University students. Pulled pork, ribs, and Brunswick stew keep 'em coming back for more. Lunch and dinner daily.

NORTHWEST GEORGIA

→

Cloudland Canyon to Georgia's Rome

Cloudland Canyon State Park, in far northwest Georgia's remote and rugged Dade County, contains one of the Southeast's most awesome natural sights. The park's namesake and centerpiece is a steep canyon cut into the western flank of Lookout Mountain by ***Sitton Creek Gulch.*** You can stand by the rim and peer into misty reaches 1,800 feet deep. Better still, lace up your hiking boots, follow woodland trails down to 3 waterfalls on the canyon floor, and get really off the beaten path on 6 miles of backcountry trails.

After you hike, unwind with a swim in the park pool or a few quick sets of tennis. Also in the heavily forested 3,488-acre park are 16 completely furnished cottages, a group lodge, and 72 tent and trailer sites, with electrical and water connections, showers, and restrooms, as well as 11 backcountry camps. For camping and cottage reservations call (800) 864-PARK. Contact the park superintendent at 122 Cloudland Canyon Park Rd., Rising Fawn, (706) 657-4050, www.gastateparks.org.

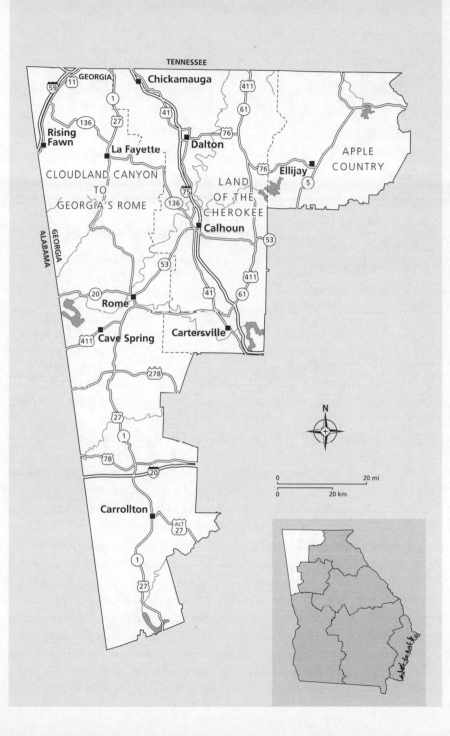

TENNESSEE

GEORGIA

Chickamauga

Rising Fawn

La Fayette

Dalton

Ellijay

APPLE COUNTRY

CLOUDLAND CANYON TO GEORGIA'S ROME

LAND OF THE CHEROKEE

Calhoun

GEORGIA

ALABAMA

Rome

Cave Spring

Cartersville

Carrollton

N

0   20 mi

0   20 km

NORTHWEST GEORGIA'S TOP HITS

Cloudland Canyon State Park	Gordon-Lee Mansion
Booth Western Art Museum	Dalton carpet outlets
James H. (Sloppy) Floyd State Park	Prater's Mill Country Fair
Capitoline Wolf	Vann House
Rome Clock Tower	Fort Mountain State Park
Chieftains Museum	Cohutta National Wilderness
Lock and Dam Park	New Echota State Historic Site
Funk Heritage Center	Etowah Indian Mounds State Historic Site
Berry College	
Martha Berry Museum and Art Gallery	Red Top Mountain State Park
John Tanner State Park	Tellus: Northwest Georgia Science Museum
Chattanooga and Chickamauga National Military Park	Ellijay's Georgia Apple Festival
	Col. Oscar Poole's Pig Hill of Fame

According to tradition, Cherokee Indians named their children for symbolic signs that caught their eye after birth. So the Cloudland community of *Rising Fawn* owes its poetic name to a chief who legend says looked out of his lodge on the happy morning his son was born and saw a newborn fawn wobble to its feet by its mother's side.

After a vigorous day in the park, make tracks for *Geneva's Restaurant* (706-398-1749). Across GA 136 from the Cloudland entrance, the homey cafe is the eating-meeting-greeting destination for folks from miles around. At breakfast, lunch, and dinner, country cooking just doesn't get any better.

Hidden Hollow Country Inn, 5 miles down the mountain from Cloudland Canyon, is one of those discoveries you can hardly wait to tell your best friends about. Tommy and Bonnie Jean Thomas preside over a gaggle of rustic but very comfortable family-size cabins around a small lake full of Canada geese. Cabins are filled with well-worn furniture, cards, board games, dog-eared magazines, and coffee, but there are no TVs or phones to ruffle your peaceful ruminations. For entertainment snag a fish in the lake, hike in the woods, and watch the sun come up and go down. Inexpensive to moderate. No meals are served, but Geneva Wooten's and other restaurants are close by.

The inn is at 463 Hidden Hollow Ln., Chickamauga. Call (706) 539-2372 or log on to www.hiddenhollowresort.com.

Be sure to bring your fishing gear when you head for *James H. (Sloppy) Floyd State Park.* Off US 27, 3 miles southeast of the Chattooga County seat of Summerville, the 270-acre park is renowned as one of the state's finest fishing places. Two stocked lakes—30 and 35 acres—offer excellent bass-fishing opportunities from the banks. Only boats with trolling motors are allowed.

Area anglers say you can expect to reel in impressive largemouth bass, as well as big catches of catfish and bream. Youngsters can learn some of the fine art of fishing during the park's annual fishing rodeo in mid-May. Admission is free, and prizes are awarded for the first, largest, and most fish caught.

Floyd State Park's 25 tent and trailer sites have water and electrical hookups and convenient showers and restrooms. You'll also find a playground, picnic areas, and hiking trails in the neighboring Chattahoochee National Forest. Contact Park Superintendent at 2800 Sloppy Floyd Lake Rd., Summerville, (706) 857-0826. Call (800) 864-PARK or log on to www.gastateparks.org for camping reservations.

Like its Italian counterpart, Georgia's *Rome* spreads over 7 green hills, in the foothills of the state's northwestern Appalachian Mountains. In the rivers department, the Georgia city of 30,000 has the edge. Instead of one mere Tiber, the Floyd County seat has three: the Etowah and Oostanaula, which join up downtown and form the Coosa. It may not have personages to match the Caesars, but a *dramatis personae* of Cherokee Indian chieftains, Southern aristocrats, cotton traders, Civil War soldiers, and riverboat paddle wheelers have made a rich and colorful cast, all the same. The city got its name quite by chance. In 1834 two traveling salesmen and a cotton planter put their choice of names in a hat. "Rome" was the fortuitous choice; otherwise, the city might be known today as Warsaw or Hamburg. A revitalized downtown, focusing on the three rivers, ensures Rome of a future as exciting as its past.

Begin your Roman holiday at the Greater Rome Visitors Center (706-295-5576 or 800-444-1834, www.romegeorgia.com), a rejuvenated Southern Railway passenger depot, circa 1900, and a retired caboose at 402 Civic Center Dr., off GA 20 and US 27 near downtown. Information is available Mon through Fri 9 a.m. to 5 p.m., Sat 10 a.m. to 3 p.m., and Sun noon to 3 p.m.

The Between the Rivers Walking Tour—it can also be driven, of course—leads you past 38 historic downtown landmarks. If you've been to the Italian Rome, you'll probably recognize the statue in front of City Hall here on Broad Street, downtown. The *Capitoline Wolf,* a replica of the Etruscan sculpture on ancient Rome's Capitoline Hill, depicts the city's mythical founders, Romulus and Remus, being nurtured by a she-wolf. It was a 1929

Root, Root, Root for the Rome Team

If you've forgotten how much fun a night at the ballpark can be, a night of minor league baseball with the Rome Braves will bring it all back. So, buy some peanuts and Cracker Jacks, hot dogs, nachos, and ice cream and find a seat in the Rome Braves' State Mutual Stadium. While the Atlanta Braves Class-A farm hands take their first steps toward the big show, the 5,200 seats in the retro-style ballpark will put you so close you can practically reach out and pat them on the back. And all for ticket and hot dog prices that won't require you to take out a second mortgage on your homestead. For tickets, phone (706) 368-9388 or visit www.romebraves.com.

goodwill gift from Benito Mussolini, a gift that was a tad embarrassing to the townspeople. In small-town Georgia, 1929, people were unaccustomed to seeing babies suckling their mother's bare breast in public, even if the mother was a wolf.

The *Town Clock,* on Clock Tower Hill, is the city's symbol and one of its most beloved landmarks. Built in Waltham, Massachusetts, in 1871, the four 9-foot-diameter clock faces rest upon a handsome 104-foot-tall brick and cypress water tower. So many people wanted to climb the 104-foot tower that the city opened it as the *Clock Tower Museum.* You can walk up the spiral staircase and take in panoramic views of the city's hills and rivers. The museum is open by appointment only or on the first Sat of each month at noon. Free admission. Phone (706) 236-4430.

Myrtle Hill Cemetery, on another of the city's 7 hills, is a beautiful tree-shaded sanctuary where the first Mrs. Woodrow Wilson, 377 Confederate soldiers, and other notables are buried. You're welcome to stroll and admire the panoramic views of Rome's rivers and green hills. Phone (706) 295-5576.

Until recently the Etowah, Oostanaula, and Coosa had to flood before Romans would pay them any attention. Nowadays the 4-mile *Heritage Trail* walking, biking, and hiking route, shaded by big trees, takes inhabitants and visitors along the Oostanaula from the *Rome–Floyd County Public Library* downtown to the Chieftains Museum and connects 4 smaller trails within the city. If you'd like to get out on the water, the visitor bureau can direct you to a canoe rental.

You can also unwind at *Lock and Dam Park,* a publicly owned camping/RV/fishing/boating park in a mountain setting beside a 1910 lock on the Coosa River. Facilities include 25 fully equipped RV campsites, a fishing pier, canoe rentals, boat ramp and docks, a bait shop, and a snack bar. Call (706) 234-5001 for information.

Rocky Mountain Recreation and Public Fishing Area is a joint venture of the Georgia Department of Natural Resources and Oglethorpe Power Corporation. The 5,000-acre retreat in northern Floyd County has 2 recreational lakes (357 and 202 acres) for swimming, fishing, and boating. You can also enjoy picnic pavilions, hiking trails, and other outdoor activities and camp out at 39 RV sites and 9 wooded tent sites. For information, call the Greater Rome Visitors Bureau at (800) 444-1834.

Rome Area History Museum (305 Broad St., Rome, 706-235-8051, www .romehistorymuseum.com) covers nearly two centuries of northwest Georgia's past. Exhibits focus on the Civil War, the Cherokees, cotton, and commerce. Original documents include maps, photographs, letters and even business records that paint a picture of Rome's history. Open Wed through Fri from 10 a.m. to 4 p.m. Admission is $3 for adults, $2 for seniors, and $1.50 for ages 6 to 12.

If golf's your game, check out the ***Stonebridge Golf Club*** (706-236-5046 and 800-336-5046, www.romestonebridge.com). Owned by the city of Rome, the 18-hole, par-72, 6,800-yard layout is at the base of Lavender Mountain, on the Berry College grounds. Rolling fairways, water, and big stands of hardwoods and pines are scenic to look at and challenging to play. The course is named for an old stone bridge over a lake on the ninth fairway. Greens fees won't handicap your budget.

The ***Chieftains Museum/Major Ridge Home*** is Rome's oldest historical landmark. Built as a frontier log cabin in 1794, Chieftains was the home of Major Ridge, the Cherokee leader who signed a treaty with the US government that partially contributed to the expulsion of the Cherokees from Georgia and the tragic "Trail of Tears." Along with Cherokee history, the museum's artifacts tell the story of Rome as a river town and its role in the antebellum South and

John Wisdom's"Midnight Ride"

Boston has its Paul Revere, and Romans remember their own courageous rider who saved the day (and their necks). Learning that Union troops were approaching the city, mail carrier John Wisdom rode off in a desperate attempt to mobilize defenders. He abandoned his mail buggy after 20 miles, begged and borrowed horses, which he changed six times, and galloped 65 miles in less than nine hours.

The approaching Union troops saw Rome's defenders armed with shotguns, squirrel guns, and muzzle-loading rifles and retreated into captivity under Confederate General Nathan Bedford Forrest. Rome's grateful citizens gave Wisdom $400 and a silver service.

the Civil War. An open archaeological dig and a 19th-century riverboat are on the grounds. It's at 501 Riverside Pkwy., Rome, off US 27. Call (706) 291-9494 or log on to www.chieftainsmuseum.org. Hours are Tues through Fri from 9 a.m. to 3 p.m. and Sat from 10 a.m. to 4 p.m. Adults $5, seniors $3, students $2.

When in Rome, shoppers from across northwestern Georgia, neighboring Alabama, Chattanooga, Tennessee, and Atlanta (65 miles north and south, respectively) do as savvy Romans do: They pass up the shopping center same-old-same-olds and hunt for unique treasures on downtown Rome's Broad Street and the Berry College campus, 10 minutes from downtown. While downtown, check out the **Historic DeSoto Theater** (530 Broad St., 706-295-7171, www.historicdesototheaterfoundation.org). Built in 1929, it was the first theater in the south to exclusively show "talkies." Beautifully restored, it is always hosting an event worth attending. At **Old Havana Cigar Company** (327 Broad St., 706-295-0546, www.oldhavanacigar.com) enjoy a glass of wine, a beer, or a cup of coffee while you choose among 230 types of cigars from Honduras, the Dominican Republic, Nicaragua, and Puerto Rico.

Born to privilege, the remarkable and very determined Miss Martha Berry founded the Berry School in 1902. Her original small school is now **Berry College,** a 4-year liberal arts college set among 28,000 acres of woodlands, forests, and fields. Automobile magnate Henry Ford funded the English Gothic–style Ford Buildings complex in 1924. As you're driving around the campus, watch out for deer impulsively crossing the roads—there are said to be 8.4 whitetails for each of the college's 2,000 students. About 90 percent of the students still work for part of their tuition.

The *Miracle of the Mountains,* as the school's story is called, is chronicled at the **Martha Berry Museum and Art Gallery,** across from the campus on US 27. Exhibits, photos, and a 28-minute film trace Miss Berry's life and her numerous honors. Nearby **Oak Hill,** a classic, white-columned Old South Greek Revival mansion built in 1847, was the Berry family's home. Students lead tours through rooms filled with antiques, art, and family memorabilia. An easygoing nature trail loops through gardens and woodlands. The Martha Berry Museum and Art Gallery and Oak Hill are open Mon through Sat from 10 a.m. to 5 p.m. Admission $5, $3 ages 6 to 12. Phone (800) 220-5504 or (706) 291-1883 or visit www.berry.edu/oakhill.

You're also invited to visit the scenic campuses of **Shorter College** (a Christian college founded in 1877) and **Darlington School** (an exclusive college prep boarding school founding in 1905), neighbors on Shorter Avenue west of downtown.

If you'd like to get a little lost in the woods, make an appointment to visit **Marshall Forest,** on Horseleg Creek Road, Rome, off GA 20, 4 miles west of downtown. The lush 170-acre preserve is the only virgin forest in the US that is located with city limits. Administered by the Georgia Chapter of the Nature Conservancy, Marshall includes 90 acres of fields and 80 acres of forests where northern red and chestnut oaks mingle with long-leaf southern pines. About 300 species of wildflowers and other plants grow on the Flower Glen Trail. The Big Pine Braille Trail offers blind visitors the opportunity to stop at 20 stations describing 53 plant species, 31 species of trees, and 19 species of vines and shrubs. Contact the Rome Visitor Center for information, (800) 444-1834, or the Nature Conservancy, (404) 873-6946 or www.nature.org/georgia.

Cave Spring, a village of 1,050 residents and 1 traffic light 16 miles south of Rome (via US 411), is pure Norman Rockwell. The *Hearn Inn* (13 Cedartown St. Southwest, 706-777-8865), a comfy community-owned inn in an 1840s schoolhouse, features 5 guest rooms with private bath and breakfast at inexpensive rates. When you're well rested, lace up your walking shoes and head across *Rolater Park* to the limestone cave that gave the town its name. The spring water flows out of the cave into a tree-shaded pond. Around the pond and the park are picnic tables and pavilions, restrooms, and a spring-fed 1.5-acre swimming pool shaped like the state of Georgia. The pool has bathhouses, snack bars, and plenty of room to spread your towels.

The Cave Springs Historical Society runs tours from Apr through Oct between 10:30 a.m. and 1:30 p.m. leaving from the Visitor's Center at 4 Rome Rd. Call (706) 777-9447 or log on to www.cavespringsgeorgia.com. The tour is $15 if you would like a meal included; otherwise it is $10.

Antiques, home decor, and gift shops and family-owned restaurants are around the square. More than 100 artists and craftspeople come for the *Cave Spring Arts Festival* the second weekend of June. For information, contact the Visitor's Center or City of Cave Spring, PO Box 365, Cave Spring 30124, (706) 777-8439 and (800) 444-1834.

John Tanner State Park, off GA 16, 6 miles west of Carrollton, is a popular getaway for west Georgians and east Alabamians. Six furnished 1-bedroom cottages, a group lodge, and 31 full-service campsites surround a lake with a sandy swimming beach, rental fishing boats, and tree-shaded picnic shelters. There is a $5 parking fee. Contact Park Superintendent: 354 Tanner Beach Rd., Carrollton, (770) 830-2222. For campsite and cottage reservations, call (800) 864-PARK, www.gastateparks.org.

Fans of Oscar–winning actress *Susan Hayward* (*I Want to Live,* 1959) can visit her gravesite at Our Lady of Perpetual Help Catholic Church, 210 Centerpoint Rd., GA 113, Carrollton. In 1957 Hayward married businessman Eaton Chalkley and moved with him to Carrollton, where they raised horses and cattle. When Chalkley died in 1966, Hayward moved back to California. When she died of brain cancer in 1972, she was buried beside him in the church cemetery across from their former home. Open daily, no admission fee. For information contact Carrollton Area Convention and Visitors Bureau at 102 N. Lake Shore Dr., Carrollton, (770) 214-9746, www.visitcarrollton.com.

Land of the Cherokee

In the hellish heat of September 19 and 20, 1863, nearly 130,000 Americans engaged in one of the bloodiest battles of the entire Civil War. When it was over, Confederate forces under the command of General Braxton Bragg had a costly and dubious victory. They had repulsed the outnumbered Union armies under General William Rosecrans but were too weakened to pursue the Federals as they fled to safety around Chattanooga, Tennessee. Subsequent Union victories at Chattanooga's Lookout Mountain and Missionary Ridge and the capture of the city's vital railway hub opened General William T. Sherman's route to Atlanta and the sea.

The 5,500-acre Chickamauga battlefield is now part of the ***Chattanooga and Chickamauga National Military Park.*** The major sites are adjacent to US 27, near Chattanooga and Chickamauga. Stop first at the National Park Service Visitors Center for the audiovisual orientation and the many exhibits. The Fuller Collection of Military Arms has more than 400 weapons from the French and Indian Wars through present-day conflicts.

Park rangers in Civil War uniforms demonstrate cannon and rifles. The Chattanooga Symphony Orchestra has free outdoor concerts here on summer Sunday evenings. Bring a blanket and a picnic supper and join the festivities!

From the visitor center, follow US 27 for 3 miles through the park. Battle sites are marked by earthworks, cannon batteries, and farm buildings. Impressive monuments have been placed by states whose sons in blue and gray died here more than 125 years ago. The park is open all the time. The visitor center is open daily from 8 a.m. to 5:45 p.m. Contact Park Superintendent at 3370 LaFayette Rd., Fort Oglethorpe, (706) 866-9241, www.nps .gov/chch.

The ***Gordon-Lee Mansion,*** on the edge of the battlefield park, invites you to spend the night in antebellum luxury. Built in 1847, the white-columned Greek Revival residence on 7 acres of gardens and grounds served as Union headquarters and a hospital during the battle. Six guest rooms, an adjoining log house, and public areas are furnished with Civil War–era antiques. Moderate rates include evening wine and cheese on the veranda and a continental-plus breakfast. Contact Gordon-Lee Mansion at 217 Cove Rd., Chickamauga, (706) 375-4728, www.gordonleemansion.com.

Before leaving the area, see *Lookout Mountain, Missionary Ridge,* and other major parts of the Chattanooga and Chickamauga National Military Park.

If you've been planning to recarpet your home or cover your pool deck or patio with Astroturf, put off that major purchase until you've been to Dalton. Seat of northwest Georgia's green and hilly Whitfield County, industrious *Dalton,* with a population of 33,000, is the long-reigning "Carpet Capital of the World."

About 90 percent of the functional carpet produced worldwide is made within a 25-mile radius of Dalton in the more than 150 modern carpet plants. If you're in a buying frame of mind or would just enjoy browsing the latest styles and colors, dozens of *Dalton carpet outlets* offer a full range of floor coverings at greatly reduced prices. The Dalton Convention and Visitors Bureau (2211 Dug Gap Battle Rd., Dalton, 706-270-9960, 800-331-3258, www.dalton cvb.com), open Mon through Sat, can provide you with an up-to-date outlets directory. You can also find out about guided tours of area mills, Civil War and Native American sites, restaurants, and lodgings.

Dalton's $15 billion carpeting industry was born around 1900, when a Whitfield County farm girl named Catherine Evans produced a hand-tufted chenille bedspread, copied from a family heirloom, and promptly sold it for the handsome price of $2.50. Encouraged by her success, she made more of the brightly colored cotton bedspreads, and these, too, were eagerly snapped up by tourists and local homemakers. Other homebound women began following her lead, and by the early 1920s, tufted bedspreads had grown into a major "cottage industry."

The bedspreads usually featured flowers and other patterns, but the brilliantly plumed male peacock was such a runaway favorite that US 41, the major highway leading into Dalton, became popularly known as "Peacock Alley."

Carpet Shopping Tips

If you're planning to do serious carpet shopping, do your homework ahead of time. Have a good idea of what you're looking for, how much you'll need, the color and style, and what you can afford to pay. Do comparison shopping in your local stores—the more than 100 outlet stores in Dalton and neighboring towns like Calhoun and Chatsworth offer prices up to 70 percent less than you'll pay in a retail store. You can get a list of the Carpet & Rug Outlet Council stores from the Dalton-Whitfield Chamber of Commerce, (706) 278-7373, and the Dalton Convention and Visitors Bureau, (800) 331-3258. Most outlets deal in "seconds," that is, those with some problems that exclude them from the "A list." It's often just a small tear or a color that doesn't match the mill's specifications. Be sure to examine it thoroughly. Having your carpet shipped will be much easier than trying to take it home yourself.

In the 1920s, a machine invented in Dalton was able to mass-produce the cotton bedspreads. Another wizard soon realized that by tufting more densely and adding a sturdy backing the same machinery could be adapted to the manufacture of carpeting. Dalton—and households the world over—were never again the same.

The original "cottage craft" of chenille bedspreads is still alive. You can find a practical souvenir with a peacock, Elvis Presley, Jesus Christ, the Confederate battle flag, and other designs at stores around Dalton and along US 41—the original "Peacock Alley"—between Dalton and the Tennessee border. Figure on paying a bit more than $2.50, however!

Some of the early chenille bedspreads are among the exhibits at Whitfield-Murray Historical Society at *Crown Gardens and Archives,* in the original Crown Cotton Mill at 715 Chattanooga Ave., Dalton, (706) 278-0217, www .whitfield-murrayhistoricalsociety.org. The museum also has historical displays, a Black Heritage room, an outdoor spring, and picnic areas. It's open Tues through Fri 10 a.m. to 5 p.m. and on Sat 9 a.m. until 1 p.m. Admission is free.

With its influx of executives and workers from across the nation and several countries, this surprisingly cosmopolitan little city is very active in the fine arts. The *Creative Arts Guild,* at 520 W. Waugh St., Dalton, (706) 278-0168, www.creativeartsguild.org, is a tastefully contemporary complex with 2 art galleries and a forum for live theater, dance, and other cultural programs. It's open daily. Admission is free.

Dalton is also a festive city. The Downtown Dalton Beer Festival each June draws thousands to sample local, American, and international brews as well as local foods. The BBQ and Music Festival each October is a bit more family friendly with arts, crafts, and music to go along with an impressive array of barbecue chefs vying for the Kansas City Barbecue Championship. Contact Downtown Dalton Development Authority in the Historic Freight Depot, 305 S. Depot St., (706) 278-3332.

On the second weekends of May and October, the *Prater's Mill Country Fair* centers on Benjamin Franklin Prater's circa 1859 gristmill. While the huge millstones turn out silky cornmeal, 185 artists and craftspeople sell their wares to the tune of bluegrass fiddlers, clog dancers, and gospel singers. There are pony rides and other special treats just for the youngsters.

Dalton Depot Restaurant & Trackside Cafe (110 Depot St., 5 minutes from I-75, 706-226-3160, www.thedaltondepot.net) is the carpet city's liveliest eating and drinking address. The cleverly regeared old wooden passenger train depot has a something-for-everyone menu: stuffed jalapeños and quesadillas, filet mignon, baby-back ribs, prime rib, rib eye and sirloin steak, chicken several different ways, fish and shrimp, sandwiches and salads, and bar drinks and 130 brands of beer. Lunch and dinner are served Mon through Sat.

Mexican and Hispanic carpet workers make up about half of Dalton's population, which accounts for the city's many Latino cafes and stores, a Spanish-language newspaper and radio station, and other services. For great Mexican food, try *Garcia's,* located at 1205 W. Walnut St. Call (706) 529-6855. The food is authentic, plentiful, and very affordable.

The *Tunnel Hill Heritage Center* (off I-75 exit 336 north, 345 south, 8 miles north of Dalton, 215 Clisby Austin Rd., 706-876-1571, www.tunnelhillheritage center.com) is a must-see for train enthusiasts. The area gets its name from the 1,477-foot Western & Atlantic Railroad Tunnel, built through the mountains in 1848–1850 to connect the port of Augusta, on the Savannah River in east Georgia, with the Tennessee River Valley. It was the focus of Civil War battles and remained in use until 1928. In the 1990s, it was restored and opened to the public. Along with the tunnel, the heritage center includes the 1848 Clisby Austin House, Civil War artifacts, and original chenille bedspreads. It's open Tues through Sat from 9 a.m. to 5 p.m., closed Sun. Adults $5, ages 12 and under $3.

Vann House was a showplace of 19th-century Cherokee accomplishment. At the junction of GA 52-A and GA 225, 3 miles west of modern-day Chatsworth, the sturdy 3-story house, with brick walls 2 feet thick, was built in modified Georgian style in 1804–1805. Owner James Vann was a half-Cherokee, half-Scot who helped create a Moravian mission for the education of young Cherokees. When Vann was murdered in 1809, his son Joseph inherited the house and surrounding farmlands. He prospered until 1830, when the state of Georgia confiscated his lands for violating a law forbidding white men to work for Indians.

AUTHOR'S FAVORITES

Cloudland Canyon State Park	Fort Mountain State Park
Booth Western Art Museum	Cohutta National Wilderness
Barnsley Gardens	New Echota State Historic Site
Hidden Hollow Country Inn	Tellus Museum
Martha Berry Museum and Art Gallery	Blue Ridge Scenic Railroad
Chattanooga and Chickamauga National Military Park	

The Georgia Department of Natural Resources has restored the house and refurnished and redecorated the rooms in early 19th-century style. An intricately carved "floating staircase" is one of Georgia's earliest surviving examples of cantilevered construction. Elsewhere are Bibles, dinnerware, and dining room and bedroom furnishings. Vann House, at the intersection of GA 52-A and GA 225, 82 GA 225 North, Chatsworth, (706) 695-2598, (800) 864-PARK, www.gastateparks.org, is open Tues through Sat from 9 a.m. to 5 p.m., Sun from 2 to 5:30 p.m. Admission $6 for adults, $3.50 for children 6 to 18; free for children under 6.

On GA 52, 7 miles east of Chatsworth, **Fort Mountain State Park** is a super-scenic park on a forested, 2,800-foot peak of the Blue Ridge Mountains' Cohutta Range. The park's namesake is a puzzling rock wall, or foundation, that winds nearly 900 feet around the mountainside. Whether it was an ancient Indian fortress, a bastion built by 12th-century Welsh explorers, or part of some other inscrutable mission is a matter of speculation. The stone observation tower nearby is no mystery. It's a legacy of the Depression-era Civilian Conservation Corps.

History lessons aside, you can relax in Fort Mountain's lake, go horseback riding, hike nature trails, play miniature golf, and set the kids loose on the playground. The 70 campsites have water, electricity, hot showers, and restrooms. Fifteen 2- and 3-bedroom cottages come with kitchen appliances, towels, sheets, and logs for the fireplace. Contact Park Superintendent at 181 Fort Mountain Park Rd., Chatsworth, (706) 422-1932. For reservations, call (800) 864-PARK or log on to www.gastateparks.org.

The 40,000-acre **Cohutta National Wilderness** in northwestern Georgia is a favorite of backpackers who really like to get away from it all. The parking area at Dally Gap, near McCaysville, is near the trailhead for Jack's River Trail, which winds through the eastern side of the wilderness. At 17 miles, Jack's River is longer than many trails in the wilderness and is one of the most scenic, with big stands of trees, ferns, and wildflowers. The Cohutta Mountains themselves rise to 4,200 feet and offer more than 87 miles of remote hiking within the wilderness area. You'll probably see white-tailed deer, beaver, and many species of birds. Be alert for black bears. Those who don't care to hike, can still see a lot on the scenic drive from Fort Mountain along GA 52 towards Ellijay. For information contact Cohutta Wildlife Management Area at (707) 635-7400.

The Cherokee assimilated themselves into the way of life established by the white settlers, then were ruthlessly crushed at **New Echota State Historic Site,** near modern-day Calhoun. In the 1820s New Echota was laid out as the capital of the Cherokee Nation that included parts of Georgia, the Carolinas, Tennessee, and Alabama. Here, the Cherokee legislature formulated laws, enforced by a series of district courts and a supreme court. The Indians wore European-style dress, used the farming methods of the white settlers, and lived in stone and frame houses with the most modern conveniences of the day. The more affluent owned black slaves. The first North American tribe to formulate its own written alphabet, the Cherokee published a bilingual newspaper, circulated as far as Europe.

Gold discovered on Cherokee lands in the late 1820s brought it all to an end. Supported by President Andrew Jackson, the state of Georgia confiscated all Cherokee lands and in 1838 forced the Indians into exile in what is now Oklahoma. Thousands perished along this "Trail of Tears."

New Echota has been meticulously reconstructed as a state historic site. Stop first to see the orientation slide show and exhibits in the reception center. Then take a self-guided walking tour that includes the supreme court building, the printing presses of the *Cherokee Phoenix* newspaper, a tavern/general store, and the home of the Reverend Samuel Worcester, a Massachusetts minister who established a mission for the Cherokee. There are 12 original and reconstructed buildings at the site, including the Council House, print shop, Worcester's home, and a host of outbuildings. Park rangers frequently demonstrate arrowhead-making and hunting techniques. Books about the Cherokee civilization are on sale at the reception center. In late October the **Cherokee Fall Festival** is a weekend of Native American crafts, cooking, and storytelling.

New Echota State Historic Site (I 75 exit 317, Calhoun, 706 624 1321, 800 864-PARK, www.gastatepark.org) is open Thurs through Sat from 9 a.m. to 5 p.m. Admission is $6.50 for adults, $4.50 for children 6 to 18; free for children under 6.

Barnsley Gardens Resort, off I-75 exit 306, 10 miles west of Adairsville, dates to 1841, when English cotton broker Godfrey Barnsley brought his wife, Julia, from Savannah and built an Italianate villa and formal gardens on 10,000 acres of former Cherokee land. More than 160 years later, Hubertus Fugger, a Bavarian prince, has complemented Barnsley's gardens with plush lodgings, a European spa, a stem-winding golf course, and other resort amenities. Thirty-three English-style guest cottages, with 1 to 4 bedrooms, have plush furnishings, private baths, wood-burning fireplaces, heart-pine floors, front porch rockers, TVs, CD players, and other luxuries. Along with the 18-hole championship golf course and multifaceted spa, guests can enjoy the outdoor pool, bratwurst and German brews in a Bavarian beer garden, fine cuisine in the formal dining room, and Godfrey Barnsley's restored gardens and the romantic ruins of his villa, where Godfrey and Julia reportedly still appear from time to time. Julia's image is on the tiered fountain in the formal gardens. The golf course, gardens, spa, and dining room are available to non-guests. Golf, tennis, romantic getaway, and other package plans are available. Barnsley also encompasses the 1,800-acre hunting estate called Springbank Plantation where guests can participate in sport clay shooting as well as quail and pheasant hunting and horseback riding. Barnsley Gardens Resort is at 597 Barnsley Gardens Rd., Adairsville. Call (770) 773-7480 or (877) 773-2447 or log on to www .barnsleyresort.com. Expensive.

While you're in the area, browse the antiques shops around Adairsville's downtown square.

Between AD 1000 and 1500, the Etowah tribe migrated into the fertile Etowah River Valley, near today's Cartersville, and created a remarkably sophisticated culture. Beans, squash, corn, and fruit that the women cultivated complemented game trapped by the men in surrounding forests and the abundant fish in the Etowah. As part of a vast trading network, the Etowahs made tools, arrowheads, axes, and household implements from Great Lakes copper and Mississippi and Ohio Valley flint. Gulf Coast seashells were fashioned into ceremonial jewelry.

Surrounded by a deep moat and log stockade, a compact city of clay and wooden houses sheltered as many as 4,000 members of the tribe. The heart of the city was a half-dozen rectangular earthen mounds. The *Etowah Indian Mounds Historic Site* was the forum for religious rites conducted by chiefs and priests and the final resting place of these dignitaries.

Stop first at the excellent small museum and reception center, where dioramas and artifacts from the mounds tell the story of this mysteriously vanished tribe. The exhibits are highlighted by a priest's burial chamber and beautifully carved busts of a woman and a warrior. A film traces the history of the Etowah. With a diagrammed map, cross the moat and explore the grass-covered mounds. Ninety-two steps take you up 63 feet to the top of Mound "A," from which the priest conducted rituals for the townspeople assembled below in the plaza. Mound "C," one of the smallest, was a principal burial site

Cassville

Just north of Cartersville on Cass White Road at Firetower Road you'll find a handful of historic buildings and a granite monument marking what used to be the grand town of Cassville. With 2 colleges, 4 hotels, and a newspaper, Cassville was the cultural center for North Georgia in the mid-1800s.

During the Civil War, the Union Army gave residents just 20 minutes notice before burning the entire town. Only a handful of buildings survived and those who fled never came back. Cassville's Confederate Cemetery holds 300 graves.

and the source of most of the artifacts in the museum. Park rangers periodically lead moonlight walks around the site.

About a 15-minute drive west of I-75 exit 288, via GA 113/GA 61, Etowah Indian Mounds Historic Site (Route 1, Cartersville, 770-387-3747, 800-864-PARK, www.gastateparks.org) is open Wed through Sat from 9 a.m. to 5 p.m. Admission is $5.50 for adults, $3.50 for children; free for children under 6.

For more insights into ancient Native American cultures, visit the *Funk Heritage Center* at Reinhardt College, in Waleska, on GA 140 northeast of Cartersville. You'll enter the Funk's John and Ethel Bennett History Museum through a 50-foot-long structure that resembles an Iroquois longhouse, where several families would have lived communally. Historians believe the northeastern Iroquois traded with Cherokees and other southeastern tribes. The left and right wings of the museum were inspired by temple mounds built at Etowah, at Cartersville, and elsewhere in the Southeast during the Mississippian period, AD 1000–1500. The Rogers Gallery of Contemporary Indian Art exhibits some 400 paintings, sculptures, and other creative endeavors. A majority were created by descendants of southeastern Cherokees, Creeks, and other tribes that were removed west of the Mississippi during the 1830s "Trail of Tears." Also on permanent exhibit, the Sellars Collection of Ancient Hand Tools includes thousands of tools and implements dating back as far as the 17th century. Funk Heritage Center (7300 Reinhardt College Pkwy., Waleska, 770-720-5600, www.reinhardt.edu/funkheritage) is open Tues through Fri 9 a.m. to 4 p.m., Sat 10 a.m. to 5 p.m., and Sun 1 to 5 p.m. Adults 18 and older, $6; seniors 65 and older, $5.50; age 18 and under, $4.

The *Booth Western Art Museum,* in downtown Cartersville (population 20,000), draws us into the once-upon-a-time America of cowboys and Indians, cowgirls and gunslingers, buffalo hunters and rodeo "bulldoggers," stagecoaches and iron horses, big skies and endless horizons, movie icons and pulp fiction heroes. Opened in August 2003, the 120,000-square-foot museum is one of the largest Western art museums anywhere in the United States.

The permanent collection's more than 350 paintings and sculptures are by some of America's leading contemporary Western artists. The Civil War Gallery's 25 paintings dramatize the conflict from the first shots at Manassas to surrender at Appomattox. The Reel West Gallery's vintage movie posters and illustrations bring back those thrilling days at the Saturday matinee, when Roy Rogers and Gene Autry quelled the bad guys and rode victoriously into the sunset just before the final credits. In the Presidential Gallery, all 44 US presidents are represented by a portrait or photograph and an original signed document. At Sagebrush Ranch, kids have a great time riding the make-believe range in a lifelike bouncing stagecoach, dressing up as cowboys and cowgirls, and creating their own Western masterpieces. The museum also hosts 6 to 10 temporary exhibits each year. Booth Western Art Museum (I-75 exit 288/Cart-ersville Main Street, 501 Museum Dr., Cartersville, 770-387-1300, www.booth museum.org) has a gift shop, cafe, and 60-seat multimedia theater with an ori-entation film about the collections. Open Tues, Wed, Fri, and Sat 10 a.m. to 5 p.m., Thurs 10 a.m. to 8 p.m., Sun 1 to 5 p.m. Adults $10; seniors $8; students and ages 13 to 18 $7; age 12 and under free.

4-Way Lunch, Main Street (corner of Gilmer Street), downtown Carters-ville, has been a landmark of swift (not "fast") food and service for more than 80 years. THIS IS NOT BURGER KING, a sign over the coffeepot advises, YOU DON'T GET IT YOUR WAY, YOU GET IT OUR WAY, OR YOU DON'T GET IT. Another cautions about the service: I CAN ONLY PLEASE ONE PERSON A DAY—AND TODAY AIN'T YOUR DAY. Crowds line up every weekday morning for bacon, eggs, grits, and biscuits, and many come back at lunch for first-class burgers, hot dogs, chopped steak, and stew. With only 11 seats at the red Formica counter, there's no lollygagging—when you're done, it's time to move on and let other hungry patrons have their 4-Way fix.

Red Top Mountain State Park, on exit 285 off I-75 south of Cartersville, is one of the nicest and prettiest in the whole system. A wealth of recreational opportunities, campsites, and cottages are spread over the wooded hillsides around 12,000-acre Lake Allatoona. During warm weather, you can sun on a sandy beach, swim, and water-ski. The rest of the year, bring tennis racquets, fishing gear, picnic supplies, and hiking shoes. Boaters may bring their own or rent houseboats and pontoon boats at the park marina. A small grocery is at the reception center.

Red Top's 18 2-bedroom cottages are completely furnished and include fireplaces. The 96 tent and RV camping sites have electricity, water, hot show-ers, and restrooms. There is also a yurt available. The park office is open daily from 8 a.m. to 5 p.m. Contact Superintendent at 50 Lodge Rd., Cartersville, (770) 975-0055. Call (800) 864-PARK for camping, cottage, and yurt reserva-tions, or log on to www.gastateparks.org for more information.

Tellus: the Northwest Georgia Science Museum is a spectacular 125,000-square-foot science museum devoted to minerals, fossils, transpor-tation technology, and hands-on science experiences. The 120-seat digital planetarium features a variety of astronomy programs, "Night at the Museum" stargazing events, and family activities. Discover how the earth was formed bil-lions of years ago in the Weinman Mineral Gallery, which showcases more than 4,000 rocks, fossils, crystals, geodes, gemstones, and minerals. "Stan," a 40-foot T-rex, is the star of the Fossil Gallery. Adults are $12, seniors $10, students and children ages 3 to 17 $8. The museum is at I-75 exit 293, at White; phone (770) 606-5000 or visit www.tellusmuseum.com.

For information about other attractions, contact the Cartersville Bartow County Convention & Visitors Bureau at 1 Friendship Plaza, Cartersville, (770) 387-1357, (800) 733-2280, www.notatlanta.org.

Apple Country

Gilmer County, in the Blue Ridge Mountains about 90 minutes due north of Metro Atlanta, is "Georgia's Apple Capital." Dozens of orchards dotting the county's green mountainsides annually produce more than 600,000 bushels of Granny Smiths, Red and Golden Delicious, Yates, Jonathans, Stayman Winesaps, Rome Beauties, and exotic Asian varieties such as Fujis and Mutsus. In the fall, when the trees are loaded with fruit, visitors by the thousands are invited into the orchards to pick their own basketsful. Those who'd just as soon leave the labor to somebody else can buy all they can haul home at farm stores that line the highways leading to *Ellijay,* the Gilmer County seat. They also can take away freshly squeezed apple cider, apple pies and cakes, and recipe books to prepare just about everything with apples.

To celebrate the harvest, *Ellijay's Georgia Apple Festival,* 2 weekends in mid-October, puts on parades, apple pie–eating and apple-cooking contests,

TOP ANNUAL EVENTS

Atlanta Steeplechase
mid-April, Kingston Downs, Kingston
(404) 237-7436
www.atlantasteeplechase.com

Historic House & Garden Pilgrimage
late April, Rome
(706) 291-7181

Kingston Confederate Memorial Day
April 22, Kingston
(770) 382-1747

Cedar Valley Arts Festival
Late April, Cedartown
(770) 748-0397

Prater's Mill Country Fair
Mother's Day Weekend, Dalton
(706) 275-6455
www.pratersmill.org

Cherokee County Indian Festival
early May, Canton
(770) 735-6275

Georgia Apple Festival
mid-October, Ellijay
(706) 636-4500
www.georgiaapplefestival.org

Chiaha Harvest Fair
Late October, Rome
(706) 235-4542
www.chiaha.org

Candles & Carols of Christmases Past
early December, Martha Berry Museum, Rome
(800) 220-5504

arts and crafts, mountain music and dancing, and a host of other festivities. Ellijay is a delightful small town with 1,600 amiable inhabitants. It may remind you of Sheriff Andy Taylor's bucolic hometown of Mayberry.

When your appetite's worked up again, get ready for some serious barbecue. As you drive into town on the 4-lane Zell Miller Mountain Parkway (GA 515), you can't help but notice *Col. Oscar Poole's Pig Hill of Fame.* For $5 you, too, can have your name painted on one of thousands of little plywood piggies that graze on the hillside beside Col. Poole's yolk-yellow *Real Pit Bar-B-Q* establishment. Call (706) 635-4100 for info. (Col. Poole is also a Methodist minister, and your $5 goes to church missions.) Inside, the barbecue is seriously delicious.

Whitewater rafters, canoeists, and kayakers flock to the Ellijay and Cartecay Rivers that flow out of the mountains, right into Ellijay. Contact the Gilmer County Chamber of Commerce, 368 Craig St., Ellijay, (706) 635-7400, www .gilmerchamber.com.

A restyled old manufacturing plant, *Hampton Square* in downtown Blue Ridge shines with studio shops that create museum-quality jewelry, stained and blown glass, pottery, paintings, wood, and fiber pieces eagerly sought by tourists and residents of this booming second-home mountain community. As you go from shop to shop, stop for a lunch-and-dinner pick-me-up at *Blue Jeans Pizza and Pasta Factory* (706-632-6503). The Ladies Dulcimer Society and other groups play for your enjoyment on Friday nights. You can satisfy your hunger for antiques and collectibles in scads of shops on downtown Blue Ridge's Main Street.

The *Blue Ridge Scenic Railroad* takes train enthusiasts in enclosed and open-air cars on a 26-mile round-trip through the mountains and along the Toccoa River between the Fannin County towns of Blue Ridge and McCaysville. The excursion operates between Mar and Dec and is especially popular in Sept and Oct when the high country's fall foliage is at its colorful peak. The Christmas Express and Halloween Haunted Express are other popular special events and you can even pay a little extra and ride on the engine. Adults, $27 to $33; senior citizens, $22 to $28; ages 3 to 12, $14 to $17. The railroad is at 241 Depot St., Blue Ridge (706-632-9833, 877-413-TRAIN, www .brscenic.com).

Places to Stay in Northwest Georgia

CAVE SPRING

Cedar Creek Park
6770 Hwy. 411 between
Rome and Cave Spring
(706) 777-3030
www.bigcedarcreek.com
Inexpensive
Fifty RV sites with full
hookups, with inexpensive
daily and weekly rates, and
24 tent sites with water,
restrooms, and showers.
Guests can enjoy a driving
range and canoeing, tub-
ing, and fishing on Cedar
Creek.

Hearn Inn Bed and Breakfast
Rolater Park
10 Georgia Ave.
(706) 777-8502
Inexpensive
Five guest rooms in a
2-story Federal-style house
that once housed 1840s
Baptist seminary students.
Rooms are attractively furnished in period style, with
private and shared baths.
TV in common area. Full
breakfast with nightly rate.

The Tumlin House Bed & Breakfast
38 Alabama St.
(706) 777-0066
www.tumlinhouse.com
Inexpensive
Three queen-size bed-
rooms and one twin bed-
room in an 1842 Victorian
country house built by
the great-aunt of cur-
rent innkeepers J. C. and
Nancy Boehm. All rooms
are furnished in comfort-
able Victorian style, with
TV and VCR. Rooms with
private bath or shared
baths, including full breakfast. On Saturday night,
the Boehms prepare a
6-course gourmet dinner,
open to guests and non-
guests for a moderate cost.
The house is a short walk
to antiques and gift shops
and eateries around Cave
Spring's picturesque downtown park.

CLOUDLAND CANYON

Hidden Hollow Country Inn
463 Hidden Hollow Dr.
Chickamauga, GA
(706) 539-2372
www.hiddenhollowresort
.com
Inexpensive to Moderate
See p. 100 for details.

CHATSWORTH

The Hearthstone Lodge
2755 Hwy. 282
(706) 695-0920
www.thehearthstonelodge
.com
Moderate
Innkeepers Pat and Phil
Cunniffe have created a
haven here in the moun-
tains with amazing views.
The lodge is situated in
a forest with nature trails
for guests to explore or
they could just choose to
sit on the porch and take
in the vista. Everything is
built for your comfort, from
the common room with its
stack stone fireplace to the
hot tub and spa. There are
3 unique rooms available.
Full gourmet breakfast and
afternoon refreshments.

ROME

Claremont House Bed & Breakfast
906 E. 2nd Ave.
(706) 291-0900
(800) 254-4797
www.theclaremonthouse
.net
Moderate
This is a showplace Victorian Gothic mansion built
in 1882. Innkeepers Chris
and Holly McHagge have
lavished their public spaces
and guest rooms with
antiques, wood-burning
fireplaces, and elaborately
carved woodwork. Cham-
pagne in the parlor, rocking
chairs on the verandas,
and full gourmet breakfast
served in the dining room
are part of the experience
of this historic downtown
home.

Places to Eat in Northwest Georgia

CARTERSVILLE

Appalachian Grill
14 E. Church St.
(770) 607-5357
www.ngeorgia.com/ang/
appalachian_grill
Inexpensive to Moderate

Fitted out like an Appalachian Mountain lodge, with stone and brick walls and aged wood, this cozy downtown Cartersville favorite features a hearty menu of prime rib, seafood, chicken, steaks, sandwiches, and salads. Crab cakes, Cajun popcorn shrimp, and French dip sandwiches are among regulars' favorites. Full bar. Lunch and dinner Mon through Sat.

D Morgan's
28 W. Main St.
(770) 383-3535
www.dmorgans.com
Expensive
Executive Chef Derek Morgan has brought sophisticated global cuisine to a renovated former storefront in Cartersville's increasingly urbane downtown area. Pork tenderloin served with traditional Southern black-eyed peas and garlicky spinach are among the standouts. Grilled scallops are given the haute cuisine treatment with caramelized fennel, caper spätzle, and almond brown butter. Desserts like tart Key lime pie are all made in-house. The wine list is strong, and there's a full bar. Dinner Tues through Sat.

Knight's 1889
24 W. Main St.
(678) 605-1889
www.knights1889.com
Moderate
Great food inside a renovated historic building

owned by the Knight family since 1889. Everything from buffalo wings (and sandwiches) to steaks and an active bar crowd. Nightly specials with a Southern flare.

ROME

City Cellar and Loft
72 S. Railroad St.
(770) 334-3170
www.thecitycellar.com
Moderate
A local favorite where the owners personally take care of you. The menu ranges from seafood to steak and pasta with inventive items like spicy grouper with grits or candied pecan bread pudding. Live music on weekends.

La Scala Restaurant & Bar
465 Broad St., downtown
(706) 238-9000
www.lascalaromega.com
Moderate to Expensive
This attractively done Italian dining room does a *bella* job with pasta, seafood, chicken, and veal dishes and offers many innovative surprises. Signature dishes include chicken Margherita, "dedicated to a beloved young woman," grilled sliced chicken with spinach, red roasted bell peppers, black olives, and ziti pasta; salmon Florentine on a bed of fresh spinach; and cioppino posillipo, a hearty stew of calamari, mussels, shrimp, and bay scallops in a tomato-based sauce, served over angel

hair pasta. Dinner Mon through Sat.

Ross's Diner
17 N. Wall St.
(770) 382-9159
Inexpensive
Ross's opened Labor Day weekend 1945 and has been serving up breakfast and lunch ever since. Good old-fashioned Southern cookin' made to order. Eat at the lunch counter and get extra attention. Closed Sun.

Swheat Market Deli
5 E. Main St.
(770) 607-0067
www.swheatmarket.com
Inexpensive to Moderate
Everything is fresh and comes from local farms and vendors so the menu changes according to season and availability. Wonderful sandwiches, soups, and salads.

DALTON

Garcia's
1205 W. Walnut St.
(706) 529-6855
Moderate
See p. 109 for details.

Dalton Depot Restaurant & Trackside Cafe
110 Depot St.
(706) 226-3160
www.thedaltondepot.net
Moderate
See p. 108 for details.

The Oakwood Cafe
201 W. Cuyler St.
(706) 278-4421
www.oakwoodcafe.net
Inexpensive to Moderate

HELPFUL WEBSITES

Dalton Convention & Visitors Bureau
www.daltoncvb.com

Northwest Georgia Travel Association
www.ngeorgia.com

Rome Convention & Visitors Bureau
www.romegeorgia.com

**Cartersville-Bartow County
Convention & Visitors Bureau**
www.notatlanta.org

Legions of Daltonians wouldn't think about starting their day without Oakwood omelets, hot cakes, and ham and sausage biscuits. They're back at lunch and dinner for steaks, chicken, chops, and seafood. Breakfast, lunch, and dinner are served Mon through Sat.

EAST ELLIJAY

Oscar Poole's Real Pit Bar B-Q
Zell Miller Parkway/GA 515
(706) 635-4100
www.poolesbarbq.com
Moderate
See p. 116 for details.

MIDDLE GEORGIA

→

Cherry Blossoms & Fried Green Tomatoes

For travelers caught in the relentless grind of interstate traffic, Macon can be a quick and refreshing retreat to a slower, easier era. Only a few minutes from the major highways, **Downtown Macon Historic District** offers a glimpse at beautifully restored Greek Revival and Victorian homes, churches, and public buildings on quiet, tree-shaded streets. Three landmark houses are open year-round. Others invite guests during the late March Cherry Blossom Festival and September Jubilee.

Your first stop should be the **Macon-Bibb County Convention and Visitors Bureau** (450 Martin Luther King Jr. Blvd., Macon, www.maconga.org, 800-768-3401 and 478-743-3401). You can pick up free maps, brochures, information, and self-guided tours.

Whether with a guide or on your own, the **Hay House** (478-742-8155, www.hayhouse.org) will be a highlight. Five years a-building, the opulent Italian Renaissance palazzo was finished in April 1861 just as Macon and Georgia were marching off to the War Between the States. Behind the stately

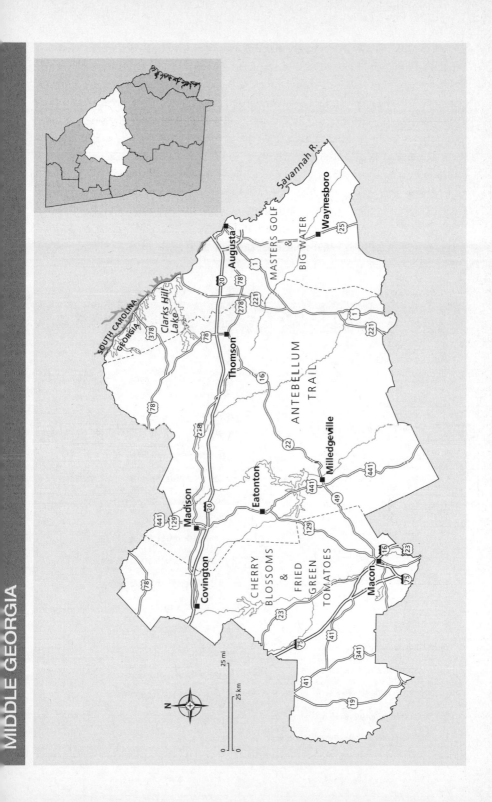

redbrick facade, the 24 rooms are a treasure trove of stained glass, statuary, European and American furnishings, silver and crystal, paintings, and silk and damask draperies and wall coverings. Long before air-conditioning, a cleverly concealed ventilation system kept the high-ceilinged rooms surprisingly cool even on the most torrid summer days. Located at 924 Georgia Ave., Macon, Hay House is open Mon through Sat from 10 a.m. to 4 p.m., Sun 1 to 4:30 p.m. Admission is $9 for adults, $8 for senior citizens, $5 for students; free for children 6 and under. They also offer behind the scenes tours.

Just around the corner at 856 Mulberry St., Macon, a white-columned Greek Revival achieved lasting notoriety when a Union shell crashed through the facade and landed in the front hallway. Walk through the *Cannonball House* and adjoining *Macon Confederate Museum* (478-745-5982, www

MIDDLE GEORGIA'S TOP HITS

Downtown Macon Historic District

Hay House

Cannonball House

The Tubman African American Museum

Ocmulgee National Monument

The Big House

Jarrell Plantation

Piedmont National Wildlife Refuge

Whistle Stop Cafe

Indian Springs State Park

High Falls State Park

Social Circle

Blue Willow Inn Restaurant

Old Governor's Mansion

Flannery O'Connor Room

Milledgeville Trolley Tour

The Uncle Remus Museum

Rock Eagle

Madison–Morgan County Cultural Center

Morgan County African-American Museum

Hard Labor Creek State Park

Rutledge antiques and craft stores

A. H. Stephens State Historic Park & Confederate Museum

Washington Historical Museum

Callaway Plantation

Kettle Creek Battleground

Old Market House

Riverwalk Augusta

Morris Museum of Art

Masters Golf Tournament

Mistletoe State Park

Elijah Clark State Park

.cannonballhouse.org) for a look at the stray missile, Civil War photos, artifacts, china, crystal, weapons, uniforms, and such rare treasures as Mrs. Robert E. Lee's rolling pin. It's open Mon through Sat from 10 a.m. to 4 p.m. Admission is $6 for adults, $5 for senior citizens, $3 for students, free for age 4 and under.

Every Georgia schoolchild learns, at least for the moment, Sidney Lanier's romantic poems "The Marshes of Glynn" and "The Song of the Chattahoochee." Poet, lawyer, linguist, and musician, Lanier was born in 1842 in the tidy Victorian cottage at 935 High St., Macon. His desk, furnishings, and personal effects are displayed at **Sidney Lanier Cottage** (478-743-3851, www.historicmacon .org) Mon through Fri from 10 a.m. to 4 p.m., Sat from 9:30 a.m. to 12:30 p.m. Admission is $5 for adults, $4 for seniors, and $3 for students.

Macon's modern musical heritage includes Rock 'n' Roll Hall of Famer "Little Richard" Penniman, soul singer Otis Redding (a life-size statue of Otis sitting on the dock of the bay can be found near the entrance of Gateway Park), and the Allman Brothers Band. Duane Allman and fellow band member Berry Oakley—both killed in 1970s motorcycle accidents—are buried in much-visited graves at **Rose Hill Cemetery.** Maconites from all the way back to the 1830s and 600 Confederate and Union soldiers are also in the historic cemetery at 1071 Riverside Dr., Macon. Call (478) 751-9119 or visit www.historicrosehill cemetery.org for information.

Allman Brothers fans can also make a pilgrimage to the place where many of their songs were created, **The Big House**. Home to the Allman Brothers Band Museum, this Tudor-style house was the place where the band lived just after they formed in 1969 and it was the center of all their early activity. The museum holds a vast array of their instruments as well and clothing, posters, and even gold records. Located at 2321 Vuine St., Macon. Call (478) 741-5551 or visit www.thebighousemuseum.com. Open Thurs through Sun 11 a.m. to 6 p.m.; adults $8, seniors and military $6, children 3 to 10 $4.

The **Tubman African American Museum** (downtown at 340 Walnut St., Macon, 478-743-8544, www.tubmanmuseum.com) displays paintings, sculpture, and other creative endeavors by black American, African, and Caribbean artists and craftspeople. The **Resources Room** has available reference materials and books on black Americans. The museum's shop sells handcrafted jewelry, paintings, posters, recordings, and books. A mural depicting contemporary black characters features Colin Powell as a military hero. Open Tues through Fri from 9 a.m. to 5 p.m., Sat 11 a.m. to 5 p.m. Admission is $6 for adults, $5 for seniors and the military, $4 for children 4 to 17; free for children under 4.

Ocmulgee National Monument, a short drive from downtown, is a must-see for anyone fascinated by ancient Native American civilization. A dozen ceremonial and burial mounds, the highest nearly 45 feet, were built by

Mississippian Indians between about AD 900 and 1100. They were succeeded at the site by Creeks, who remained here until their expulsion to Oklahoma in the 1830s.

Stop first at the National Park Service Visitors Center and see a short film, artifacts unearthed from the mounds, and dioramas on the cultures that flourished here. You can climb steep wooden stairs to the flat top of the 45-foot-high *Great Temple Mound* and to the crest of the surrounding smaller mounds. You may also see them from the comfort of your car. A sound-and-light presentation brings the circular *Earthlodge* back to life, as tribal elders discuss plans for a war, the effects of a drought, and other important issues. The monument is at 1207 Emery Hwy., Macon (478-752-8257, www.nps.gov/ocmu). Hours are (daily) 9 a.m. to 5 p.m. Free admission.

The *Georgia Sports Hall of Fame* (301 Cherry St., Macon, 478-752-1585, www.georgiasportshalloffame.com), a 43,000-square-foot museum, showcases heroes of golf, football, baseball, basketball, and other endeavors. You'll be able to test your skills on interactive and virtual reality games. Open Mon through Sat 9 a.m. to 5 p.m., Sun 1 to 5 p.m. Admission is $8 for adults; $6 for military personnel, college students with ID, and senior citizens 60 and older; $3.50 for children 6 to 16; free for children 5 and under.

Douglass Theatre (335 Martin Luther King Jr. Blvd., Macon, 478-742-2000, www.douglasstheatre.org) was built in 1921 by African-American businessman Charles Douglass. The downtown Macon theater hosted many of the country's most acclaimed performers. Among the talents that delighted audiences for more than three decades were Duke Ellington, Bessie Smith, Cab Calloway, Nat King Cole, Billie Holliday, James Brown, "Ma" Rainey, and Macon's own Otis Redding and "Little Richard" Penniman. Restored and reopened in 1996, the Douglass now has state-of-the-art facilities for movies and live performances and an archive of black history in music, film, and drama. Open for tours Mon through Sat from 9 a.m. to 5 p.m., Sun from noon to 5 p.m. Donations accepted.

To get in the proper antebellum spirit, make reservations at the *1842 Inn* (353 College St., Macon, www.1842inn.com, 478-741-1842 or 800-336-1842). The 22 guest rooms in the circa-1842 Greek Revival showplace and an adjacent cottage are decorated with antiques, fresh flowers, fireplaces, and all the contemporary comforts. Some rooms have whirlpool baths. Double rates (expensive) include continental breakfast and afternoon wine and hors d'oeuvres.

During the last 10 days of March, more than 300,000 Japanese cherry trees set the stage for the city's annual *Cherry Blossom Festival* highlighted by concerts, home and garden tours, parades, and other activities. You won't be in town very long before proud Maconites tell you that in sheer numbers of blossoming trees, if nothing else, their festival is bigger than Washington, D.C.'s.

Cherry blossom season or not, you'll still enjoy a drive by the stately homes on north Macon's "Cherry Blossom Trail," several miles of streets marked by pink and white signs. For information: www.cherryblossom.com or (478) 751-7429.

Twila Faye's Tea Room & Soda Fountain (US 41, off I-75/Bolingbroke, 478-994-0031) is a sweet old-fashioned retreat from the crass commercialism and junk food of I-75. The soda fountain and cafe is a delightful place to sip sodas; sundaes; phosphates; cherry, vanilla, and lemon Cokes; a big choice of teas (served English style with finger sandwiches, scones, and shortbread tea cakes); and lunch and dinner on salads, house-made soups, and a variety of nutritious sandwiches and Southern cooking. It's open from 11 a.m. to 5 p.m. Mon through Fri, and 11 a.m. to 9 p.m. Sat.

Jarrell Plantation State Historic Site is a homespun juxtaposition to the romanticized Old South of Tara and Twelve Oaks, dashing beaux and ladies fair. At the end of a tree-shaded graveled road off GA 18 between Forsyth and Gray, you enter a world where unrelenting hard work—not flirtation and idle mint juleps—was the rule of society. From the early 1840s, when John Fitz Jarrell built the first dwelling, until 1958, when the last direct heir died, the plantation was worked by three generations of Jarrells. They planted cotton, ran gins and gristmills, and battled boll weevils, depressions, and General William Tecumseh Sherman himself. Nowadays, the dwellings, work buildings, barnyards, and fields are maintained by the Georgia Department of Natural Resources as a living memorial to the state's agricultural heritage.

Harlem's Oliver Hardy

One of the silver screen's most popular and recognizable comedians was born in 1892 in the small eastern Georgia town of Harlem. Rotund fussbudget Oliver Hardy left home when he was 8 years old and joined a traveling show as a boy soprano. Weary of the road, he attended Georgia Military Academy and studied law at the University of Georgia.

But greasepaint was apparently in his blood. He opened Milledgeville's first movie house and was so intrigued by the films, he became a comic villain in a theater company. In the mid-1920s, he went to Hollywood and teamed up with his sidekick and foil, Stan Laurel. It was a match made in the stars. They appeared together in more than 100 pictures and performed on radio, stage, and TV. Hardy died in 1957, and his memory lives on at Harlem's *Laurel and Hardy Festival* in early October. Visitors enjoy a Laurel and Hardy film fest and a look-alike contest (www.laurelandhardy.org). You can also visit the ever popular Laurel and Hardy Museum at 250 N. Louisville St.; for more information call (706) 556-0401 or visit www.laurelandhardymuseum.org, Tues through Sat 10 a.m. to 4 p.m.

You'll enter the plantation through the scuppernong arbor, whose juicy fruit Jarrell women turned into pies and jellies. A flock of guinea fowl, squawking like so many feathered burglar alarms, alerted the family that visitors were approaching. These days, the guinea fowl still sound off, and an assortment of barnyard animals—a goat, a horse, a brown milk cow, a burro, a couple of sheep—press against the fence for the hay held out by children.

At the modern visitor center, you can watch a film on the plantation's history and pick up a self-guided walking-tour map.

At the 1847 plantation's plain first dwelling, you can visualize the womenfolk sitting in a circle, busily making quilts and clothes while hearty stews bubbled on the wood-burning stove. At the mill complex down the hill from the house, workmen get the steam engine ready to grind the sugarcane into syrup. The site was donated to the State of Georgia by his descendents.

Jarrell Plantation (Route 1, Box 40, Juliette, 478-986-5172, 800-864-PARK, www.gastateparks.org) is open Thurs through Sat from 9 a.m. to 5 p.m. Admission is $6 for adults, $3.50 for children 6 to 18; free for children 5 and under. It's 18 miles south of I-75 exit 185 at Forsyth, 18 miles north of I-75 exit 171 at Macon.

The *Piedmont National Wildlife Refuge,* a 35,000-acre preserve 10 miles down the graveled road from the plantation, has a visitor center and hiking trails. You can bring your fishing gear and try your luck in the Ocmulgee River. Phone (478) 986-5441 or visit www.fws.gov/piedmont.

If you saw the movie *Fried Green Tomatoes* or read the Fannie Flagg novel it was based on, you'll be glad to know it wasn't pure fiction. After the movie's highly successful 1991 run, enterprising folks in the almost-ghost town of *Juliette* bought up the store that served as the movie's cafe and reopened the "new" *Whistle Stop Cafe* (478-992-8886, www.thewhistlestopcafe.com). Fried green tomatoes are served, along with barbecue, fried chicken, meat loaf, pork chops, and other home-cooked favorites. Southern-style breakfast is also served. The block of stores and the white frame depot around the cafe have also been revived as antiques and gift shops. Adding to the atmosphere, local kids dive off the dam near the textile mill, just as they did in the film. The Whistle Stop Cafe is open Mon through Fri 11 a.m. to 4 p.m. It's in downtown Juliette, 10 miles off I-75 north and south exit 186. Inexpensive.

A quiet and peaceful recreation place now, *Indian Springs State Park,* near Jackson, has a long, colorful, and tragic history. For many centuries Creeks and other tribes gathered at a sulfur spring whose waters were believed to have magical powers to cure ailments and restore vitality. In the spring of 1825, Creek Chief William McIntosh signed an illegal treaty ceding all tribal lands to the state of Georgia. The fraudulent treaty so enraged the dispossessed natives that they murdered McIntosh and several of his followers. A valid treaty in 1828 finally ended Creek dominion, and the town of Indian Springs was founded, along with what's believed to be the oldest state park anywhere in the United States.

Nowadays people still flock to the sulfur springs and take home jugs of the strong-smelling water. They swear by its ability to restore health and vitality and offer this advice to those who quail at the rotten-egg smell: Just let it sit for 2 to 3 days, and the aroma will vanish, but not the curative strength of the minerals.

The handsome fieldstone buildings in the park were built during the Great Depression by the Civilian Conservation Corps. Along with the mineral waters, artifacts and historical displays are on view at the *Indian Museum*. Around a 105-acre lake are a swimming beach, fishing, rental boats, nature trails, and picnic areas. Campsites with electrical and water hookups are $25 a night. Completely furnished 2-bedroom cottages, with log-burning fireplaces, are available. There is a $5 per visit parking fee. Contact Park Superintendent at 678 Lake Clark Rd., Flovilla, (770) 504-2277. For reservations, call (800) 864-PARK or log on to www.gastateparks.org.

Fresh Air Bar-B-Que (770-775-3182, www.freshairbarbque.com), on GA 42 between Jackson and Indian Springs State Park, is one of the holy grails of this savory Georgia art form. Except for wooden planking that covered the old sawdust floor a few years ago, and one change of ownership more than 50 years ago, this rambling, wooden barbecue shack has changed only marginally since it served its first platter in 1929.

The pine board tables have been in place for more than 40 years. Pork is slowly cooked over hickory and oak coals right behind the ordering counter. It's sweet and succulent, with a tangy pièce de résistance provided by a secret sauce prepared by the family that has operated the place since the early 1940s. Along with barbecued pork, the simple menu includes only Brunswick stew, coleslaw, slabs of starchy white bread, soft drinks, and iced tea. It's open Mon through Thurs from 7 a.m. to 7:30 p.m., Fri and Sat until 9:30 p.m., and Sun until 8:30 p.m. During the summer, it usually remains open a half hour to an hour later.

High Falls State Park, off GA 36 (I-75 exit 198), about 12 miles south of Indian Springs, is another rustic off-the-beaten-path retreat. The centerpiece is a series of scenic whitewater cataracts of the *Towaliga River* rushing over mossy rocks. According to legend, Creek Indians "cured" their victims' scalps around the Towaliga—hence the name, which means "roasted scalp."

Two hiking trails offer views of the falls, the river, and adjacent woodlands. You can wade into the river, but be extremely careful of the slick, mossy rocks.

Also in the 995-acre park, you'll find a 650-acre lake for fishing and boating, a swimming pool, and 142 tent and trailer sites, with water and electrical hookups. There is a $5 per visit parking fee. Contact Park Superintendent: Route 5, 76 High Falls Park Dr., Jackson, (478) 993-3053, (800) 864-PARK, www.gastate parks.org. Open 7 a.m. to 10 p.m. For reservations call (800) 864-PARK. It's 1.8 miles east of I-75 exit 198/High Falls Road.

The little Walton County town of *Social Circle,* about 8 miles west of Hard Labor Creek on GA 11, is a delightful place to stroll and browse. The 19th-century storefronts have been brightly repainted, and three are antiques shops. The wooden shelves in Claude T. Wiley's Store are stacked to the ceiling with canned goods, overalls, farm products, and household necessities. The town allegedly got its name when a stranger happened onto a cluster of idling locals and found them so friendly he proclaimed, "Why, this is sure some social circle."

The *Blue Willow Inn Restaurant* (294 N. Cherokee Rd., GA 11, Social Circle, 770-464-2131, www.bluewillowinn.com) is like a nostalgic Sunday dinner at Grandma's. The dining room of the 1890s Victorian house is filled with a bountiful buffet that includes fried chicken, pork chops, chicken and dumplings, baked ham, an array of vegetables (including state-of-the-art fried green tomatoes), congealed salads, cake, and fruit cobbler—all at astonishingly modest prices. After your feast, sit on front porch rockers, walk in Billie Van Dyke's gardens, and stroll down Social Circle's Main Street. Open Mon through Fri from 11 a.m. to 2:30 p.m. and 5 to 8 p.m., Sat from 11 a.m. to 2:30 p.m. and 4:30 to 9 p.m., and Sun from 11 a.m. to 7 p.m. Adjacent to the inn is the *Blue Willow Village,* a specialty shopping area.

Lake Oconee, a mammoth Georgia Power Company impoundment of the Oconee River, is a major destination for outdoor recreation. The 19,000-acre lake, with a 375-mile shoreline, has numerous marinas, campsites, picnicking areas, and swimming beaches. The Georgia Power Company office at the lake (800-886-LAKE, www.visitlakeoconee.com) can supply further information about recreational facilities. The lake is easily accessible from I-20.

The *Ritz-Carlton Lodge at Reynolds Plantation* (1 Oconee Lake Trail, Greensboro, 800-241-3333, 706-467-0600, www.ritzcarlton.com/reynolds plantation) brings high luxury to Lake Oconee's shores. The Adirondacks-style lodge's 251 guest rooms and suites have all the deluxe bells and whistles. Guests enjoy fine wining and dining; water sports, tennis, 4 superb golf courses; and pampering in the wellness center. Expensive.

The Ritz-Carlton and other upscale developments around the lake have been a boon to nearby Greensboro. Antiques shops around the courthouse square attract browsers and buyers, who can also visit a couple of historic curiosities. The **Old Rock Gaol,** a fortress-like jail built in 1807 and in use until 1895, bears a grim resemblance to Paris's notorious Bastille, on which it was allegedly modeled. Granite walls 2 feet thick, with small barred windows and a rooftop gallows, warned citizens to stick to the straight and narrow. Or else. It can be toured by appointment with the Greene County Chamber of Commerce, 111 N. Main St., Greensboro, (706) 453-7592, (866) 341-4466, (800) 886-5253, www.greeneccoc.org. After visiting the Gaol and downtown shops, enjoy lunch and dinner at **The Yesterday Cafe** at 114 N. Main St., www.the yesterdaycafe.com, (706) 453-0800. See "Where to Eat in Middle Georgia," p. 146, for details.

The Iron Horse, visible in a pasture on GA 15 at the Oconee River Bridge, was originally a public sculpture placed on the University of Georgia campus in 1954. But after students looked the gift horse in the mouth, then shamefully vandalized it, the 2,000-pound scrap-iron sculpture was relocated in a cornfield where he safely grazes in sight but out of harm's way.

Antebellum Trail

Milledgeville was Georgia's capital city from early after the American Revolution until after the War Between the States. Laid out in 1803–1804 on a precise grid of broad streets and public squares, it was the only American city other than Washington, D.C., specifically planned as a capital. In its own way, it was to post-Revolutionary Georgia what Brasilia was to mid-20th-century Brazil: a magnet intended to lure settlers away from the comforts of the Atlantic coast.

Statesmen and public officials eased the burdens of the wilderness by building palatial Greek Revival mansions filled with the finest American and European furnishings, books, and art. Halcyon days ended in the fall of 1864, when General William T. Sherman's Union army, marching from Atlanta to Savannah, captured the city.

According to which legend you choose to believe, Milledgeville was spared Sherman's torch because (a) he was met at the outskirts by fellow brothers of the local Masonic lodge, who pleaded for leniency; (b) he didn't want to burn a town he'd chosen as temporary headquarters; or (c) he had a local lady friend and did not wish to break her heart.

The real reason was that Milledgeville had no military significance. Union troops burned the military arsenal and stoked molasses down the pipes of the Episcopal church, which was used as a horse stable. When the "March to the Sea" resumed, the Governor's Mansion and everything of nonmilitary importance was left unharmed. The Reconstruction government moved the capital to Atlanta, an action ratified by the state's voters in 1868.

The Old State Capitol and Old Governor's Mansion are the most tangible landmarks of Milledgeville's tenure as Georgia's capital city from 1838 to 1868. When Union troops occupied the city in 1864, they held a mock session of the state legislature in the Gothic-style capitol and "revoked" the Ordinance of Secession that took Georgia out of the Union in 1861. Recently restored, the building, at 301 E. Greene St., Milledgeville (478-453-1803, www.oldcapitol museum.org), is now a classroom building for Georgia Military College. Cadets lead tours Mon through Fri, 10 a.m. to 4 p.m. and Sat noon to 4 p.m. that include a historical museum and the antebellum House Chamber. Adults $2, students $1.

The **Old Governor's Mansion,** built in 1838 in Palladian Greek Revival style, underwent a $10 million restoration, completed in 2005, that returned it to its 1850s grandeur. The Marquis de Lafayette danced the minuet in the mansion's ballroom during his 1825 farewell to America tour. One of Georgia's most beautiful public buildings, the rose-hued mansion with four Ionic columns and a wealth of antiques, art, and unique architectural features, is at 120 S. Clark St., Milledgeville. Call (478) 445-4545 or visit www.gcsu.edu/mansion. Open Tues through Sat from 10 a.m. to 4 p.m., Sun 2 to 4 p.m. Adults $10, seniors $7, students $2.

American literature fans should also visit the **Flannery O'Connor Room** (478-445-4047, www.library.gcsu.edu) in the library of Georgia College and State University. The late author wrote her two novels (*The Violent Bear It Away* and *Wise Blood*) and short story collections while living here. She died in 1964 and is buried in Memory Hill Cemetery. The Flannery O'Connor Room at her alma mater displays first editions, manuscripts, gifts from admirers, memorabilia, and drawings she did as a hobby. It's in the Georgia College and Instructional Technology Center, Georgia College, Milledgeville. Tours are self-guided but guided tours are available by appointment. Open Mon through Sat 10 a.m. to 4 p.m. Donations are accepted.

O'Connor's fans shouldn't miss **Andalusia,** the author's 544-acre farm on US 441, 4 miles northwest of Milledgeville, where she wrote many of her stories. A self-guided tour includes the gently rolling farmland that inspired so much of her fiction, the main house, barns, equipment and milk-processing sheds, horse stable, and 3 tenant houses. On your tour, you'll probably encounter some of the "residents": white-tailed deer, wild turkeys, red-tailed hawks, beavers, raccoons, opossums, birds, reptiles, and amphibians. In the main house, rooms open to the public include O'Connor's bedroom, the dining room, and the kitchen. Guests are invited to view the video production of O'Connor's story, *The Displaced Person,* which was filmed on location at Andalusia in 1976. Andalusia is open for tours on Mon, Tues, Thurs, Fri, and Sat from 10 a.m. to 4

TOP ANNUAL EVENTS

Macon Cherry Blossom Festival
mid- to late March
(800) 768-3401

Madison's Spring Tour of Homes
mid-April
(706) 342-4743

Washington-Wilkes Tour of Homes
early April, Washington
(706) 678-2013

Masters Golf Tournament
early April, Augusta
(800) 726-4067

Riverwalk Bluegrass Festival
early May, Augusta
(706) 592-0054

Oliver Hardy Festival
early October, Harlem
(706) 556-3448

Blind Willie McTell Blues Festival
early October, Thomson
(706) 595-5584

Ocmulgee Indian Celebration
late September, Ocmulgee National
Monument, Macon
(800) 768-3401

Green Tomato Festival
Late October, Juliette
(478) 992-8886

Twelve Days of Christmas
mid-November to end of December,
Millodgovillo
(800) 653-1804

Christmas at Callaway Plantation
early December, Washington
(706) 678-7060

p.m. Admission is free, but there is a suggestion of a $5 donation. For information, call (478) 454-4029 or log on to www.andalusiafarm.org.

The best way to enjoy the town's heritage is on a 2-hour motorized *Milledgeville Trolley Tour,* which covers the major landmarks and includes a visit to the Governor's Mansion. Guides weave a wealth of humor and anecdotes into their historical narrative. Tours leave the Milledgeville Convention and Visitors Bureau (200 W. Hancock St., Milledgeville), Tues and Fri at 10 a.m. and Sat at 2 p.m. Adults are $10; children 6 to 12, $5. The tourism office (478-452-4687 and 800-653-1804, www.visitmilledgeville.org) also has free maps and information for self-guided walking tours. It's directly across the street from the handsome *Baldwin County Courthouse.*

Milledgeville is a "high-spirited" town. If you'd like to hear about some of its specters, join the *Milledgeville Grits* (132 Hardwick St., downtown Milledgeville, 478-453-2520), where ravenous students and other townsfolk satisfy their craving for perfectly prepared fried chicken, fish, sweet potato casserole, turnip and collard greens, squash soufflé, pecan pie, and other Southern comfort food. Lunch every day except Sat. Inexpensive. Also downtown, you'll find sushi bars, Chinese buffets, Mexican, Italian, and barbecue restaurants.

Antebellum Inn, in Milledgeville's downtown historic district (200 N. Columbia St., Milledgeville, 478-454-5400, www.antebelluminn.com) has 5 guest rooms and suites, with private bath, cable TV, phone, pool, and wraparound verandas, all in an 1890s Victorian home. Moderate rates include full breakfast.

After Milledgeville's history lesson, you'll probably be ready for some quiet relaxation. **Lake Sinclair,** a 15,330-acre, 420-mile shoreline impoundment of the Oconee River, has plenty of stretching room. Marinas, fishing docks, and campgrounds are off US 441 north of Milledgeville.

Milledgeville's literary lioness was Flannery O'Connor. Eatonton, about 15 miles north on US 441, was the birthplace in 1848 of Joel Chandler Harris, who turned the slave legends he heard as a youngster on a Putnam County plantation into the *Uncle Remus: Tales.*

The **Uncle Remus Museum** (706-485-6856, www.uncleremus.com/museum), on US 441, Eatonton, south of the town of 4,800, has Harris's personal mementos and illustrations of the tales of the devilish Br'er Rabbit, sly-but-perpetually-outwitted Br'er Fox, dumb ole Br'er Bear, and, of course, the Tar Baby. Also in the log cabin, which was created from 3 original slave cabins, you'll see first editions, a diorama of an antebellum plantation, and other historical artifacts. The museum is open daily during the summer from 10 a.m. to 5 p.m. and closed on Tues Nov through Mar. Adults are $1; children, 50 cents. Eatonton also is the home of Alice Walker, Pulitzer Prize–winning author of *The Color Purple.* With the **Alice Walker Driving Tour** brochure from the Putnam County Chamber of Commerce office (105 S. Washington Ave., Eatonton, 706-485-7701, www.eatonton.com), see the church she attended, her parents' graves, the house where she grew up, and other landmarks of her life.

As you drive past the Putnam County Courthouse in the center of Eatonton, look for the little likeness of Br'er Rabbit on the lawn facing US 441. Many well-kept antebellum homes are on the shady streets leading off the courthouse square. Putnam County is also the center of Georgia's dairy industry, so you'll spot several contented herds as you drive out of town.

Rock Eagle, 4 miles north of Eatonton, is a relic of Indian civilizations that flourished here more than 6,000 years ago. A creamy white quartz effigy—about 10 feet high, 103 feet from its head to its tail, 32 feet from wingtip to wingtip—the great bird seems poised for flight. Archaeologists believe Rock Eagle was a focus for Indian tribal rituals. The best views are from an observation tower. It's located in a 4-H Club Center, on GA 74, off US 441. Call (706) 484-2800 or visit www.rockeagle4h.org for more information.

Morgan County, between Augusta and Atlanta, claims **Madison** (I-20 exit 114/US 441), one of Georgia's prettiest antebellum towns. In 2007, *Money* magazine named Madison one of "The Best Places to Live." Years later, it's as beguiling as ever. Before leaving, you can relax at a state park with an 18-hole golf course and fish and swim at a 19,000-acre lake.

Strolling along the tree-shaded streets and picturesque town square, admiring Madison's treasury of glorious antebellum architecture, we should say "thank you" to a United States senator who put himself between the town and General William T. Sherman's torch. In late 1864, Atlanta in ruins 60 miles away and the cruel "March to the Sea" in full stride, Sherman's Union army approached Madison's outskirts. They were met by former Senator Joshua Hill, a foe of secession who'd been acquainted with Sherman in Washington. He peacefully surrendered the town, which was miraculously spared war's ravages.

Your first stop should be the **Madison–Morgan County Chamber of Commerce Welcome Center** (115 E. Jefferson St., Madison, 706-342-4454, 800-709-7406, www.madisonga.com). In this former 1880s fire station on the courthouse square, you can load up on walking-tour maps and brochures and get any information you may need on festivals, bed-and-breakfasts, and restaurants. Stop next at the **Madison–Morgan County Cultural Center** (434 S. Main St., Madison, 706-342-4743, www.mmcc-arts.org). The Romanesque-style redbrick schoolhouse, circa 1895, is now the hub for regional arts, theater performances, and the source of walking-tour maps of the fetching little town of 3,000. The former schoolrooms now show pottery, weaving, paintings by Georgia artists and traveling exhibitions, 19th-century furniture, farm implements, clothing, and Civil War artifacts. You can also see a log cabin from the early 1800s and an 1890s schoolroom, complete with pot-bellied stove and hickory switch. The center's August theater festival features everything from Shakespeare to Tennessee Williams. The center is open Tues through Sat from 10 a.m. to 4:30 p.m., Sun from 2 to 5 p.m. Admission is $3 for adults, $2.50 for seniors, $2 for students; 6 and under free. No charge on Wed.

With a self-guided tour map, walk through the **Madison National Historic District** and admire more than three dozen gorgeous Greek Revival, neoclassical, Victorian, Federal, and Romanesque homes, many of them graced by gardens and stately trees. A number of these old beauties are open to the public during Madison's May and December festivals.

The **Morgan County African-American Museum** (156 Academy St., Madison, 706-342-9191, www.mcaam.org) documents the contributions blacks have made to the area's cultural and social life. Located in the 1895 Horace Moore House, the museum has rooms with period furnishings, a reference library, paintings, books, and exhibits. Open Tues through Sat from 10 a.m. to 4 p.m. Admission is $4 for adults, $3 for students.

You can take a guided tour of **Heritage Hall** (277 S. Main St., Madison, 706-342-9627, www.friendsofheritagehall.com), a white-columned 1830s Greek Revival showplace near the courthouse square. Look for romantic messages etched on the windows, and be mindful of a mysterious presence that sometimes evidences itself in an upstairs bedroom. Open Mon through Sat from 11 a.m. to 4 p.m. and Sun 1:30 to 4:30 p.m. Adults are $5; students, $2.

Madison's town square is one of Georgia's most delightful, and the **Morgan County Courthouse** one of the grandest in the 159 counties. Several antiques and handicraft stores will draw your attention as you stroll around the square. When hunger strikes, head for the cafeteria line at **Ye Olde Colonial** (Courthouse Square, Madison, 706-342-2211), a unique dining landmark on the square. Once upon a time the building was a bank, which accounts for the high ceilings, tiled floors, and a small dining room in the one-time vault. These days you can cash in on excellent fried chicken, barbecue, fish, Southern-style vegetables, and hearty breakfasts with biscuits and buttery grits. Service is continuous from breakfast through lunch and dinner Mon through Sat (11 a.m. to 8 p.m.).

Several of Madison's loveliest homes welcome bed-and-breakfast guests: **Brady Inn** (250 N. 2nd St., 706-342-4400, www.bradyinn.com), **Southern Cross Guest Ranch B&B** (1670 Bethany Church Rd., 706-342-8027, 800-342-8027, www.southcross.com), **The Farmhouse Inn** (1051 Meadow Ln., 706-342-7933, www.thefarmhouseinn.com), **Reese-Bourgeois Cottage** (444 N. Main St., 706-342-4603, wwww.reesebourgeoiscottage.com), and **Madison Oaks Inn and Gardens** (766 East Ave., 706-343-9900, www.madisonoaksinn .com).

The **Steffen Thomas Museum and Archives,** near the rural Morgan County community of Buckhead, houses hundreds of oil and watercolor paintings, mosaics, and sculptures by late German-born expressionist artist Steffen Thomas, who did most of his work in Atlanta. Like many artists, Thomas was his own model: *The Goat of Mentelle* is the self-portrait sculpture of the artist as a billy goat. (He lived on Mentelle Street in Atlanta.) The museum is at 4200 Bethany Rd., 3 miles from I-20 exit 121. Open Tues through Sat 11 a.m. to 4 p.m. Phone (706) 342-7557 or log on to www.steffenthomas.org. Adults $6, students free.

Hard Labor Creek State Park, 12 miles west of Madison, near the small community of Rutledge, is a nice place to relax for a day, or several days. The recreational possibilities include a very good 18-hole golf course and a lake for swimming, boating, and fishing. Plenty of picnic tables are spread among the pines, and there's a playground for the youngsters. If you're planning to play the 6,682-yard, par-72 course (www.georgiagolf.com/the-creek), bring your own clubs. You may rent an electric cart in the clubhouse, which has showers and a snack bar. The park's 50 campsites have water, electricity, restrooms, and showers; 20 2-bedroom cottages are completely furnished, including towels, sheets, and kitchen utensils. There is a $5 per visit parking fee. The park office is open daily from 8 a.m. to 5 p.m. Contact Superintendent: 5 Hard Labor Creek Rd., Rutledge, (706) 557-3001. For reservations call (800) 864-PARK or log on to www.gastateparks.org.

Until recently *Rutledge* (I-20 exit 105, www.rutledgega.us) was a couple of blinks as you passed through on the way to Hard Labor Creek. During the past few years, a group of citizens has bought up much of the town of 650 and attracted a cadre of artists and craftspeople from as far away as New England. You'll see why their motto is "Small but Special." *Rutledge antiques and craft stores* on the main street sell handmade quilts, handcrafted furniture, original artwork, pottery, and antiques. At *Red Door Studio* (706-557-9020, www.reddoorstudio.com) Molly Lesnikowski crafts birdhouses from Victorian textile spindles, and also sells watercolor paintings and painted furniture. *Rutledge Hardware* (706-557-1770) has been in continuous operation since the late 1800s and changed only marginally the past half century. Paul Jones fills orders for galvanized tubs, cast-iron cookware, tools, seed, farm implements, and chamber pots "like my great-grandpa used." Its shelves are filled with gifts and collectibles, bath products, and lotions. When it's time for a break, many shoppers enjoy ice cream, colorful shaved ices, sandwiches, and salads at *The Caboose* (706-557-9021), a revamped 1910 railroad car. The entire delightful town is now on the National Register of Historic Places.

For breakfast and lunch locals and visitors take tables and booths at *Yesterday's Cafe* (706-557-9337). Kris Bray's delicious repertoire includes Southern breakfast, highlighted by blueberry and buttermilk pancakes, grits, and country ham. At lunchtime the menu features burgers, sandwiches, soups, and the cafe's signature dish, buttermilk pie. Open for breakfast and lunch daily. Inexpensive to moderate.

A. H. Stephens State Historic Park, on GA 22, Crawfordville, outside the small town of Crawfordville, includes the home and gravesite of Alexander Hamilton Stephens, governor of Georgia and vice president of the Confederacy. *Liberty Hall,* the 2-story frame house Stephens built around 1830, is filled with his furnishings, personal effects, and the wheelchairs to which he was bound much of his life.

The adjoining *Confederate Museum* (706-456-2602, 800-864-PARK, www .gastateparks.org) is highlighted by a bronze statue of Stephens by Gutzon Borglum, sculptor of the US presidents on Mount Rushmore, South Dakota. This

Sunshine & Sunflowers

Just seeing a sunflower brings a smile to my face, and showing up at the **West-Holt Family Farm** outside of Rutledge is enough to leave me grinning for days. Drive just south of I-20's Rutledge exit and you'll find 15 acres of sunflowers. The scene is just breathtaking.

The farm was started as a cotton farm, and in 1936 W. W. West and his wife Pauline bought it as a place to raise their five (and eventually eight) children. It wasn't until the 1980s that West's son decided to start growing sunflowers to help provide Pennington Seed company with seeds for their birdfeed.

All of those bright yellow flowers were too much to pass up. People started stopping by and asking if they could cut some flowers and take pictures. Wes Holt, grandson of W. W., set up cut-your-own stations that proved so popular, the family decided to hold a festival.

In late June and much of July the flowers are in full bloom and it is a guaranteed happy place to be.

Around the Fourth of July, the family (fifth generation) hosts the **Sunflower Festival.** It's good, clean, old-fashioned fun in a spectacular setting. Events include an antique tractor parade, hayrides, an artist's market, local music, and tours of the 1811 McCowan-McRee farmhouse and 1891 Sharecropper's Market.

Oh, and as with any gathering out in the country, there is plenty of food to go around as well.

The best part is that everyone gets to cut their own bouquet of sunflowers to take home with them. The farm is located at 1430 Durden Rd. For more info, call (706) 557-2870 or visit www.sunflowerfarmfestival.com.

If you somehow miss the festival, there are usually plenty of flowers remaining for you to stop by and cut your own.

fine collection of memorabilia also includes dioramas of soldiers in the heat of battle and the quiet of the campfire; rifles and shot; field gear; battle flags; and touching personal belongings—Bibles, prayer books, and bloodstained photos of wives and sweethearts.

As in all wars, Civil War soldiers used sharp-edged humor to help blunt the insidious enemies of fear and homesickness. "In this army," a Confederate foot soldier wrote, "one hole in the seat of the breeches indicates a captain, two holes is for a lieutenant, and the seat of the pants all out is for us privates." Liberty Hall and the Confederate Museum are open Mon and Wed through Sat from 9 a.m. to 5 p.m., Sun from 2 to 5:30 p.m. Closed Tues. Admission is $4 for adults, $2.75 for children 5 to 18; free for children under 5.

After your history lesson, relax at the park's recreation area. Located 0.25 mile from Liberty Hall, you'll find a swimming pool, 2 fishing lakes, picnic shelters, 4 cottages, and 22 tent and trailer sites, with water and electrical hookups, showers, and restrooms. The museum and park are 2 miles from I-20 exit 148, Crawfordville. There is a $5 per visit parking fee. On a more modern note, scenes from the 2002 Reese Witherspoon film *Sweet Home Alabama* were filmed in Crawfordville.

Incorporated in 1780, the picture-book little town of **Washington** was the first American community named in honor of the father of our country. Skirted by General William T. Sherman's rampaging "March to the Sea" and treated kindly by progress and time, the town of about 4,000 is today like a living Williamsburg. More than 30 Greek Revival homes, churches, and public buildings predate 1850. Most of them are still well-maintained residences. Three antebellum landmarks are open to visitors year-round.

The **Robert Toombs House State Historic Site** (216 E. Robert Toombs Ave., Washington, 706-678-2226, www.gastateparks.org) was the home of Georgia's "Unreconstructed Rebel," US senator, and Confederate secretary of state. At odds with the Confederacy—he was resentful of Jefferson Davis's presidency—as well as the Union, he fled to the Caribbean and Europe after the war. Returning in 1880, he scorned political pardon. "I am not loyal to the government of the United States," he declared, "and do not wish to be suspected of loyalty." The guided tours of his Greek Revival house include a documentary film, anecdotes, historical exhibits, and several rooms with period furnishings. Open Tues through Sat from 9 a.m. to 5 p.m. Admission is $3 for adults, $2 for children 6 to 18; free for children under 5.

The **Washington Historical Museum** (308 E. Robert Toombs Ave., Washington, 706-678-2105, www.museum.washingtonga.net) houses an outstanding collection of Civil War artifacts, including Jefferson Davis's camp chest (given to him by English sympathizers), weapons, uniforms, signed documents, photographs, and furnishings. The main floor of the circa 1835–1836 2-story frame house is furnished as a typical 19th-century double parlor, dining room, and bedroom. The ground floor has been restored as a period kitchen. The grounds are noted for beautiful landscaping and one of Georgia's largest camellia gardens. Hours are Tues through Sat from 10 a.m. to 5 p.m., Sun from 12:30 to 3 p.m. Admission is $3 for adults, $2 for children ages 5 to 12, under age 5 free.

Callaway Plantation (5 miles west of Washington on US 78, 2160 Lexington Rd., Washington, 706-678-7060, www.callaway.washingtonga.net) is a living heritage museum rich in lessons about Southern antebellum life. Three restored homes and the adjoining farm are like a walk back in time. The redbrick, white-columned manor house was the heart of a 3,000-acre cotton plantation. Rooms are furnished with period antiques and many unique architectural features. The outbuildings include a hewn log cabin, circa 1785, with early domestic and agricultural tools and primitive furniture and a smokehouse, barn, pigeon house, and cemetery. Surrounding fields are planted with cotton, corn, cane, and vegetables, just as they were in the mid-19th century. The plantation has been owned by the same family since the late 18th century, and it's open Tues through Sat from 10 a.m. to 5 p.m., Sun from 2 to 5 p.m. Admission is $4 for adults, $2 for children 5 to 12.

The *Mary Willis Library* (204 E. Liberty St., Washington, 706-678-7736) is an architectural gem, with a place in history and a mystery in its foyer. Georgia's first free public library, the redbrick high-Victorian landmark with its stately round tower was founded in 1888 by Dr. Francis T. Willis in honor of his daughter, Mary, whose likeness is the centerpiece of a priceless Tiffany Studios stained-glass window. The mystery revolves around an old iron trunk in the foyer. Did it once hold part of a shipment of "Lost Confederate Gold" that still attracts fortune hunters to Wilkes County? It's keeping a tight lid on the secret. The building is now the regional library for Wilkes, Taliafero, and Green Counties.

Washington also figured in the Revolutionary War. A marker at *Kettle Creek Battleground,* 8 miles south of town on GA 44, Washington,

Where, Oh Where, Can Jim Williams Be?

The quiet, final resting place for the protagonist of the best-selling book *Midnight in the Garden of Good and Evil* is surprising given the flamboyant lifestyle of the fastidious Savannah antiques dealer. For the uninitiated, Jim Williams withstood three mistrials for the 1981 murder of his gay lover before dying of a heart attack following being acquitted in the fourth. I happened to be living across the street from Williams but was lucky enough to be out of town the night of "the incident." The book by John Berendt chronicled the eccentric people he met when he covered the story— people I somehow avoided during my time in Savannah.

Williams was from the Wilkinson County town of Gordon and now lies outside of town, in a vast garden of stone a few yards from the prim, white-frame Ramah Primitive Baptist Church. His black granite marker, inscribed JAMES ARTHUR WILLIAMS, DEC. 11, 1930, JAN. 14, 1990, is well-kept and weedless. The bucolic country churchyard is 200 miles from his old compadres, many of whom are still reaping the benefits of fame from the book. No doubt he'd love to get his manicured hands on whoever keeps putting pots of plastic flowers on his stone. But in case he's tempted to break out and have another fling at his glamorous old life, his mama is right there to rein him in. If you'd like to drop by, he's on the left side of the cemetery, on GA 57 at GA 18, between Macon and Irwinton.

commemorates the patriots' 1779 rout of the British and the Redcoats' subsequent withdrawal from this area of Georgia. Picnic tables are at the site. Call (706) 678-2013.

When hunger overwhelms your hunt through history, head for **Washington Jockey Club** (5 East Sq., 706-678-1672), an attractive cafe on the courthouse square. Midday fare includes sandwiches, soups, salads, plate lunches, and homemade desserts Mon through Sat. Fine-dining dinner is served Tues through Sat. Inexpensive to moderate.

Many of Washington's most magnificent homes are open during the early April **Washington-Wilkes Tour of Homes.** Contact Washington Wilkes Chamber of Commerce at PO Box 661, Washington, (706) 678-2013, www .washingtonwilkes.org.

Stop by the Thomson–McDuffie County Tourism Bureau in the restored train depot at 149 Main St., Thomson (706-567-1000, www.thomson-mcduffie .com) for information on some of Georgia's best off-the-beaten path secrets. You'll discover places like the **Rock House,** a 1785 fieldstone farmhouse that was an old trading post and is one the oldest structures in Georgia; **Alexandria,** a stately Virginia-influenced brick plantation house and boxwood gardens from 1805; and the site of November's **Belle Meade Fox Hunt.** You'll also find traces of Wrightsboro, a 1768 settlement of Quakers. The church and the cemetery provide the best representation of that period. A number of gracious antebellum homes line Thomson's tree-shaded streets.

You can stay overnight at the quaint **Woodall House** (324 W. Main St., 706-647-7044, www.woodallhousebb.com). The beautifully restored Victorian home with its wraparound porch is a great place to stay while exploring. It has 4 guest rooms and provides a full breakfast each day. Inexpensive.

The **Old Market House** is a souvenir of the period from 1796 to 1805 when little Louisville ("Lewis-ville") was Georgia's capital. Built in the 1790s, the Market's weathered timbers are held together by 1-inch-diameter wooden pegs. The Market's bell was cast in France in 1722 and was on its way to a New Orleans convent when it was hijacked by pirates and somehow ended up in Louisville. Louisville's tenure as state capital was immortalized by the Great Yazoo Land Fraud of 1795, which cost Georgia the territory that later became the states of Alabama and Mississippi. Contact the Jefferson County Chamber of Commerce at 302 E. Broad St., Louisville, (478) 625-8134, www.ourlouisville.com.

Masters Golf & Big Water

Augusta, a metro area of 450,000, traces its heritage to 1736, when General James Edward Oglethorpe, founder of the Georgia Crown colony, laid it out as the state's second city, after Savannah. Fought for during the Revolutionary War and skirted by General William T. Sherman's "March to the Sea," Augusta has mild winters and a genteel Old Southern lifestyle that caught the attention of post–Civil War Northern aristocrats, who found the right formula for golf—a pastime that symbolizes this city to people around the world.

For many years Augusta almost forgot that the Savannah River ran by its doorstep. All that has changed since *Riverwalk Augusta* has become the center of downtown activity. The main entrance to Riverwalk is at Eighth and Reynolds Streets, a block off Broad Street (www.augustariverwalk.com). The top of the old river levee has been turned into an inviting brick esplanade with seating clusters overlooking the river, historical displays, and playground and picnic areas. Major hotels, shops, and dining are along the Riverwalk. Stop first at the Augusta Visitor Information Center, inside the Augusta Museum of History (560 Reynolds St., Augusta, 706-724-4067, 800-726-0243, www.augustaga.org) for information and historic exhibits on Augusta's once-lucrative trade in "white gold." It's open Mon through Sat from 10 a.m. to 5 p.m., Sun from 1 to 5 p.m. Self-guided walking and driving tours as well as group tours are available at the welcome center.

The *Augusta Museum of History* is part of Riverwalk's excitement. The 60-year-old "municipal attic" lays out the city's past in a 48,000-square-foot home at Sixth and Reynolds Streets. The 23 permanent galleries are filled with Revolutionary and Civil War weapons and uniforms, Native American culture, natural history (including a major dinosaur exhibit), space exploration, communications, vintage photographs, and a tribute to the city's and Georgia's founder, General James Edward Oglethorpe. Savannah River marine life inhabits a small aquarium. Train buffs shouldn't miss "Old No. 302," the Georgia Railroad's last steam engine. Contemporary times are represented by exhibits on the 1960s Civil Rights movement and stage costumes worn by the late James Brown, Augusta's flamboyant "Godfather of Soul." The museum is at 560 Reynolds St., Augusta. Open Tues through Sat from 10 a.m. to 5 p.m., Sun from 1 to 5 p.m. Adults are $4, seniors $3, children 6 to 18 $2. Phone (706) 722-8454 or visit www.augustamuseum.org.

The *Jessye Norman Amphitheater* (9th Street Plaza, 706-821-2300) down by the water is often the scene of festivals and outdoor concerts.

Morris Museum of Art is at Riverfront Center, 1 10th St. at Riverwalk, Augusta (706-724-7501, www.themorris.org). Two centuries of Southern art are represented in this museum designed like a private home. The permanent collection includes works by Augusta native Jasper Johns and mixed media artist Robert Rauschenberg. Special exhibits are held throughout the year. Open Tues through Sat from 10 a.m. to 5 p.m., Sun from noon to 5 p.m. Admission is $5 for adults, $3 for students and senior citizens.

AUTHOR'S FAVORITES

Cherry Blossom Festival

Hay House

Indian Springs State Park

The buffet tables at the Blue Willow
Inn Restaurant

Old Governor's Mansion

Antebellum Milledgeville

Antebellum Madison

Antebellum Washington

Riverwalk Augusta

Laurel and Hardy Museum

Whistle Stop Cafe

Augusta Canal boat rides

Woodrow Wilson's Boyhood Home has been beautifully restored to his time here as a young child with his family. In 1858, when the future 28th president was 1 year old, his father became pastor of Augusta's First Presbyterian Church. The family lived 13 years in the church-owned manse in downtown Augusta. Wilson's earliest memory was hearing of Abraham Lincoln's 1861 election. In 1865 he saw Federal troops escorting captive Confederate President Jefferson Davis through the streets. In 1871 he met Robert E. Lee, a guest of the city. He scratched his name, "Tom," (his first name was Thomas)—which is still visible—on a parlor window and left scuff marks from his shoes on the dining room table, one of 13 church-owned pieces in the house when the Wilsons lived there. The only item that belonged to the Wilsons and that is still in the house is a butter dish, part of a silver service given to the family their first Christmas in Augusta. In 1991 Historic Augusta, Inc., purchased the house from owners who'd used it as a flower shop and beauty shop. Following a $2 million restoration, the 2-story redbrick house is open for guided tours Tues through Sat, 10 a.m. to 4 p.m. Adults $5, seniors $4, students $3. The home is at 419 E. 7th St., Augusta. Phone (706) 722-9828 or log on to www.wilson boyhoodhome.org.

New York has its Erie Canal; Georgia has the **Augusta Canal National Heritage Area.** Built in 1845 to harness the waterpower of the Savannah River, it's the nation's only industrial canal still used for its original purposes. The Heritage Area offers history, recreation, and unique experiences at its Interpretive Center and boat tours on 8.5 miles of waterway and towpath. Located inside Enterprise Mill, a colossal 19th-century redbrick textile mill once powered by the harnessed waters of the Savannah River, the Interpretive Center's film and exhibits explain the canal's construction by African-American, Irish,

Chinese, and Italian laborers and also the mechanics and physics of turning water into industrial power. Large windows reveal the working 1920s-era electrical turbines that are once again generating hydroelectric power. Artifacts and audiotape interviews with former mill workers enhance the experience that's culminated with hour-long tours in shallow-draft, 19th-century, Petersburg-style canal boats. The Interpretive Center (Enterprise Mill, 1450 Greene St., Augusta, 888-659-8926, 706-823-0440, www.augustacanal.com) is open Mon through Sat 10 a.m. to 6 p.m., Sun 1 to 6 p.m. Boat tours are Tues and Thurs 11 a.m. and 1:30 p.m., and Sat 11 a.m. and 1:30 and 3 p.m. Tickets to the Interpretive Center and boat tour can be purchased separately or in combination: $6 interpretive center, $12.50 for the combo. There are also 3-hour sunset cruises during the summer for $21 and Moonlight Music Cruises on Fri in the summer for $25.

Ezekiel Harris House (1840 Broad St., Augusta, 706-724-0436) is Augusta's second-oldest structure. In 1797, the prominent tobacco merchant Harris came to the area from South Carolina with plans to build a town to rival Augusta as a tobacco market. On a hill overlooking Augusta, the house is an outstanding example of post-Revolutionary architecture. The gambrel roof and vaulted hallway are reminiscent of New England. Tiered piazzas are supported by artistically beveled wooden posts. Rooms are furnished with period antiques. It's open by appointment Mon through Fri from 1 to 4 p.m., Sat from 10 a.m. to 1 p.m. Adults are $2; students, $1.

Meadow Garden (Independence Drive near the intersection of Walton Way and 13th Street, Augusta, 706-724-4174, www.historicmeadowgarden.org) was the home of George Walton, one of Georgia's signers of the Declaration of Independence. Built around 1791, it's the city's oldest documented structure and has been restored and refurnished by the Georgia Society, Daughters of the American Revolution. Hours are Mon through Fri from 9 a.m. to 4 p.m., Sat and Sun by appointment. Admission is $4 for adults, $1 for children and seniors.

Gertrude Herbert Institute of Art (506 Telfair St., Augusta, 706-722-5495, www.ghia.org) is an architecturally unique early 19th-century residence that showcases regional and Southeastern contemporary art. Built in 1818 by Augusta Mayor Nicholas Ware, the elliptical 3-story staircase, Adam-style mantels, and other rich ornamentation earned it the name "Ware's Folly." Hours are Tues through Fri from 10 a.m. to 5 p.m., Sat from 10 a.m. to 2 p.m. Admission is $2 for adults, $3.50 for seniors, $3 for students, $1 for children.

The *Lucy Craft Laney Museum of Black History* (1116 Phillips St., Augusta, 706-724-3576, www.lucycraftlaneymuseum.com) honors the beloved late educator, born in slavery, who established Augusta's first black secondary schools and a nurses' training school. Her former home has exhibits and photos on her remarkable life and many contributions to African-American culture.

Open Tues through Fri 9 a.m. to 5 p.m., Sat 10 a.m. to 4 p.m., Sun by request. Adults $5, seniors $3, children $2.

Until the 1960s, Broad Street, America's second widest main street after New Orleans's Canal Street, was downtown Augusta's hub. When suburban malls suffocated its retail trade, Broad nearly died of neglect. Happily, it's coming back to life as the *Broad Street Artist Row* (www.artistsrowaugusta .com). More than a dozen art galleries, antiques and gift shops, and fun little restaurants have taken over deserted mercantile stores. Have lunch or dinner at *Nacho Mama's* (976 Broad St., 706-724-0501, www.nachomamasaugusta.com) for killer burritos, tacos, and margaritas. Or stop at *Luigi's* (590 Broad St., 706-722-4056, www.luigisinc.com) which has seen Broad Street through good and bad times since 1946. Spin your favorite Bing Crosby, Andrews Sisters, and Glenn Miller platters on your personal booth jukebox while you tuck into good old Italian-American spaghetti and meatballs, lasagna, and ravioli.

Kids and adults who love wild things will have a wonderful time exploring *Phinizy Swamp Nature Park* (Lock-and-Dam Road, Augusta, 706-828-2109, www.phinizyswamp.org). The park's 1,100 acres of uncorrupted wetlands, swamps, nature trails, boardwalks, and observation decks put you in sight of herons, egrets, red-shouldered hawks, otters, alligators, amphibians, and other free-ranging creatures. Open daily. Free.

For golfers around the globe, Augusta is Christmas, the World Series, the rainbow's end. In late Mar and early Apr, fortunate faithful congregate along the dogwood- and azalea-rimmed fairways of storied *Augusta National Golf Club* to hail the game's elite as they pursue the Green Jacket, symbolic of the *Masters Golf Tournament* championship. Unless you know a player or a club member, tickets to the championship rounds will be impossible to find. But don't despair. You can see all the greats up close—even take their pictures—during the practice rounds preceding the tournament. The bad news is the *Masters Practice Rounds* have become so popular that tickets must

That Green Jacket

Those green jackets with the Augusta National emblem on the pocket that are awarded to winners of the Masters were originally created not for the winners, but for the club members to wear during the tournament. In 1937, when the contest began, members wanted to be identified so that guests and spectators would know who they were and could ask them any questions about the course or the contest. They decided a green jacket would help them stand out. When Sam Snead won the Masters in 1949, he was presented his own jacket and the tradition stuck.

now be purchased in advance. To receive an application form, write to Masters Tournament Practice Rounds, PO Box 2047, Augusta 30903-2047, or go to www .masters.com.

If you'd like to play, the *Jones Creek Course,* an 18-hole public layout at 777 Jones Creek Dr., Evans (706-860-4228, www.jonescreekgolfclub.com), is considered the "poor man's" Augusta National. Designed by renowned golf architect Rees Jones, it has an excellent practice facility and professional instructors. Rental clubs and carts are available.

Bass anglers and those seeking more off-the-beaten-path relaxation should look into a minivacation at *Mistletoe State Park.* About 35 miles north of Augusta, on 76,000-acre Clarks Hill Reservoir, this very tranquil park reputedly commands some of America's finest bass fishing waters. You may also swim and boat in the lake, hike 5 miles of woodland trails, and ride rental bikes around the 1,920 acres. Ten 2-bedroom furnished cottages and 96 camping sites with water, electricity, showers, and restrooms are available. There is a $5 per visit parking fee. Contact Park Superintendent at 3723 Mistletoe Rd., Appling, (706) 541-0321. For camping and cottage reservations, call (800) 864-PARK or log on to www.gastateparks.org.

Elijah Clark State Park, north of Mistletoe, is another wooded retreat on the western shores of Clarks Hill Lake. Twenty furnished cottages and 175 tent and trailer sites are a few steps from the water. You'll also find marinas, docks, boat ramps, a swimming beach, nature trails, and plenty of picnic areas. The park was named for Revolutionary War hero Elijah Clark. A Colonial museum displays relics from the period. The park is 7 miles east of Lincolnton at 2959 McCormick Hwy. Phone (706) 359-3458 for information. For reservations, call (800) 864-PARK or log on to www.gastateparks.org.

Burke County, between Augusta and Savannah, hails itself as "The Bird Dog Capital of the World." You can test its veracity with an organized bird and game hunt at the 5,000-acre *Boll Weevil Plantation* (Route 2, Box 356A, Waynesboro, 706-570-2715, www.bollweevilplantation.com). Contact the Burke County Chamber of Commerce at 828 Liberty St., Waynesboro, (706) 554-5451.

Places to Stay in Middle Georgia

MACON

Macon Marriott City Center

250 Coliseum Dr.
(478) 621-5300
www.marriott.com
Moderate to Expensive
Located in the heart of historic downtown Macon, the new Marriott complex offers 120,000 square feet of event space as well as 211 rooms, a business center, indoor pool, and fitness center. Comfortable, clean, and in a great location.

1842 Inn

353 College St.
(478) 741-1842
(877) 452-6599
www.1842inn.com
Expensive
See p. 124 for details.

MADISON

See p. 134 for B&Bs.

MILLEDGEVILLE

Antebellum Inn

200 N. Columbia St.
(478) 454-5400
www.antebelluminn.com
Moderate, includes full breakfast
See p. 132 for details.

JULIETTE

The Jarrell 1920 House

715 Jarrell Plantation Rd.
(888) 574-5434
(478) 986-3972
www.jarrellhouse.com
Inexpensive to Moderate
Philip and Amelia Haynes's 1850s-style plantation house, built in 1920, was originally part of what's now Jarrell Plantation State Historic Site. There are 2 large guest rooms with private baths. Rate includes full breakfast. The Friday and Saturday weekend package includes Saturday breakfast at the Whistle Stop Cafe in nearby Juliette. Guests are also given a tour of the neighboring Jarrell Plantation State Historic Site. The house is 18 miles east of I-75 exit 185.

WASHINGTON

Fitzpatrick Hotel

16 W. Public Sq.
(706) 678-5900
www.thefitzpatrickhotel .com
Inexpensive to Moderate, includes continental breakfast
Seventeen handsomely renovated guest rooms in a restored 1898 hotel on downtown Washington's public square.

Holly Ridge Country Inn

2221 Sandtown Rd.
(706) 285-2594
Inexpensive

Lafayette Manor Inn

219 E. Robert Toombs Ave.
(706) 678-5922
www.lafayettemanor.com
Moderate to Expensive

Southern Elegance Bed and Breakfast

115 W. Robert Toombs Ave.
(877) 678-4775
www.southernelegance bandb.com
Inexpensive to Moderate
Two blocks from downtown in the restored historic Fitzpatrick Hotel, this B & B offers an elegant style in a relaxing atmosphere. Beautifully decorated, guest will also enjoy hearty country breakfasts. Gourmet dinners are available.

Washington Plantation Bed and Breakfast

15 Lexington Ave.
(706) 678-2006 or (877) 405-9956
www.washingtonplantation .com
Moderate
Parts of the historic inn date back to 1814 when it used to be part of a 3,000 acre plantation. The seven acres it now occupied are beautifully manicured with magnolias and azaleas. Fully modern with a touch of history, the inn's rooms have private baths, gas fireplaces and comfortable bedding.

HELPFUL WEBSITES

Macon Convention & Visitors Bureau
www.maconga.org

Milledgeville Visitors Center
www.visitmilledgeville.org

Augusta Convention & Visitors Bureau
www.augustaga.org

Madison-Morgan County Chamber of Commerce
www.madisonga.org

Washington–Wilkes Chamber of Commerce
www.washingtonwilkes.org

AUGUSTA

Partridge Inn
2110 Walton Way
(706) 737-8888
(800) 476-6888
www.partridgeinn.com
Moderate to Expensive
This full-service inn, beautifully updated in 2007, has 155 executive, studio, and deluxe suites. Many have kitchens and balconies. Dining room serves upscale American and continental lunch and dinner; there's also a full bar. Rates include Southern buffet breakfast.

Queen Anne Inn
406 Greene St.
(706) 723-0045
www.queenanneinnaugusta.com
Moderate
This 3-story Victorian inn looks like a wedding cake. It offers beautiful Southern elegance. Spa packages are available.

Places to Eat in Middle Georgia

MACON

Natalia's
2720 Riverside Dr.
(912) 741-1380
www.natalias.net
Moderate to Expensive
Natalia's has satisfied Macon's hunger for classical Italian cooking since 1984. Grilled veal chops, risotto, osso bucco, seafood, pasta, and chicken dishes are complemented by light, delicate sauces (no heavy red sauces). French, Italian, and American wines are available by the glass. Dinner is served Mon through Sat.

Tic Toc Room
408 Martin Luther King Jr. Blvd., downtown Macon
(478) 744-0123
Moderate to Expensive

New Southern, Italian, and American cuisines are showcased in a stylishly revamped former downtown Macon music club, where Macon native "Little Richard" Penniman got his start. Before and after dinner, enjoy live music and a full bar in the upstairs lounge. Dinner Mon through Sat.

AUGUSTA

French Market Grille
Surrey Center, 425 Highland Ave.
(706) 737-4865
www.frenchmarketaugusta.com
Moderate to Expensive
Chuck and Gail Baldwins' spicy Louisiana Cajun cooking has kept Augustans coming back for more than 15 years. They can't seem to get enough of the Baldwins' delectable gumbo, Cajun crawfish étouffée, jambalaya, and pecan praline pie. Lunch and dinner are served daily.

La Maison
In a restored mansion in the Old Town Historic District at 404 Telfair St.
(706) 722-4805
www.lamaisontelfair.com
Moderate to Expensive
La Maison prepares the city's most sophisticated cuisine. Chef Heinz Sowinski's repertoire includes a wide range of French, German, Swiss, and other specialties. Magnificent desserts reflect Sowinski's European culinary heritage. Cocktails and a large selection of American, Australian, and European wines round out the menu. For more casual dining, visit the Tapas Lounge and Wine Bar. Dinner is served Mon through Sat.

Luigi's
590 Broad St., downtown Augusta
(706) 724-0501
www.luigisinc.com
Inexpensive
Enjoy spaghetti and meatballs, lasagna, ravioli, and other hearty Italian-American dishes while you play your favorite 1940s and 1950s tunes on your booth jukebox. Dinner Mon through Sat.

MADISON

Ye Olde Colonial
Courthouse Square, downtown Madison
(706) 342-2211
Moderate
See p. 134 for details.

GREENSBORO

The Yesterday Cafe
114 N. Main St.
(706) 453-0800
www.theyesterdaycafe.com
Inexpensive to Moderate
Teri Bragg, former owner of Yesterday's Cafe in Rutledge, has opened a casual restaurant in downtown Greensboro's historic Bickers & Goodwin Building. Fans of her Rutledge restaurant will be pleased to see many familiar items on the lunch and dinner menus, ranging from burgers and sandwiches, soups and salads to steaks, chicken, seafood, and pasta dishes. Be sure to save room for her signature buttermilk pie. The restaurant is popular with residents of upscale communities around Lake Oconee. Lunch Mon through Sat and dinner Tues through Sat.

Historic Savannah

Founded in 1733, **Savannah** is one of America's truly special cities. Not long after founding father General James Edward Oglethorpe came ashore on Yamacraw Bluff and dispersed his 144 settlers, he set about planning Savannah in a style befitting the capital of a Crown colony named for King George II. He hunkered down in his damask tent on the bluffs and with military precision laid out a grid of straight, broad streets, braided at 2-block intervals by spacious public squares. Initially, the 24 squares were mustering places for troops and convenient locales for citizens to draw water and exchange news.

In 1793 Eli Whitney, a visiting New Englander given to tinkering with gadgets, devised a mechanized way to separate cotton seeds from the fluffy white bolls. His cotton gin revolutionized Southern planting. On the tragic downside, it also perpetuated the waning practice of slavery and indirectly led to the Civil War. Soon, real gold earned from "white gold" enabled planters, merchants, and shipbuilders to embellish Oglethorpe's squares with English Regency, Georgian, Federal, and Gothic Revival showplaces, filled with fine furniture and

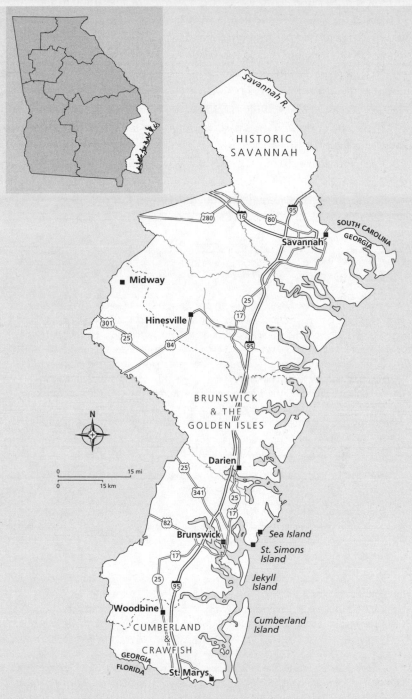

COASTAL GEORGIA

HISTORIC SAVANNAH

Savannah R.

280
16
80
95

Savannah

SOUTH CAROLINA
GEORGIA

Midway

25
17

301
Hinesville

25
84
95

N

BRUNSWICK
& THE
GOLDEN ISLES

0   15 mi
0   15 km

25
Darien

341
25
17

82
Brunswick
17

Sea Island
St. Simons
Island

25
95

Jekyll
Island

Woodbine

CUMBERLAND
&
CRAWFISH

Cumberland
Island

GEORGIA
FLORIDA
St. Marys

art objects shipped from Europe. As "front yards" for the affluent, the squares were dressed up with trees, flowering plants, benches, fountains, and memorials to Revolutionary heroes and other notables.

In the 1950s, much of the city's heritage teetered on the brink of extinction. Scores of venerable landmarks, even a couple of Oglethorpe's squares, were crunched in the jaws of progress before the Historic Savannah Foundation rode in like the cavalry and saved the day. To date, more than 1,500 historic structures have been restored in the 2.2-square-mile *Savannah National Historic District,* the nation's largest.

Before you leave home, phone the Savannah Convention & Visitors Bureau, (877) 728-2662, for advance information. When you arrive, stop first at the Savannah Visitors Center (303 Martin Luther King Jr. Blvd., Savannah,

A Prophecy Fulfilled

Savannah is full of ghosts and tales of ghosts. Jack Richards, an artist fascinated by the subject, leads true believers and the openly skeptical on "Ghost Talk, Ghost Walk" tours of the historic district (www.ghosttalkghostwalk.com). He relates tales of apparitions at the Pirates House and Olde Pink House restaurants, cemeteries, and private homes. One of his favorites is a romantic story about the mother of Girl Scouts founder Juliette Gordon Low. In the 1890s, when workers were digging the foundation in Wright Square for the monument to William Washington Gordon, founder of the Georgia Railroad and grandfather to Juliette Gordon Low, they inadvertently dug up the remains of Tomochichi, the Indian chief who had befriended General James Edward Oglethorpe. They reported the discovery to Eleanor Kinsey Gordon, Gordon's daughter-in-law and Juliette Gordon Low's mother.

Embarrassed by the incident, she ordered the big granite stone now on Tomochichi's grave in Wright Square. Although she asked for a bill several times, the Stone Mountain Granite Company never sent one.

After a decade of repeated requests, she finally got a bill for a dollar, "Due on Judgment Day." She sent a check for a dollar, with a curt note: "I'll be much too busy on Judgment Day to pay my debts."

On the day she died, her prophecy apparently came true. She called her deceased husband's name, as if she were seeing an apparition. He was known as "The Old Captain," his rank in the Confederate Army. Minutes later, as her daughter-in-law, Margaret, rested in the downstairs parlor, a man in a Confederate officer's uniform walked down the stairs and out the front door. He was followed by Margaret's husband, who announced Mrs. Gordon's death. He hadn't seen the mysterious officer. When they walked outside, the family servant was crying. He said, "I just saw the Old Captain and he said, 'I'm taking Miss Eleanor for her afternoon ride.'" Just as she predicted, Mrs. Gordon was too busy on Judgment Day to worry about her debts.

912-238-1779, www.savannahvisit.com). Inside the former 1860s Central of Georgia Railway depot, you'll find everything you need: free brochures, tour and restaurant information, lodging reservations, and an orientation film. The center adjoins the **Savannah History Museum,** with displays, multimedia presentations, a steam locomotive, and homage to famous citizens like songwriter Johnny Mercer ("Moon River," "Moonlight in Vermont," and countless other standards). You can also see the movie prop bus stop bench where Tom Hanks told his tale in the Oscar-winning film *Forrest Gump.* Outside the Visitors Center, take one of the many guided orientation tours in an open-air tram or air-conditioned van or minibus. The museum is open Mon through Fri from 8:30 a.m. to 5 p.m., and Sat and Sun from 9 a.m. to 5 p.m. Adults $5; age 6 and under free.

When you're ready to head off on your own, **River Street,** a wide brick pedestrian esplanade also known as Riverfront Plaza, is the best place to start. An elevator at Bay and Bull Streets next to the Hyatt Regency Savannah Hotel will take you down to a Savannah Convention & Visitors Bureau Welcome Center, with restrooms, water fountains, and attendants ready to load you up with information (101 E. Bay St., 912-644-6400, 877-SAVANNAH). As a major plank in the restoration movement, the antebellum brick cotton warehouses were refashioned as seafood restaurants, taverns, touristy shops, and art galleries. Recessed benches are great places to sit and watch the cargo ships cruising to the Georgia Ports Authority docks and heavy industries upriver and the open Atlantic 20 miles downriver.

Browse the shops, have a drink and a bite, then take the elevator or climb up the cobblestoned steps to Bay Street and you're ready for your walk on Savannah's most beautiful street. Few cities are fortunate to be blessed by a thoroughfare as charming as the 10 blocks of **Bull Street** from Savannah's gold-domed City Hall to the green bower of Forsyth Park. Five of Oglethorpe's most picturesque squares are set like gems on this glorious avenue named for a British colonial officer. It divides the historic district into east and west halves. Before you leave, you'll be drawn back time and again to this wonderful, old-worldly street. Revolutionary hero General Nathanael Greene is buried under the granite shaft in Johnson Square. Wright Square honors the founder of the Central of Georgia Railroad, William Washington Gordon.

At Bull Street and Oglethorpe Avenue, Girl Scouts and students of American history should pause at the *Juliette Gordon Low Girl Scout National Center* (912-233-4501, www.juliettegordonlowbirthplace.org). Designed by noted early 19th-century English architect William Jay, the dignified English Regency mansion was the 1860 birthplace of "Daisy" Low, granddaughter of William Washington Gordon and founder of the Girl Scouts of America. Her

COASTAL GEORGIA'S TOP HITS

Savannah National Historic District	Fort King George State Historic Site
Midnight in the Garden of Good and Evil tours	Sapelo Island Tours
	Hofwyl-Broadfield Plantation State Historic Site
Mighty Eighth Air Force Museum	
Fort Jackson/Oatland Island Education Center	Jekyll Island Historic District
	Fort Frederica National Monument
Tybee Lighthouse and Museum	Christ Church
Skidaway Island State Park	St. Simons Lighthouse
Wormsloe State Historic Site	Cumberland Island National Seashore
Midway Church	Woodbine Crawfish Festival

paintings and sculpture, personal effects, and GSA mementos are in the high-ceiling rooms. The museum is at 142 Bull St., Savannah. It's open Mon through Sat from 10 a.m. to 4 p.m., Sun from 11 a.m. to 4 p.m.; closed Wed. Admission is $8 for adults, $7 for registered adult Girl Scouts and students, Girl Scouts ages 6 to 18 $6; children 5 and under are free.

A bronze statue of General Oglethorpe, by Daniel Chester French (who sculpted the seated statue at Washington's Lincoln Memorial), looks south from its pedestal in ***Chippewa Square,*** daring the Spanish in Florida to move against his city. Sergeant William Jasper, killed in the 1779 British siege of the city, brandishes the flag atop the monument in the center of Madison Square.

The tree-shaded benches are usually filled with earnest-looking young people who've drifted over from the Savannah College of Art and Design. Chartered in 1979, with 71 students and four faculty, SCAD has grown from the redbrick, late-1800s Guards Armory on the square's east side into an internationally known institution with 10,000 students and 750 faculty and staff. SCAD has restored almost six dozen buildings in the historic district, and all those students infuse the area with electrifying energy.

When Savannah peacefully surrendered to the Union army in December 1864, General William T. Sherman lodged in the Gothic Revival ***Green Meldrim House*** (now St. John's parish house) on Madison Square's west side, 14 W. Macon St. (912-233-3845, www.stjohnssav.org). From the house, he sent a telegram to his commander in chief: "Dear Sir, President Lincoln: I beg to present you as a Christmas gift, the city of Savannah with 150 heavy guns and also about 25,000 bales of cotton." You're welcome to walk in and admire magnificent Gothic wood carvings, plasterwork, and spacious rooms. Open Tues, Thurs, and Fri from 10 a.m. to 4 p.m., on Sat 10 a.m. to 1 p.m. Adults, $7; students, $2.

If you're starting to flag a bit, pep up with a cappuccino or latte at *Gallery Espresso's* indoor or sidewalk tables at 6 E. Liberty St. (912-233-5348, www .galleryexpresso.com), across from the DeSoto Hilton Hotel. You can also tuck into shepherd's pie and a pint of something from the bar at *Six Pence Pub,* a bit of Olde England at 245 Bull St. (912-233-3156, www.sixpencepub.com).

Patriotic Savannahians named *Monterey Square* for an American victory in the 1840s Mexican War. The monument in the center of the square salutes Count Casimir Pulaski, a Polish nobleman who gave his all for the American cause during the 1779 British siege. *Temple Mickve Israel* (912-233-1537, www.mickveisrael.com), on the east side, is Georgia's oldest Jewish congregation. Spanish and German Jews, who landed five months after Oglethorpe, brought Torahs and other sacred objects and documents that are now part of a collection you're welcome to see. Just knock on the side door Mon through Fri from 10 a.m. to noon; no charge.

Savannah's most famous house is directly across the square. Some tour guides used to tell visitors that the *Mercer Williams House Museum* was songwriter Johnny Mercer's boyhood home. Mercer's grandfather built it after the Civil War, but the family never lived in the stately redbrick Italianate mansion at 429 Bull St., Savannah. Antiques dealer, social arbiter, and arts patron

Savannah's First Big Scandal

The founder of Methodism had Savannah tongues wagging some 250 years before Jim Williams shot Danny Hansford in the scandal immortalized in *Midnight in the Garden of Good and Evil.* According to John Duncan, book dealer and raconteur extraordinaire, the parson's tale went something like this:

"John Wesley came to Savannah in the 1730s to minister to the Indians, but he became pastor of Christ Anglican Church. His undoing was falling in love with the original Hard-Hearted Hannah, Vamp of Savannah. It was one of those May-December romances—he was 36, Sophia Hopkey was 18. They'd walk hand-in-hand in the moonlight, and read poetry together, but when he asked her to marry him, she dropped him like a hot potato and married another man. After the marriage, when Sophia and her new husband came to services at Christ Church, Wesley refused to give his ex–lady friend communion. Sophia's in-laws sued Wesley for defamation of character. He was indicted, but never came to trial. It was Savannah's first big public scandal, of which we've had many ever since."

Jim Williams lived there until he shot his companion to death in 1981 and became fodder for John Berendt's international bestselling nonfiction book *Midnight in the Garden of Good and Evil,* loosely made into a 1997 movie. The house is open for tours of about 30 to 35 minutes Mon through Sat 10:30 a.m. to 4 p.m., Sun 12:30 to 4 p.m. Purchase tickets, $13.25 for adults, $8.48 for students, at Mercer House Gift Shop, behind the main house. Phone (912) 236-6352 or (877) 430-6352 or go to www.mercerhouse.com for info. Jim Williams's sister, Dorothy Kingery, lives full-time in the house.

Another 2 blocks and you're in Forsyth Park. The centerpiece of the 20-acre sanctuary is an ornate, wrought-iron fountain that looks a bit like a 3-tiered wedding cake decorated with swans and water-spouting tritons.

Squares east and west of Bull Street are blessed with landmarks in a variety of styles. ***Isaiah Davenport House*** (324 E. State St., Savannah, 912-236-8097, www.davenporthousemuseum.org), on Columbia Square, played a pivotal role in the restoration crusade. Built between 1815 and 1820 and considered one of America's most perfect Georgian mansions, the redbrick house was threatened with demolition in the 1950s to make space for a funeral home parking lot. The Historic Savannah Foundation came to the rescue and went on to help save hundreds of other imperiled structures. The restored Davenport House gleams with Chippendale and Sheraton furnishings, woodwork, and plaster crown moldings. It's open Mon through Sat from 10 a.m. to 4 p.m., Sun from 1 to 4 p.m. Admission is $8 for adults, $5 ages 6 to 18. As for the funeral home, it's now Kehoe House, one of the city's grandest historic inns.

The ***Owens-Thomas House, Telfair Academy of Arts & Sciences,*** and the new ***Jepson Center for the Arts*** are part of the same cultural family, with the same hours, fees, and website, www.telfair.org. Each is open Mon from noon to 5 p.m.; Tues through Sat 10 a.m. to 5 p.m.; Sun 1 to 5 p.m. Admission for the 3-site combination is: adults $20, seniors and AAA $18, college students $5, ages 5 and under are free. Family pass $40.

The Jepson Center for the Arts, dedicated in spring 2006, is a dramatically contemporary expansion of the Telfair Museum in downtown Savannah. With 64,000 square feet in 2 buildings that are connected by a glass bridge over a historic lane, the glistening white Portuguese stone–clad Jepson, with floor-to-ceiling windows and abundant natural light, includes 2 galleries for traveling exhibits; dedicated galleries for African-American art, Southern art, and photography and works on paper; a 2-level hands-on "experience" gallery for young people; 2 outdoor sculpture terraces; and an auditorium and cafe.

The $24.5 million Jepson was the first major expansion of the 120-year-old Telfair, designed in 1819 by renowned architect William Jay, whose other Savannah landmarks include the Owens-Thomas House. The Regency-style

Dashing Through the Spanish Moss

Born in Boston, James Lord Pierpont wrote the popular Christmas song "Jingle Bells" in Savannah in 1857. A distant kin of financial baron J. P. Morgan, Pierpont arrived in Savannah in 1852 and played the organ at the Unitarian church, where his brother was pastor. He married the daughter of Savannah's Civil War mayor and, with visions of New England's snowy landscapes dancing in his head, gave the world the tune that's been played ad infinitum ever since. A historical marker in downtown Savannah's Troup Square commemorates his contribution to the holiday repertoire.

building was originally the home of the Telfairs, a distinguished Savannah family, and became the South's oldest public art museum in 1875. The stately rooms and a ballroom where the Marquis de Lafayette danced minuets during his 1825 visit to Savannah house collections of American and European paintings, sculpture, and decorative arts. You can also view the original *Bird Girl* statue, featured on the book cover of *Midnight in the Garden of Good and Evil*. The Telfair and Jepson are at 121 Barnard St., Savannah. Call (912) 232-1177.

The Marquis de Lafayette slept at the Owens-Thomas House on Oglethorpe Square, 124 Abercorn St., Savannah (912-233-9743), during his 1825 farewell-to-America tour. He addressed the populace from the wrought iron side balcony. William Jay's elegant Regency-style urban villa is filled with art, antiques, and intriguing architectural details.

King-Tisdell Cottage/Black History Museum, an 1890s Victorian cottage at 514 E. Huntington St., Savannah (912-234-8000, www.kingtisdell.org), displays documents, furniture, and artifacts of Low Country black heritage. It's the headquarters for Negro Heritage Tours, which includes landmarks of black history going back to the first slaves. Open Tues through Sat noon to 5 p.m. Admission for all ages is $2.50.

Ships of the Sea Maritime Museum (41 Martin Luther King Jr. Blvd., Savannah, 912-232-1511, www.shipsofthesea.org) has moved its extensive collections of sailing ship models, ships in bottles, scrimshaw art, maritime paintings, ornamental figureheads, and other nautical artifacts into spacious galleries in the 1819 Scarbrough House. Open Tues through Sun from 10 a.m to 5 p.m. Adults, $8; students and senior citizens, $6.

The role Savannahians played in the 1960s Civil Rights movement is portrayed with memorabilia, photos, documents, and displays at the ***Ralph Mark Gilbert Civil Rights Museum*** (460 Martin Luther King Jr. Blvd., Savannah, 912-231-8900, www.visit-historic-savannah.com). It's open Mon through Sat from 9 a.m. to 5 p.m. Admission is $4 for adults and senior citizens, $2 for students.

City Market, once-neglected blocks of brick warehouses on West Congress, West St. Julian, and Barnard Streets, 2 blocks from River Street, has been given reviving doses of adrenaline. You can browse about two dozen artists' studios and enjoy casual dining and nighttime entertainment in a growing number of venues. Several have outdoor tables. Horse-drawn carriage tours begin and end at the market.

Some of the city's most intriguing sights are outside the historic district. The *Mighty Eighth Air Force Museum* (175 Bourne Ave., Pooler, I-95 exit 102 at US 80, 15 minutes west of downtown, 912-748-8888, www .mightyeighth.org) pays tribute to the juggernaut that was born in Savannah in January 1942. Although its headquarters soon moved to England for the duration of the war, Savannah has always had an affectionate place in its heart for "The Mighty Eighth," which won the WWII air war over Europe. Hundreds of high-tech exhibits, artifacts, films, and dioramas take you on a time trip through harrowing years. *The Darkest Hour,* a documentary film, recounts the Battle of Britain, the Japanese attack on Pearl Harbor, the Holocaust, and other atrocities. Through a doorway, displays trace the US entry into the conflict; the buildup of men, women, and war machines; and the Eighth Air Force's birth. Through another door, you're on a 1943 English airfield. In a small hut, you sit in on a briefing session for crews about to take off on a bombing raid over Germany. Leaving the hut, you're in front of a 2-story control tower, similar to hundreds that dotted the English countryside during the war. Original 16 mm color combat film and the sounds of flak, antiaircraft guns, and German fighter planes re-create the terrors Allied crews experienced.

A following exhibit shows the tide of war turning in favor of the Allies, the coming of D-Day, V-E Day, and the atomic bombs on Japan that brought the Pacific war to a close. Open daily from 9 a.m. to 5 p.m. Admission is $10 for adults, $9 for seniors and AAA or AARP members, $6 ages 6 to 12; free for children under 6.

Old Fort Jackson (on US 80/Islands Expressway, Savannah, 3 miles east of downtown, 912-232-3945, www.chsgeorgia.org) was constructed on the Savannah River between 1808 and 1879. All shipping bound for Savannah's port had to pass by the fort's heavy guns. A tidal moat still guards the stout brick walls. Artifacts include cannon, small arms, machinery, and tools demonstrated at annual events. In summer, uniformed soldiers conduct cannon firings and military drills. Open daily from 9 a.m. to 5 p.m. General admission is $6, children 6 and under free.

Oatland Island Education Center (711 Sandtown Rd., Savannah, off the Islands Expressway east of the Wilmington River, 912-898-3980, www.oatland island.org) is a fascinating nature experience for all ages. Operated by the Chatham County Board of Education, the center is a focus of nature education programs and special events. You can walk a nature trail and see an astonishing variety of wildlife secured in natural habitats, including gators, wolves, bobcats, bears, panthers, deer, bald eagles, egrets, and heron. Open daily from 10 a.m. to 5 p.m. Admission is $5 for adults; $3 ages 3 to 17 and 65 and over. Free for age 3 and under.

Bamboo Farm and Coastal Gardens (2 Canebrake Rd., Savannah, off US 17, 10 miles south of Savannah, 912-921-5460, www.bamboo.caes.uga.edu) exhibits what's purportedly the world's largest living collection of bamboo varieties. It began in 1890, when Mrs. H. B. Miller planted three bamboo canes in her farm garden. By 1915, Mrs. Miller's trio covered more than an acre of the Miller farm with tall, sturdy stalks that towered 30 to 70 feet high, with a girth of several inches. By and by, the farm was sold to the US Department of Agriculture as an experiment station, with bamboo types and other plants brought from around the world to test their compatibility with coastal Georgia soil and climate. Experiments were made to develop paper from bamboo. During WWII, goldenrod and dog fennel were tested as substitutes for rubber trees. During the Vietnam War, bamboo did its patriotic duty as material for mock villages to train soldiers at Fort Benning, Georgia. When the USDA closed the station in 1978, the University of Georgia took it over as a research and education center. UGA added palms, black walnut, crape myrtle, Chinese elm, and fruit and nut trees. In summer, strawberry fields host you-pick-'ems and the public is invited to fish-and-fry the stocked ponds. A pavilion built by Friends of the Coastal Gardens holds weddings, family reunions, gardening classes, and conferences. You may roam through the bamboo free of charge.

Fort Pulaski National Monument (912-786-5787, www.nps.gov/fopu), off US 80, Savannah, a half hour east of downtown Savannah, guards the Savannah River's entrance from the Atlantic. The star-shaped fortress took 18 years to construct. A young West Point engineering grad named Robert E. Lee lent his talents—but it surrendered to Union forces on April 11, 1862, following a devastating attack by new cannon rifles. Historical exhibits, weapons, and uniforms are displayed. Open daily from 9 a.m. to 6 p.m. Extended summer hours. Admission for adults is $5; free for children under 16.

There's not one iota of chic or glamour anywhere on **Tybee Island.** In truth, it's the antithesis of rich and trendy Hilton Head Island, just across the water in South Carolina. Therein lies the charm of this comfortable old shoe of a beach and summer home retreat 20 miles east of downtown Savannah. Many

Savannah families spend the torrid summers in cottages near the beach, where the mild Atlantic surf laps 3 miles of hard-packed sand. Stop first at the Tybee Visitor Center, US 80, Tybee Island, as you enter the island. For info call (912) 786-5444 or (800) 868-2322 or visit www.tybeevisit.com.

In warm weather, you'll probably want to make a beeline for the Tybee beaches. The most popular stretch for swimming and sunbathing is the commercial area around Butler Avenue and 16th Street—a quirky time warp straight out of Coney Island, circa 1940. Here's where you'll find ice cream and fudge shops, hot dog stands, beer joints, old department stores, convenience stores, chair and beach umbrella vendors, motels, condos, and public restrooms. The Tybee Island Pier & Pavilion, jutting far out into the water, is a fine place to cast your fishing line. It was modeled after the old Tybrisa Pier, where young swains and their belles used to dance to the Dorseys and Benny Goodman.

Don't be disappointed that the Atlantic on the Georgia coast isn't Caribbean blue-green. The grayish-green surf isn't polluted—rivers like the Altamaha flowing down from Georgia's interior leave a silt bottom, rather than a sand bottom that would reflect the sunlight and create more translucent colors.

Tybee Lighthouse and Museum (30 Meddin Dr., Tybee Island, 912-786-5801, www.tybeelighthouse.org) are must-see landmarks. You can climb 178 spiraling steps to the 154-foot top of Tybee Light, which first guided ships in between the river and ocean in 1773. Partially destroyed by Confederate raiders during the Union occupation, it was rebuilt after the war. An extensive restoration was completed in 1998. Tybee Island Museum is across from the lighthouse, inside Fort Screven, a Spanish-American War coastal artillery battery. Inside the fort's old bunkers are uniforms, weapons, and displays that reflect the fort's active service through World War II. The museum and lighthouse are open daily except Tues from 9 a.m. to 5:30 p.m. Adults $8, ages 62 and over and ages 6 to 17 $6.

Skidaway Island, south of downtown, also has a trove of off-the-beaten-path adventures. **Skidaway Island State Park** (52 Diamond Causeway, Savannah, 912-598-2300, www.gastateparks.org) is a 490-acre preserve that's relaxed and quiet even in busy seasons. The 87 tent and trailer camping sites have electrical and water connections, showers, and restrooms. Amenities include a swimming pool, picnic shelters, nature trails, and a playground. No fishing areas or beaches are inside the park, but they are plentiful nearby. There's a $5 per visit parking fee. For camping reservations, call (800) 864-PARK or log on to www.gastateparks.org.

The **UGA Marine Education Center and Aquarium** (30 Ocean Science Circle, located on Skidaway Island, Savannah, 912-598-2496, www.marex.uga.edu/aquarium) operated by the University of Georgia, has a 12-tank aquarium with an array of coastal marine life, including moray eels, barracuda, catfish, pigfish, monkfish, and 50 or so others. Open Mon through Fri 9 a.m. to 4 p.m., Sat from 10 a.m. to 5 p.m. Adults $6, ages 3 to 12 $3.

At **Wormsloe State Historic Site** (7601 Skidaway Rd., Savannah, 912-353-3023, 800-864-PARK, www.gastateparks.org) a 1.5-mile avenue of live oaks leads to the ruins of the colonial estate built by Noble Jones, one of the contingent of settlers who arrived with General Oglethorpe in 1733. A physician and carpenter in Surrey, Jones was one of the first Georgians to fully realize the American dream. He became a constable, soldier, surveyor, rum agent, and member of the Royal Council. Between 1739 and 1745, he built his fortified tabby home on the Isle of Hope. Tabby was a popular building material made by pouring equal parts of water, lime, sand, and oyster shells into wooden molds. When the substance hardened, the wooden molds were removed and the next layer was poured. It was designed to last forever, but alas it didn't. You can see a model of it in the visitor center, along with artifacts found on the estate and an audiovisual show about the Georgia colony's early years.

Walk a nature trail to the Jones family grave site and the ruins of Noble Jones's great house. During Christmas season, Memorial Day, Labor Day, and Georgia Week in February, staff in period dress demonstrate colonial crafts and skills. Open Tues through Sun from 9 a.m. to 5 p.m. Adults $8; children $4.50.

The **Isle of Hope** is a photogenic place for a drive or walk. Go to the end of LaRoche Avenue (off Skidaway Road, southeast of downtown Savannah) and follow Bluff Drive along the Wilmington River. Many lovely homes and a Roman Catholic church are set off by towering live oaks and banks of azaleas.

Fort McAllister State Historic Park (I-95 exit 90), in Bryan County, 25 miles south of Savannah, has some of the South's best preserved earthwork

Beards in Trees

The gray Spanish moss you see draped across branches of oak trees along the Georgia coast (and beyond) have no real connection to Spain except through legend. Native Americans called the plant "tree hair." One legend has it that when the Spaniards arrived with their long beards, the Natives were fascinated. French explorers as an insult to their rivals started called the gray flowing plant Spanish Beard, which evolved to its present name.

Yet another legend says an early settler and his Spanish fiancée were attacked by a Cherokee warrior who was less than pleased they were taking his land. He cut off her hair and flung it into a tree, where it shriveled and turned gray before hopping from tree to tree.

fortifications. Built on bluffs above the south bank of the Great Ogeechee River, the earthworks withstood seven Union land and sea assaults before finally surrendering in December 1864. It was the last major obstacle on General William T. Sherman's "March to the Sea" and led to Savannah's peaceful surrender a few days later. The earthworks and heavy guns have been restored to their wartime appearance. The museum and visitor center has Civil War weapons and other artifacts.

Fort McAllister's recreation area has 3 cottages, 65 tent and trailer camping sites with electricity, water, restrooms, showers, picnic tables, and grills; 5 miles of hiking trails; and boat ramps and docks. Adult admission $6.50, children $3.75. There's a $5 per visit parking fee. It's at 3984 Fort McAllister Rd., Richmond Hill. Drive GA 144 for 10 miles east of I-95. Phone (912) 727-2339 or (800) 864-PARK for reservations or log on to www.gastateparks.org.

As you drive US 17 between Savannah and Brunswick, *Midway Church* looms out of the gnarled arms of a live oak grove, like a New England meeting house that's lost its way. The white clapboard church, with its gabled roof and square belfry, traces its heritage to Massachusetts Puritans, who established the Midway Society in 1754. The church dates from 1792. Illustrious parishioners have included two signers of the Declaration of Independence and Theodore Roosevelt's great-grandfather. The fathers of Oliver Wendell Holmes and Samuel F. B. Morse have served as pastor.

Pick up the big iron church key at the neighboring *Midway Museum* (Midway, 912-884-5837, www.themidwaymuseum.org). The sanctuary's unadorned interior has straightback pews and a slave gallery. The churchyard across the highway is the resting place of the church's founders and Revolutionary heroes. Midway Museum has colonial furnishings, documents, and exhibits. Open Tues through Sat from 10 a.m to 4 p.m. Adults, $3; children 12 and under, $1.

The Midway area also has two other historic sites. A biracial community effort is restoring *Seabrook Village,* (660 Trade Hill Rd., Midway, 912-884-7008, www.discoverlibertyga.com), a post–Civil War African-American community that thrived until the 1930s. Descendants of original former slave settlers lead tours of the one-room schoolhouse, homes, and outbuildings. Open Tues through Fri, 10 a.m. to 4 p.m. Group rates are available.

At the 67-acre *Fort Morris State Historic Site,* (2559 Fort Morris Rd., Midway, 7 miles east of I-95 exit 76/Midway, 912-884-5999, 800-864-PARK, www.gastateparks.org) a film and museum tell the story of Sunbury, a pre-Revolutionary port that rivaled Savannah and died after the British captured it in 1778. A cemetery is the only physical remains of the town. A marked trail goes around the earthworks of Fort Morris, which failed to protect the town from invasion. A nature trail with excellent bird-watching goes through the

Blame it on the General

It's ironic that the city's founder, General James Edward Oglethorpe, may have inbred Savannah's love of hard drink. Although he tried unsuccessfully to prohibit rum (and lawyers) from his colony, Oglethorpe was the first person in the colony to brew beer. He did it, he wrote, "to keep the soldiers satisfied." Like the Puritans and Pilgrims in New England, Oglethorpe also believed that drinking beer was a far healthier and more godly endeavor than partaking of polluted water whose very sip was an invitation to disease.

woodlands and along the marshes. Open Thurs through Sat 9 a.m. to 5 p.m., Sun 9:30 a.m. to 5:30 p.m. Adult admission $4.50, children $3; $5 parking fee.

McIntosh County, between Savannah and Brunswick, was the site of a British fort that predated Georgia's founding as a colony in 1733. Marshy bays and coastal islands are home to national marine and wildlife refuges and fleets of fishing boats and shrimping trawlers.

Stop first at the McIntosh County Welcome Center (105 Fort King George Dr., Darien, 912-437-6684, www.mcintoshcounty.com) on US 17 at the Darien River bridge for general information. The **Fort King George State Historic Site** (a mile off US 17, Darien, 912-437-4770, 800-864-PARK, www.gastateparks .org) marks an earthwork and palisaded log fortress South Carolinians built in 1721 to fend off hostile advances by the Spanish in Florida. It is the oldest English fort remaining on Georgia's coast. Most of the fort was destroyed by fire in 1726. A state visitor center and museum has displays, artifacts, and a film about the fort and early Georgia life. Open Tues through Sun from 9 a.m. to 5 p.m. Admission is $6.50 for adults, $3.75 for children 6 to 12. On the way to the fort, you can stop and photograph Darien's shrimp fleet and **St. Cyprian's Episcopal Church** (1870), McIntosh County's first black house of worship. It's located at 301 Fort King George Dr. Call (912) 437-4562 or log on to www.standrewsstcyprians.org.

Christ's Memory Chapel, purportedly "America's Smallest Church," was built in 1949 by McIntosh County grocery store owner Agnes Harper, who apparently thought travelers on US 17 needed divine guidance as they traveled the coastal highway between the northeastern United States and Florida. The 10-by-15-foot wooden chapel, with a steeple and imported stained glass windows, seats 13, just large enough, it's said, to accommodate Christ and his 12 Apostles. It's open to the public daily. Donations appreciated. Just switch off the lights when you leave. Take I-95 to the US 17/South Newport exit. The chapel is right beside the highway.

Unlike its neighboring states, most of Georgia's barrier islands have remained undeveloped. **Sapelo Island Tours,** conducted by the Georgia State Park system, take you through the fascinating ecology of the state's fourth largest barrier island. It accessible only by private boat or the state-run ferry and because access is limited, you may want to make prior arrangements. The ferry leaves from the visitor center/museum at the little fishing community of Meridian. On the 30-minute voyage, you'll skirt wavering stands of cord grass and scores of small islets and hammocks.

Touring the 10-mile-long, 16,000-acre island on a bus or tram, you'll see marine, bird, and animal life in the Sapelo Island National Estuarine Research Reserve (SINERR), the University of Georgia Marine Institute, and the R. J. Reynolds State Wildlife Refuge. You'll also pause at the exterior of the mansion North Carolina tobacco baron Reynolds got when he purchased the island from Hudson Motors executive Howard Coffin during the Great Depression. Naturalists will show you how to seine a flounder, explain some of the mysteries of the marshes, and point out deer, wild turkey, and many species of waterfowl that call the island home. You'll have time to walk the beaches and collect shells. Sapelo Island's historic lighthouse has been restored. About 1 percent of the island is owned by Hog Hammock, a black community of slave descendants who operate a small store with sandwiches, cold drinks, and insect repellent.

Tours are conducted year-round Tues through Fri 7:30 a.m. to 5:30 p.m., Sat 8 a.m. to 5:30 p.m., and Sun 1:30 to 5 p.m. Tickets are $15 for adults, $10 for those 6 to 18; free for children under 6. Sapelo Island Visitors Center is at 1 Landing Rd., Meridian. Phone (912) 437-3224 or visit www.sapeloislandgeorgia.org

Hofwyl-Broadfield Plantation State Historic Site (5556 US 17, Brunswick, 6 miles south of Darien, 912-264-7333, 800-864-PARK, www.gastateparks .org) is the last vestige of the rice culture that once flourished along the Altamaha River. Developed by South Carolinian William Brailsford in 1806–1807, the plantation grew to 7,300 acres, largely on the backs of 350 black slaves who labored in hellish conditions of heat and disease. A path takes you by the tabby ruins of the rice mill and along the top of the rice field dikes to the antebellum plantation house, furnished as it was in the early 1970s, when it was willed to the state by the last owner. Open Thurs through Sat from 9 a.m. to 5 p.m. Adults, $6.50; children, $3.75.

Brunswick & the Golden Isles

"The Golden Isles" are a necklace of lush, subtropical barrier islands snaking languidly along Georgia's 120-mile Atlantic coast. Several of the principal islands are part of Glynn County. Even the most developed islands—St. Simons

TOP ANNUAL EVENTS

St. Patrick's Celebration
downtown Savannah, for several days
leading up to March 17
(800) 444-2427
www.savannahsaintpatricksday.com

Jekyll Island Arts Festival
Goodyear Cottage, mid-March
(912) 635-3920

Savannah Tour of Homes & Gardens
late March
(912) 234-8054
www.savannahtourofhomes.org

Savannah Music Festival
late March
(877) 728-2662
www.savannahmusicfestival.org

N.O.G.S. Tour of Hidden Gardens
walled gardens north of Gaston Street,
downtown Savannah
mid-April
(912) 238-0248
www.gardenclubofsavannah.org

Great Golden Easter Egg Hunt
Jekyll Island Historic District, Easter
Sunday
(912) 635-3636
www.jekyllisland.org

Sapelo Island Cultural Festival
mid-October
(912) 485-2197
www.sapeloislandbirdhouses.com

Christmas in Savannah
throughout December
(800) 444-2427

Historic St. Marys Christmas Tour
mid-December
(912) 927-4976
www.stmaryswelcome.com

and Jekyll—are low-key, laid-back, and lightly commercialized compared to other resort islands on the Eastern Seaboard.

Blessed with long stretches of hard-packed beaches, marshes, inlets, rivers, and Spanish moss–veiled live oak trees, the islands are inviting places to get off the beaten path and commune in solitude with unsullied nature.

Brunswick, the Glynn County seat and a center of Georgia's shrimping and fishing industry (population 16,000), is the gateway to St. Simons, Jekyll, Sea Island, and Little St. Simons Island. Chartered in 1771, Brunswick was named for King George II's German ancestral home. Like Savannah, it was laid out on a precise grid of broad straight streets and public squares named for English places and nobility. Albany, Amherst, Dartmouth, Egmont, George, Gloucester, London, and Newcastle Streets, and Halifax, Hanover, and Hillsborough Squares kept their names after the Revolution. They're in the Old Town National Historic District. Queen Anne, Neo-Gothic, Italianate, Mansard, and Jacobean homes are enhanced by towering live oaks and banks of azaleas, camellias, and dogwoods. Several are charming bed-and-breakfast inns. See "Places to Stay in Coastal Georgia."

Get advance information from the **Brunswick–Golden Isles Convention & Visitors Bureau** (4 Glynn Ave., Brunswick, 912-265-0620, 800-933-2627, www.goldenisles.com). When you get here, pick up maps and information at the Brunswick–Golden Isles Visitors Center at US 17 and the F. J. Torras/St. Simons Island Causeway. Open daily except holidays from 9 a.m. to 5 p.m. Also visit the Brunswick I-95 Visitors Center, north of the city on I-95.

In downtown Brunswick, the turreted Queen Anne–style City Hall was built in 1883. Around the corner, the Glynn County Courthouse, at Reynolds and G Streets, is a good place to rest a spell. The classical, cupolaed building sits in a botanical garden of moss-draped oaks, Chinese pistachio, magnolia, and swamp trees and flowering shrubbery.

Get off the beaten path and walk the **Earth Day Nature Trail,** a self-guided tour that takes you on wooden boardwalks over a wading-bird habitat. You'll also see an osprey/eagle nesting platform and wildlife observation decks. The wavering salt marshes, where your favorite seafood begins its life cycle, was immortalized in Sidney Lanier's 1878 poem "The Marshes of Glynn," which goes in part: " . . . Sinuous southward and sinuous northward the shimmering band of the sand beach fastens the fringe of the marsh to the folds of the land." Lanier was inspired by the same view you'll see from **Marshes of Glynn Overlook Park.** The trail starts at the DNR Coastal Resource Division Headquarters, 1 Conservation Way. Call (912) 264-7218 for information.

If you'd like to go deep-sea fishing or just get out on the open water for a spell, many charter boats are at the Brunswick docks at the end of Gloucester Street. Get information at the Brunswick–Golden Isles Convention & Visitors Bureau.

Jekyll Island

Jekyll Island is connected to Brunswick by a 6-mile causeway and a high-span bridge ($3 per car) that allows boats to go under while you head unimpeded for your holiday. You can fish from the remains of the mothballed, nearly 60-year-old adjacent bridge. Stop first at the Jekyll Island Welcome Center at the island end of the bridge; find it at 901 Downing Musgrove Causeway, Jekyll Island, (912) 635-3636 or (877) 4-JEKYLL, www.jekyllisland.com. Open daily from 9 a.m. to 5 p.m. On the island, the Jekyll Island Museum Visitors Center (100 Stable Dr., 912-635-4036, 877-4-JEKYLL, www.jekyllisland.com) has exhibits on the island's "Millionaires' Era" and carriage tours and Sea Turtle Walks.

Between 1886 and 1942, Jekyll was the winter home of many of America's richest and most famous families. From the Gilded Age until early in World War ll, Astors, Pulitzers, Vanderbilts, Morgans, Rockefellers, Cranes, Goodyears, and other aristocrats lived in secluded luxury on their remote Georgia island. Shortly after Pearl Harbor, they boarded up their elegant "cottages" and left the island for the last time.

After the war, the state of Georgia paid $675,000 for the island and turned it into a state park. Although the purchase price now seems a pittance, Governor M. E. Thompson, who championed it, was widely lambasted for what political enemies labeled "Thompson's Folly."

According to the legislation creating the state park, only 35 percent of the island can be developed. That's a blessing for vacationers, who can hike and bike and bird-watch in a wilderness as pristine as when it was created, and enjoy amenities the old plutocrats could never have imagined. One side of the island is skirted by nearly 10 miles of hard-packed Atlantic beaches, washed by a usually mild surf perfect for young children and waders and the family dog. A rock wall intended to stop erosion prevents your Fidos from racing off the beach into woods where they're hard to find. Free showers, restrooms, and changing rooms are at regular intervals along the beachfront. Even on the busiest holiday weekends, there's plenty of room to get away from everybody else. The island's mainland side is washed by the Intracoastal Waterway and scenic salt marshes. Deer, raccoon, armadillo, wild turkey, and many species of waterfowl roam the marshes, live oak, and pine forests.

Tours of the *Jekyll Island Historic District* start at the Visitors Center. You can see a video presentation about Jekyll's colorful history, and guided tram tours take you inside several of the millionaires' restored cottages. Indian Mound Cottage, Standard Oil director William Rockefeller's shingled Cape Cod–style cottage, has been furnished as it was when the family began wintering

125 Years of History

The grand Jekyll Island Club Hotel at 371 Riverview Dr. (800-678-8946) was originally built as a hunting retreat in 1886 where the likes of the Rockefellers, the Vanderbilts, and the Astors would come and play away. Since the entire island was purchased by the State of Georgia in 1947, the hotel has gone through several major incarnations. It was fully restored to its splendor in 1987 and today is again considered an exclusive retreat, only now available to the public. The year 2012 was celebrated as not just its 125th anniversary, but the 25th anniversary of the Jekyll Club being open to the public. Guests can dine in the once-exclusive dining room or take part in up to 50 different island activities ranging from golf to horseback riding.

here in 1917. You'll probably wonder why there's no kitchen in most of the houses. The Club House, now the Jekyll Island Club Hotel, was the social center, where members gathered for meals, cards, and other activities. Other stops on the tour include Mistletoe Cottage, a Dutch Colonial Revival with a collection of sculpture by noted artist Russell Fiore, a longtime Jekyll resident. Cypress-shingled Faith Chapel is illuminated by Louis Comfort Tiffany and D. Maitland Armstrong stained-glass windows. Jekyll's recreational riches include 63 holes of golf that wind through marshes and woodlands, indoor and outdoor tennis, a fishing pier, marinas, a water slide park and wave pool, rental bikes, picnic grounds, and hiking trails.

Former shop buildings and servants' quarters now house an array of unique shops. Nature's Cottage, built in 1916 for the island's engineer, has hand-carved wooden ducks, bears, birds, and other wildlife. The Servants Dining Hall, from 1900, now sells beautiful sterling silver jewelry and Native American crafts. The Island Design Store, in the 1905 butlers' and valets' dormitory, specializes in casual clothes and decorative arts. For a rainy day at the beach, check out the new, used, and rare books at Jekyll Books and Antiques in the 1890s Furness cottage.

Jekyll hosts 114 monitored sea turtle nests, so it's only natural that the **Georgia Sea Turtle Center** is available to monitor the turtles and assist in care of turtles throughout the year. Located in the former 1903 power plant, the facility has a museum-style learning center, a state-of-the-art rehabilitation center, and a veterinary clinic. Guided turtle walks are conducted nightly from May through Aug. Located at 214 Stable Rd. (912-635-4444, www.georgiasea turtlecenter.org), the center is open year-round Tues through Sat 9 a.m. until 5 p.m. From Mar until Nov, it is also opened Mon 10 a.m. until 2 p.m. Adults are $7, seniors $6, and children ages 4 to 12 are $5.

St. Simons & Sea Islands

The toll-free F. J. Torras Causeway takes you to **St. Simons Island.** The most developed of the four Glynn County "Golden Isles" has seen a big increase in hotels, condos, restaurants, and shopping areas in recent years, but that hasn't dimmed the natural glories of the Manhattan-size island's salt marshes, beaches, and live oak forests wrapped in Spanish moss. You can swim and sunbathe on long strands of beach—all Georgia beaches are public domain—fish, ride horseback, play golf and tennis, and visit historic sites dating back to the early 18th century.

Fort Frederica National Monument, Frederica Road, St. Simons Island, at the island's northern end, includes remnants of a tabby fortress the British built in the 1730s as a bulwark against Spanish invaders from Florida. Leading up to the fort are foundations of homes and shops once occupied by 1,500 troops and civilians. The fort was never tested. The Spanish attacked in 1742, and their defeat at the nearby Battle of Bloody Marsh kept England firmly in control of Georgia's coast. Stop first at the National Park Service Visitors Center (912-638-3639, www.nps.gov/fofr) for a film and historical displays. Bring insect repellent, and don't step on the fire ant mounds! Open daily from 9 a.m. to 5 p.m. Admission is $3; free for children 16 and under.

Christ Church, a Gothic wooden sanctuary on the road to Fort Frederica, is the island's most beloved (and most photographed) landmark. The site of services John and Charles Wesley conducted for Frederica's garrison, the original church was built in 1820. Desecrated by Union soldiers, it was rebuilt in 1884 by the Reverend Anson Phelps Dodge, whose life was chronicled by late St. Simons novelist Eugenia Price in *Beloved Invader.* The church is framed by an arbor of live oaks, dogwoods, and azaleas. The interior is illuminated by stained-glass windows. The church is at 6329 Frederica Rd., St. Simons Island (912-638-8683, www.christchurchfrederica.org). Open daily, donations appreciated. Episcopal services are conducted every Sunday.

ghostlylight

If you stand outside the walls of Christ Church burying ground late at night, you might see a light flickering through the darkness. Legend says a young woman with a terrible fear of the dark was buried there. To ease her spirit, her husband brought a lighted candle to the grave site every night, and long after his own death, the candle still burns.

St. Simons Lighthouse (St. Simons Island, 912-638-4666, www.saintsimonslighthouse.org) at the island's southern end, has been a landmark since 1872. The present 104-foot brick sentinel—still maintained as an operational beacon by the US Coast Guard—stands on the site of an 1810 lighthouse that was destroyed by retreating Confederate troops in 1861. The old lightkeeper's cottage houses the **Museum of Coastal History,** with collections of colonial furniture, shipbuilding tools, and changing exhibits of coastal art. Open Mon through Sat from 10 a.m. to 5 p.m., Sun from 1:30 to 5 p.m. Admission for adults is $10; ages 6 to 11 $5; under 6 free.

Neptune Park, around the lighthouse, has seaside picnic tables, a playground, and steps down to the beach. You can fish from the beach or take a cooler and lawn chair onto the Municipal Pier and angle for flounder and whiting, even pull up a startled hammerhead shark or barracuda. No license is required for saltwater fishing. The pier, lighthouse, and Neptune Park are in The Village, around Mallery Street, St. Simons's original commercial area, where you'll find restaurants, shops, and lodgings.

Massengale Park, on Ocean Boulevard, between the King & Prince Hotel and the Coast Guard Station, has several miles of public beach, picnic areas, and restrooms.

Whatta you do on a rainy day at the beach? The *Maritime Center at the Historic Coast Guard Station* on St. Simons's East Beach, opened in April 2006, invites visitors to learn about life as a "Coastie" in the early 1940s. "Ollie," a fictional Coast Guardsman from the 1940s, is the "tour leader." Through his "letters home" and his field journal entries, we learn the ropes of being a Coastie and explore the beaches and marshes that surround his base. The museum's 7 galleries are filled with hands-on exhibits that include "Coasties in Training," life-saving techniques, "Digging for Fossils," a radar training school, the area's marine life, shrimping and fishing, weather and hurricanes, and the perils of German U-boats off the Georgia coast in the early days of WWII. The Maritime Center is open Mon through Sat from 10 a.m. to 5 p.m. Adults $10, $5 ages 6 to 11.

For information about any sites of activities on the island, contact St. Simons Island Visitors Center at 530 B Beachview Dr., St. Simons Island, (800) 933-2627, www.goldenisles.com. The website includes information about all the Golden Isles.

By the time you've made the 20-minute launch crossing from "big" St. Simons to *Little St. Simons Island,* the world's problems will have vanished in the sunlight of another glorious Low Country morning. A fortunate set of circumstances has left the island—6 miles long by 2 to 3 miles wide—very nearly as nature created it.

Through the 1800s, the 10,000 acres were the domain of one rice planter family. In 1903 a pencil company bought the island, but when the red cedars proved too wind-gnarled for writing instruments, it became an off-the-beaten-path retreat, now open to the public.

AUTHOR'S FAVORITES

Savannah National Historic District	St. Simons Island
Telfair Art Museum	Isle of Hope
Tybee Island	Little St. Simons Island
Midway Church	St. Marys Submarine Museum
Sapelo Island	Cumberland Island National Seashore
Jekyll Island	Breakfast and lunch at Mrs. Wilkes Dining Room

Congenial hosts at *The Lodge* on Little St. Simons Island will put you up in rustic but comfortable, air-conditioned guest rooms and cottages that accommodate up to 32. At mealtime, sit at a communal table and relive your day's adventures. Things to do are bountiful: horseback riding, sunbathing, and swimming in a pool or in 7 miles of wild beaches, boating, canoeing, crabbing, bird-watching, fishing, and walking through forests inhabited by deer, raccoon, armadillos, pelicans, red-tailed hawks, great blue heron, egret, and more than 200 other species of birds. Gators cruise like ironclad vessels in marshes and rivers. All meals and activities are included in expensive double occupancy daily rates. Phone (912) 638-7472 or (888) 733-5774 or visit www.littlestsimons island.com. Write PO Box 21708, St. Simons Island 31522.

Accessible only through a gated causeway, only *Sea Island* homeowners and guests at the exclusive Cloister Resort are allowed on the island (www .seaisland.com).

Cumberland & Crawfish

Cumberland Island National Seashore is an intricate web of nature's rarest, most wondrous gifts. Maintained by the National Park Service, the island—18 miles long and 1 to 2 miles wide—preserves astonishing treasures of marshes and dunes, pristine beaches, live oak forests, lakes, ponds, estuaries, and inlets. "Natives" include great blue heron, wood storks, egrets, and dozens of other bird species, many rarely seen beyond these shores; giant sea turtles, which plod over the beaches to regenerate their endangered kind; fiddler, hermit, and ghost crabs; shrimp, oysters, and flounder; deer, armadillo, mink, wild horses, and wild boar; playful otters; and gators that cruise the waterways like men o' war.

Mankind's 4,000-year habitation began with ancient Guale Indians, followed by 16th-century Spanish missionaries, 18th-century British troops, and pre–Civil War indigo and cotton planters. Thomas Carnegie, of the Pittsburgh Carnegies, bought the entire island in the 1880s. His family's splendid estates were mostly abandoned when the Gilded Age gave way to the Roaring Twenties, and high society discovered more fashionable wintering places. With only a few intrusions, the island has passed into public trust largely as it was created.

Unless you own your own boat, the only way to enjoy Cumberland's glories is via a 45-minute ride on the **Cumberland Queen** from St. Marys. With a capacity of 150, the *Queen* departs St. Marys daily from Mar 1 to Nov 30 at 9 a.m. and 11:45 a.m., arriving at Cumberland at 9:45 a.m. and 12:30 p.m., respectively. The rest of the year, it operates at the same times daily except Tues and Wed. Including taxes, fares are $20 for adults, $18 for those 65 and older, $14 for children 12 and under. You must check in 30 minutes beforehand or they will cancel

The Downside of Spanish Moss

Spanish moss, which isn't a moss at all, but an air plant loosely related to pineapple, hangs in wispy picturesque veils from live oak trees in the southern and coastal parts of the state. It's lovely to look at, but the very devil to touch. Chiggers (aka redbugs) are voracious little pests that make their home in Spanish moss. They enjoy nothing better than feasting on a fresh, tasty smorgasbord of anybody unwary enough to think the moss would be picturesque in a home garden or stuffed in a pillow. Chiggers attack en masse and make you itch and scratch until you think you'll lose your sanity. Modern medications like Benadryl can relieve the torture, but many Southerners prefer old-fashioned remedies like Epsom salt baths, nail polish, and Chapstick. It's best to avoid the scenario altogether no matter how tempting it may be to take some home.

your reservations. When you arrive on the island, the National Park Service will collect a $4 per person user fee. For information and reservations, phone (912) 882-4336 or (877) 860-6787 or go to www.nps.gov/cuis. The NPS visitor center on the St. Marys waterfront is open daily from 8 a.m. to 4:30 p.m. Bear in mind that sailing times are as precise as Swiss trains. If you miss the last ferry from the island, you'll have to hire a boat from St. Marys or Florida's Fernandina Beach. Campers have a choice of developed and primitive campgrounds available for a small cost, which varies according to the site you choose. Sea Camp, 5 minutes' walk from the ferry dock, has bathrooms and showers ($4 per person per day, plus $4 one-time day-use fee); primitive campsites, a 3.5- to 10-mile hike from the dock, have trench latrines and cold water spigots ($2 per person per day, plus $4 one-time day-use fee). If you're a day-tripper, you can walk several nature trails, or swim and sun and view the remains of Dungeness, the Carnegies' fabulous estate destroyed by fire in the 1950s. Park Service rangers lead history and nature walks. There's nothing at all for sale on the island, so remember to bring food, cold drinks, insect repellent, and sunscreen.

The *Greyfield Inn* is Cumberland's only hotel-type accommodation. The late John F. Kennedy, Jr., and his wife, Carolyn, had their wedding reception in the Carnegie family's old Georgian-style mansion after taking their vows at the island's African-American chapel. Staying overnight is a one-of-a-kind experience. Guests sleep in 17 air-conditioned rooms with four-poster beds, bathe in claw-footed tubs, and relax amid family portraits and mementos. All meals, boat transportation from Fernandina Beach, Florida, and walks with naturalists are included in the expensive rates. Contact Greyfield Inn at PO Box 900, Fernandina Beach, FL, (904) 261-6408, (866) 410-8051, www.greyfieldinn.com.

St. Marys Submarine Museum (102 St. Marys St., St. Marys, on the St. Marys waterfront, 912-882-2782, www.stmaryssubmuseum.com) will tell you everything you ever wanted to know about submarines, with special emphasis on the nuke fish at nearby Kings Bay Submarine Base. You can also see diving equipment, research documents, uniforms, and a re-created sub interior. Looks pretty cozy, eh? Imagine spending several months in these quarters without seeing the surface of the seas you're cruising under. Open Tues through Sat from 10 a.m. to 5 p.m., Sun from 12 to 5 p.m. Admission is $5, $4 for military and seniors, $3 children 6 to 18. Contact the St. Marys Tourism Council at PO Box 1291, St. Marys, (912) 882-4000, (800) 868-8687, www.stmaryswelcome.com.

The Cumberland Island National Seashore Museum in downtown St. Marys tells the story of the War of 1812's "forgotten invasion." In the early morning hours of January 13, 1815, five days after Andy Jackson's backwoodsmen and Jean Lafitte's French pirates bested the British at New Orleans, effectively ending the war, 600 British sailors landed at Point Peter, a fort guarding St. Marys. They overwhelmed the 130 American defenders in what was the war's belated last battle. Nearly two centuries later, musket balls, uniform buttons, pottery shards, cooking utensils, and other artifacts recovered at Point Peter are on display at the National Seashore Museum. The museum also exhibits artifacts and photos of Cumberland Island's human history, from ancient Guale Indians, through the Gilded Era of the Carnegies and the island's acquisition as a national seashore in 1972. The museum is on Osborne Street, a few steps from St. Marys's waterfront. Open Wed through Sun 1 to 4 p.m. Free admission. Located at 113 St. Marys St. Phone (912) 882-4336 or go to www.nps.gov/cuis.

The *Woodbine Crawfish Festival* takes over the tiny Camden County seat the last weekend of April. The chance to see beauty queens, marching bands, parades, and arts and crafts and put away mountains of delicious crustaceans—fried, gumbo'd, étouffléed, jambalaya'd, and boiled in savory Cajun herbs—lures crowds from all over the Georgia coast, even down into Florida. Phone (912) 576-3211 or visit www.woodbinecrawfish.com for information.

Aaron Burr Slept Here

After being indicted for murder for killing popular founding father Alexander Hamilton in an 1804 pistol duel, US Vice President Aaron Burr fled south, first to Cumberland Island, where he was unwelcome, then to the home of his Princeton law school classmate, Major Archibald Clark, in St. Marys. Mistress Clark reportedly didn't cotton to an accused murderer under her roof, so Burr, who was never tried for Hamilton's death, returned to Washington and resumed his duties as Thomas Jefferson's veep. A bronze plaque on the front of the Clark-Bessant House on Osborne Street (St. Marys's oldest house, 1801) notes Burr's visit and that of Gen. Winfield Scott, who R&R-ed on returning from Indian wars in Florida. The house's current occupants are descendants of Archibald Clark.

Places to Stay in Coastal Georgia

SAVANNAH HISTORIC DISTRICT

Bed & Breakfast Inn
117 W. Gordon St.
(912) 238-0518
(888) 238-0518
www.savannahbnb.com
Moderate
History and charm at moderate prices. A pair of 1835 Federal-style townhouses have 15 guest rooms. A garden suite and 2 cottages have kitchens and sitting areas. Full Southern breakfast included.

Foley House
14 W. Hull St.
(912) 232-6622
(800) 647-3708
www.foleyinn.com
Expensive
This elegant 1896 Victorian townhouse has 19 guest rooms, several with oversize whirlpool tubs and working fireplaces. Continental breakfast, afternoon tea, and cordials included.

The Gastonian
220 E. Gaston St.
(912) 232-2869
(800) 322-6603
www.gastonian.com
Expensive
Sumptuous 17-room inn in a matched pair of 1868 townhouses. Georgian and Regency antiques and all the modern comforts. Honeymooners prefer the

Caracalla Suite, with an antique four-poster bed and a draped whirlpool bath as big as Cleopatra's barge. The rate includes gourmet breakfast.

Mansion on Forsyth Park
700 Drayton St.
(912) 238-5198
www.mansiononforsyth park.com
Expensive
The Savannah Historic District's newest luxury hotel blends a restored 1890s redbrick mansion with a seamless new addition. Overlooking beautiful Forsyth Park, the hotel's Victorian exterior is contrasted with more than 400 pieces of original contemporary art, Brazilian mahogany, Italian marble, antique mirrors, and other materials. The 126 guest rooms have many deluxe amenities. Guests and visitors may enjoy the eclectic 700 Drayton Restaurant, cooking school, lounges, and spa.

Mulberry Inn
601 E. Bay St.
(912) 238-1200
(877) 468-1200
www.savannahhotel.com
Expensive
The 121-room historic district hotel, in a onetime Coca-Cola bottling plant, is a Holiday Inn franchise, but you'd never guess it from the antiques and other Old Savannah decor and furnishings. Full restaurant and bar.

The President's Quarters
225 E. President St.
(912) 233-1600
www.presidentsquarters .com
Moderate to Expensive
Consistently voted "Best Savannah Inn," this boutique hotel is located on Oglethorpe Square in the heart of the historic district. Originally constructed in 1855, these twin towered mansions now offer 16 spacious suites. An elegant breakfast is included.

TYBEE ISLAND

If you'd like to rent a condo or a beach house, contact Tybee Island Rentals, PO Box 1440, Tybee Island 31328, (800) 755-8562. Tybee's chain motels include Days Inn, (800) 325-2525 and (912) 786-4576; Econo Lodge Beachside, (912) 786-4535; and Best Western Dunes Inn, (912) 786-4591. For general information, contact Tybee Island Visitor Center at (800) 868-2322.

Lighthouse Inn Bed & Breakfast
16 Meddin Dr.
(912) 786-0901
(866) 786-0901
www.tybeebb.com
Moderate, includes full breakfast
Innkeeper Susie Morris's 3 guest rooms in a tree-shaded 1910 beach house have private entrances, phone, minifridge, clawfoot tubs, and coffeemakers. The inn is close to

Historic Accommodations

More than three dozen historic bed-and-breakfast inns surround you with the aura of Old Savannah. For information and reservations, phone Bed & Breakfast Reservations of Savannah, (800) 729-7787 and (912) 232-7787 (RSVP), and Savannah Historic Inns and Guest Houses, (800) 262-4667. Chain hotels and motels are also abundant.

beaches, Tybee Lighthouse, and restaurants.

Tybee Island Inn
24 Van Horne St.
(912) 786-9255
(866) 892-4667
www.tybeeislandinn.com
Moderate
The number one bed-and-breakfast inn on Tybee, the inn features 7 rooms, each with its own bath. The inn was built in 1902 and has been impeccably restored. Just a 5-minute walk from the beach, it is in the island's Fort Screven Historic District. Innkeepers Cathy and Lloyd Kilday were married at the inn and have owned it since 1995.

BRUNSWICK

Brunswick Manor
825 Egmont St.
(912) 265-6889
www.brunswickmanor.com
Moderate, includes full breakfast and high tea
Built in 1886 as the home of a former Union Army officer, the redbrick Romanesque mansion is decorated with antiques and period furnishings. Four suites have queen-size beds and private

baths. Two have kitchens and breakfast nooks. A separate cottage sleeps 8.

McKinnon House
1001 Egmont St.
(912) 261-9100
(866) 261-9100
www.mckinnonhouse
bandb.com
Inexpensive to Moderate
Victorian splendor in a handsomely restored Queen Anne mansion with elaborate woodwork and fine New Orleans and Charleston furniture. Full breakfast and afternoon refreshments. Three guest rooms with private baths.

JEKYLL ISLAND

Jekyll Island Campground
N. Beachview Drive
(912) 635-3021
(866) 658-3201
www.jekyllisland.com
Inexpensive
Eighteen wooded acres with full hookups, restrooms, showers, laundry, and camp store. Pets allowed on leash. Near beaches, fishing, and golf courses. Nightly, weekly, and monthly rates available.

Jekyll Island Club Hotel
371 Riverview Dr.
(912) 635-2600
(800) 535-9547
www.jekyllclub.com
Expensive
The millionaires' turreted, 4-story former clubhouse has been transformed into a deluxe hotel graced by stained glass, plaster molding, and other rich architectural details. Swim in the outdoor pool, take carriage rides, and play croquet on the emerald lawns. The 134 guest rooms and suites have all the first-class comforts.

Villas by the Sea Resort
175 N. Beachview Dr.
(912) 635-2521
(800) 841-6262
www.villasbythesearesort
.com
Moderate to Expensive
As the name suggests, this is right on the water with some beautiful views. There are 160 1- to 3-bedroom villas with fully equipped kitchens. A full conference center is designed for those seeking to have meetings by the sea.

ST. SIMONS ISLAND

Days Inn
1701 Frederica Rd.
(912) 634-0660
(800) 870-3736
www.daysinn.com
Inexpensive
Complimentary continental breakfast and microwave and refrigerator in all 101 rooms. Bike rentals on site.

Epworth-by-the-Sea
100 Arthur Moore Dr.
(912) 638-8688
www.epworthbythesea.org
Inexpensive
Methodist conference center, spiritual retreat, and vacation center has 223 modern motel rooms, 12 family apartments, an inexpensive cafeteria, a swimming pool, tennis courts, and fishing piers. No alcohol or unmarried couples allowed.

King & Prince Beach & Golf Resort
201 Arnold Rd.
(912) 638-3631
(800) 342-0212
www.kingandprince.com
Expensive
On its own Atlantic beach, the K&P has been catering to St. Simons vacationers since its original building opened in 1935. Now a deluxe, full-service resort, its 187 accommodations include guest rooms and suites, oceanfront cabanas, and 2- and 3-bedroom villas. Amenities include an indoor pool, spa, restaurants and bars, tennis courts, and golf privileges at nearby courses.

St. Simons Inn by the Lighthouse
609 Beachview Dr.
(912) 638-1101
www.stsimonsinn.com
Moderate, includes continental breakfast
Thirty-four modern, attractive guest rooms and pool around the corner from the Village shops, restaurants, pier, and lighthouse. Microwaves and refrigerators in every room.

Village Inn and Pub
500 Mallory St.
(912) 634-6056
(888) 635-6111
www.villageinnandpub.com
Moderate
This beautifully restored 1930s beach cottage has 28 unique rooms, some with balconies. Breakfast is included. The main lobby features a pub with a stone fireplace and a courtyard. In-room massages are available.

ST. MARYS

Since its establishment in 1979, the Kings Bay Nuclear Submarine Base—home port for 8 Trident missile nuclear subs—has mushroomed St. Marys's population from 2,000 to nearly 9,000. A flood of fast-food outlets, video rental stores, and chain stores has grown up on the outskirts, but the historic old town on the St. Marys River is as quaint and unchanged as ever.

Crooked River State Park
GA Spur 40, 7 miles north of St. Marys
(912) 882-5256
Inexpensive
Has campsites and cottages, swimming pool, fishing areas, and playgrounds. There's a $2 per visit parking fee. For camping and cottage reservations, call (800) 864-PARK, www.gastateparks.org/crookedriver.

Emma's Bed & Breakfast
300 W. Conyers St.
(912) 882-4199
www.emmasbedandbreakfast.com
Inexpensive to Moderate, includes full breakfast
Beautifully decorated inn, with southern pine floors and working fireplaces, has 4 main house guest rooms and 5 others in an adjacent cottage, each with private bath. The Honeymoon Suite has a red heart-shaped Jacuzzi and a private deck. Picnic lunches can be packed for Cumberland Island trips. The house is on 4 wooded acres, with deer, birds, and other wildlife.

Goodbread House Bed and Breakfast
209 Osborne St.
(912) 882-7490
(877) 205-1453
www.goodbreadhouse.com
Inexpensive to Moderate, includes full breakfast

This bed-and-breakfast has 4 guest rooms with private baths in an 1870s Victorian house. Children are welcome, and pets can stay in the fenced yard.

Spencer House Inn
200 Osborne St.
(912) 882-1872
(888) 840-1872
www.spencerhouseinn
.com
Inexpensive, includes full breakfast
The 1872 National Register House is a short walk from the Cumberland Island ferry. Fourteen rooms have private baths, claw-foot tubs, TV, and phone. Guests relax in the library and on verandas with cypress rockers.

Places to Eat in Coastal Georgia

SAVANNAH HISTORIC DISTRICT

Belford's
315 W. St. Julian St.
(912) 233-2626
www.belfordssavannah
.com
Moderate to Expensive
Local and imported seafood and steaks in one of City Market's newest upscale restaurants. Full bar. The breakfast and Sunday brunch menus feature eggs Benedict and a variety of omelets.

Breakfast, lunch, and dinner daily.

Garibaldi Cafe
315 W. Congress St.
(912) 232-7118
www.garibaldisavannah
.com
Moderate to Expensive
Located in an historic fire station, Garibaldi's has been a local favorite for years. Food ranges from seafood to pastas and steaks. The specialty is their crispy flounder which has been on the menu since the early 1980's.

Goode Feathers
39 Barnard St.
(912) 233-4683
www.goosefeathers.com
Inexpensive
Popular City Market drop-in serves sandwiches, soups, salads, pastries, and croissants in a cheerful black-and-white-tiled former drugstore.

Gryphon Tea Room
337 Bull St., at Madison Square
(912) 238-2481
Inexpensive
A century-old pharmacy has been transformed into a romantic European tearoom. Sit back and enjoy your tea, coffee, soups, sandwiches, and desserts amid the beauty of Honduran mahogany, 14 original stained-glass windows, Tiffany-style globes, and lace curtains. Open daily morning to night.

The Lady and Sons
102 W. Congress St.
(912) 233-2600
www.ladyandsons.com
Moderate to Expensive
You've seen her on TV, bought her cookbooks, and tried her recipes at home. Now you're in Savannah, so here's the chance to feast at her table. Maybe the lady—food guru Paula Deen—and her sons will be there to great you. Gorge yourself on the Mon through Sat buffet, laden with fried chicken, chicken and dumplings, baked ham, collard greens, corn bread, cobblers, etc. Or go "light" by picking from the menu, which isn't available on Sun. Whenever you come, get there real early and be prepared to wait in line. Or have somebody hold your place while you check out the gift shop. It's open Mon through Sat from 11 a.m. to 3 p.m. and Sun 11 a.m. to 5 p.m.

Lulu's Chocolate Bar
42 Martin Luther King Jr. Blvd.
(866) 462-8681
www.luluschocolatebar
.com
Inexpensive to Moderate
Ditch your diet at the door of this late-night dessert and martini bar in a rejuvenated downtown area. The Dessert Bar features such tempting "waistline disasters" as chocolate-covered strawberries, cappuccino brownies, layer cakes, tarts, and

handmade truffles. The house specialty drink is the LuLutini, real chocolate, chocolate vodka, crème de cacao, and Godiva chocolate liqueur. It's open Mon through Sat.

Mrs. Wilkes Dining Room
107 W. Jones St.
(912) 232-5997
www.mrswilkes.com
Inexpensive
Mrs. Wilkes Dining Room is a treasure hidden away in a historic district townhouse. You know you're there by the long lines waiting outside. Family-style lunch fills the tables with bottomless platters of fried chicken, fried fish, Southern-style vegetables, corn bread, biscuits, and dessert. Come for breakfast and you'll be treated with feather-light biscuits, eggs, sausage, and buttery grits. Mon through Fri, breakfast and lunch only. No credit cards.

The Olde Pink House
Reynolds Square,
23 Abercorn St.
(912) 232-4286
Expensive
This is the ticket for a romantic, candlelight dinner. The stunning 18th-century mansion's dining rooms are graced by colonial paintings and decor, a perfect dress-up place for Low Country she-crab soup, crispy flounder, sautéed shrimp, country ham served over grits, and Vidalia onion stuffed with sausage. Before or after

dinner, sit by the fireplace and enjoy the pianist in the cozy downstairs tavern. Dinner daily.

Six Pence Pub
245 Bull St.
(912) 233-3156
www.sixpencepub.com
Inexpensive to Moderate
General Oglethorpe might feel at home in this cozy British pub in downtown Savannah's historic district. Locals and tourists meet for shepherd's pie, fish and chips, soups, salads, sandwiches, and a raft of imported and domestic brews and a full bar. Lunch and dinner daily.

TYBEE ISLAND

AJ's Dockside
1315 Chatham Ave.
(912) 786-6109
Inexpensive
Overlooking the Back River, AJ's is off the beaten path and a local favorite, serving up fresh seafood along with live music. Conch fritters, po' boys, and platters are just some of the fare. Open for lunch and dinner, it serves 46 different types of beer and is a great happy hour spot to people watch.

The Crab Shack
40A Estill Hammock Rd.
(912) 786-9857
www.thecrabshack.com
Inexpensive
As the sign of the happy crab says, THE PLACE WHERE THE ELITE EAT IN THEIR BARE FEET, the Crab Shack epitomizes Tybee's laid-back

ambience. Sit on a big open deck by the water or in the screened-in dining room, and tuck into monster platters of fried and broiled shrimp, oysters, crabs, and fish at very moderate prices. Open continuously for lunch and dinner daily.

North Beach Grill
41A Meddin Dr.
(912) 786-4442
Inexpensive to Moderate
Behind the Tybee Museum, across from the lighthouse, this longtime Tybee favorite delivers a flavorful blend of Southern and Caribbean cooking. Genial owner/chef George Spriggs wows his patrons with Jamaican-style jerk (marinated) chicken, pan-seared snapper, eggplant parmigiana, crab cake sandwiches, Cuban-style pot roast, and many other wonderful creations. Open daily for lunch and dinner.

Fannie's on the Beach
1613 Strand Ave.
(912) 786-6109
www.fanniesonthebeach
.com
Inexpensive
With open-air seating on the second floor and air-conditioning on the first, you can't beat the views of the beach from Fannie's. Great beach food fare ranging from fish sandwiches to burgers to crab legs.

Marlin Monroes
404 Butler St.
(912) 786-4745
www.marlinmonroessurf
sidegrill.com
Moderate
The beachside bar and
grill is the sort of place you
could stay all day. In addition to the restaurant there
is a pool with live entertainment. Fresh seafood
includes fish tacos to grilled
platters.

Spanky's Beachside
165 Strand, across from
the Tybee Pier
(912) 786-5520
Inexpensive
A popular drop-in for cold
beer, seafood, and sand-
wiches, and casual meeting
and mingling. Open daily.

BRUNSWICK

The Georgia Pig
2712 US 17 South
(912) 264-6664
Inexpensive
The place for Brunswick
stew at the source, plus
delectable barbecue pork
plates with all the trim-
mings. Lunch and dinner
daily.

Oyster Shak
2027 Stacy St.
(912) 265-2850
www.oystershak.com
Inexpensive to Moderate
Fresh variety of seafood
right off the docks and
the largest raw bar in
Glynn County. A local
hangout that is a sight to
behold inside. Have your
oysters raw or by the

steamed bucket. Casual
atmosphere.

SUNBURY

Sunbury Crab Company
541 Brigantine-Dunmore
Rd.
(912) 884-8640
www.sunburycrabco.com
Inexpensive
A well-off-the-beaten
path gem that's worth the
detour, this seafood shack
overlooking the coastal
rivers and marshes serves
shrimp, oysters, fish, and
blue crab just out of the
water. Crab cakes, fresh
steamed crabs, and fried
shrimp are house special-
ties. Full bar. Open Wed
through Fri 5 to 10 p.m.,
Sat and Sun from noon to
10 p.m.

JEKYLL ISLAND

Blackbeard's
200 N. Beachview Dr.
(912) 635-3522
Moderate
Fresh Low Country seafood
dishes are the specialties
at this popular beachfront
eatery.

Cafe Solterra
Jekyll Island Club Hotel
371 Riverview Dr.
(912) 635-2600
www.jekyllclub.com/dining/
cafe-solterra
Inexpensive
Pick up sandwiches, sal-
ads, pizza, and desserts,
and enjoy them inside or at
outdoor tables.

The Grand Dining Room
Jekyll Island Hotel
(See "Places to Stay.")
Expensive
Dine in the splendor of the
Gilded Age, amid candle-
light, fine crystal, china, and
silver. The extensive menu
includes innovative continental cuisine, steaks, fresh
seafood, and pasta. The
yards-long Sunday brunch
shouldn't be missed.

**SeaJay's Waterfront Cafe
& Pub**
Jekyll Harbor Marina, 1
Harbor Rd.
(912) 635-3200
www.seajays.com
Moderate
Low Country seafood,
steaks, and Brunswick
stew in a casual dining
room overlooking the
shrimp and pleasure boats
at the Jekyll Harbor Marina.
Enjoy sunset on the
marshes.

ST. SIMONS ISLAND

Barbara Jean's
214 Mallery St.
(912) 634-6500
and 138 Johnny Mercer
Blvd., Wilmington Island
near Savannah
(912) 898-4424
www.barbarajeans.com
Inexpensive to Moderate
Family-run restaurants skill-
fully combine Low Country
seafood and Southern
home cooking. Crab cakes,
she-crab soup, and fried
shrimp are right up there
with from-scratch fried
chicken, chicken-fried
steak with cream gravy,

vegetables, and other Southern classics. Follow it up with Barbara Jean Barta's "Chocolate Stuff" dessert and you'll be planning your next visit before you're out the door.

Bennie's Red Barn
5514 Frederica Rd.
(912) 638-2844
www.benniesredbarn.com
Moderate to Expensive
Fresh coastal seafood and steaks grilled over a wood fire have made this rustic off-the-beaten-path old barn a dining landmark since 1954.

Fourth of May Cafe & Deli
321 Mallery St., at the main Village corner
(912) 638-5444
www.4thofmay.com
Inexpensive
The cafe features daily potluck specials—meat or seafood with 2 fresh

vegetables, for inexpensive prices, and also has huge deli sandwiches and desserts. Lunch and dinner daily.

J. Mac's Island Restaurant & Bistro
407 Mallery St.
(912) 634-0403
www.jmacsislandrestaurant.com
Moderate
A cool, classy place for rack of lamb, soft-shell crabs, lobster, steaks, pasta, cocktails, wine, and live musical entertainment. Dinner Mon through Sat.

ST. MARYS

Pauly's Cafe
102 Osborne St.
(912) 882-3944
www.paulyscafe.com
Inexpensive
On the St. Marys waterfront, a few steps from the Cumberland Island Visitors Center, the snug little cafe serves local seafood, Italian dishes, subs, steaks, and beer and wine at lunch and dinner daily. A cold beer or a glass of wine with almond-crusted fresh grouper or lobster scampi (baby lobster tails sautéed in garlic butter) is a perfect way to celebrate a Cumberland Island adventure.

NORTHEAST GEORGIA →

Depending on which direction you've pointed your hiking boots, the 2,015-mile **Appalachian Trail** either begins or ends with 79 miles of northeastern Georgia mountainland. Many AT veterans acclaim the Georgia section as the most beautiful in all the 14 states between here and Mount Katahdin, Maine.

The AT's southern terminus is atop 3,782-foot **Springer Mountain,** in Dawson County, 75 miles northeast of Atlanta. An 8-mile approach trail begins at Amicalola Falls State Park. There hikers can camp out, get their gear together, and have their packs weighed by park rangers.

From Springer Mountain the AT's Section I is a 22.3-mile easy-to-strenuous hike to GA 60 at Woody Gap. Section II, 10.7 miles from Woody Gap to Neels Gap, has just one long uphill stretch and is popular with one-day and weekend hikers. At Neels Gap, the trail crosses US 19/US 129 and goes "indoors" as it passes through a covered breezeway of the **Mountain Crossing/Walasi-Yi Center.** At this stone-and-log legacy of the 1930s Civilian Conservation Corps, hikers can get trail information and replenish supplies of dehydrated foods and camping gear, do their laundry, and enjoy a hot shower.

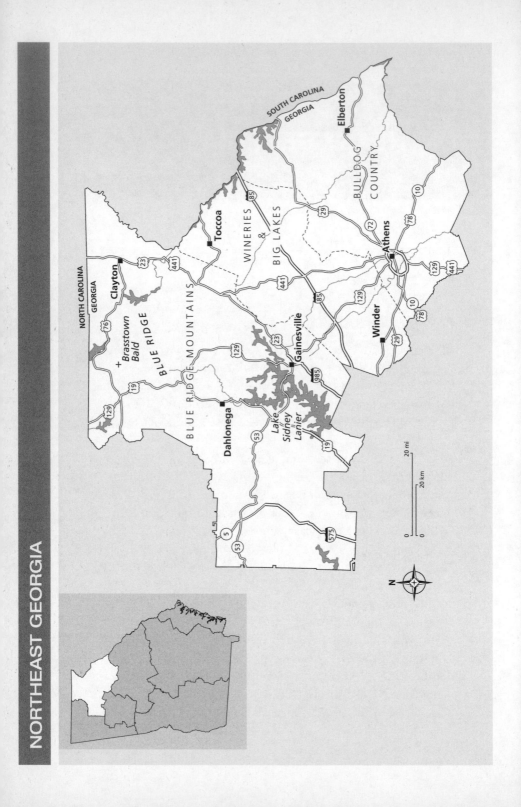

NORTHEAST GEORGIA'S TOP HITS

Appalachian Trail

Chattooga River rafting

Lake Rabun Hotel/Rabun Beach Recreation Area

Tallulah Gorge Park

Foxfire Museum

Black Rock Mountain State Park

Moccasin Creek State Park

Georgia Mountain Fair

Lake Chatuge

Chattahoochee National Forest

Brasstown Valley Resort

Richard B. Russell-Brasstown Scenic Highway

Vogel State Park

Lake Winfield Scott Recreation Area

Mark of the Potter

BabyLand General Hospital

Old Sautee Store/Stovall Covered Bridge

Alpine Helen

Unicoi State Park

Anna Ruby Falls

Dahlonega Courthouse Gold Museum

Amicalola Falls State Park

Lake Lanier Islands

Georgia Mountains Museum

Elachee Nature Science Center

Hart State Park

Tugaloo State Park

Victoria Bryant State Park

Travelers Rest

Château Élan Winery & Resort

Fort Yargo State Park

Crawford W. Long Museum

Elberton Granite Museum
Georgia Guidestones

Bobby Brown State Park

Richard B. Russell State Park

University of Georgia

Oconee Cultural Arts Foundation

Northeast Georgia Folk Pottery Museum

Motorists stop by for mountain handicrafts and short hikes on the trail. Phone (706) 745-6095 or (888) 689-4647 or log on to www.mountaincrossings .com. Open daily from 9 a.m. to 5 p.m.

From Walasi-Yi, Section III is a moderately difficult 5.7 miles to Tesnatee Gap on the Richard Russell Scenic Highway (GA 348). Sections IV–VI carry the trail upward and onward. At Bly Gap, near the Rabun County/Towns County border, you bid adieu to Georgia and cross into the North Carolina Great Smokies. Mount Katahdin, here we come!

Blue Ridge Mountains

In Georgia's far northeast corner, up against the North Carolina and South Carolina borders, Rabun County is the heart of the state's dramatically rugged Blue Ridge Mountain country. About 80 percent of the county is included in national forests and state parks. Outdoor adventures range from tranquil trout fishing in mountain streams, canoeing, swimming, off-the-beaten-path hiking, and browsing for handmade crafts at country stores to the ultimate heart-pounding adventure: ***Chattooga River rafting.***

Until the early 1970s, when Jon Voight, Burt Reynolds, and the rest of the *Deliverance* movie crew let the world in on the secret, the Chattooga River was the remote domain of mountain folk along the Georgia–South Carolina border. Nowadays daredevils come from early spring through late fall to test their courage against the river's steep sluices, whirlpools, and roller-coaster rapids. To see that they accomplish their missions safely, the US Forest Service licenses professional outfitters to conduct the trips, which are made in sturdy 6-person rubber rafts and are led by guides who know every rock and rill along this tempestuous waterway.

Outfitters offer a variety of Chattooga experiences. Beginners usually test their wings on Section III, a 7-hour, 6-mile ride that sweeps them through many of the *Deliverance* landmarks. At lunchtime guides pull a small deli out of their waterproof packs and spread the feast at the foot of a waterfall.

Section III is a mere warm-up for "The Ultimate Challenge," the Chattooga's wild and woolly Section IV. Suggested only for well-seasoned white-water hands in top physical condition, this rip-snorting 7-hour cruise carries you through swiftly moving currents; steep, wooded gorges; up and over, down and around such potential perils as Seven Foot Falls, Corkscrew, and Jawbone. At day's end, the Chattooga finally turns you loose, into the peaceful waters of Tugaloo Lake.

For those who really want to get to the heart of the river, outfitters offer 2-day trips, which include overnight camping, a steak dinner, and a bountiful breakfast. Some packages offer the option of lodgings at rustic inns and cabins.

Day trips on Section III are about $94, $15 higher on weekends. For Section IV, figure on paying around $99, $124. You'll be supplied with all the necessary equipment and transportation to and from river access points. You'll also get a briefing on paddling techniques and safety rules, expert guide service, lunch, and a place to shower and change clothes at the end of your ride. Half-day trips are also offered. Contact Nantahala Outdoor Center at (888) 905-7238, www.noc.com; Wildwater Limited at (800) 451-9972, www.wildwaterrafting.com; and Southeastern Expeditions at (800) 868-7238, www.southeasternexpeditions.com.

Bald Peanuts

A drive through the mountains is your chance to experience an indigenous culinary treat. You'll catch the savory aroma of boiled peanuts as you approach roadside stands and country stores, where the goobers are boiling in brine in big iron kettles. Some of the tastiest are billed as "balled," "bald," "biled," or "bolled." City slickers and other greenhorns pry open the mushy shells and pluck out the soft, salty fruit with their fingers. Real fans eat the shell and all. Like grits and chitlins, it's an acquired taste.

If the Chattooga sparks memories of *Deliverance*, **Lake Rabun,** near the little town of Tallulah Falls, may remind you of the film *On Golden Pond*. Ringed by the soft green humps of the Blue Ridge Mountains and unpretentious summer cottages, some dating back to the 1920s and 1930s, this small, off-the-beaten-path lake is the embodiment of peace and quiet.

Built in 1922, the **Lake Rabun Hotel** is the perfect complement to the lake. New owners have spruced up the 16-room wood-and-stone lodge, polished the mountain laurel and rhododendron furniture, added baths to all the rooms, and put in queen-size beds and heat for spring and fall guests. TVs are in the lobby and bar. What the Lake Rabun does offer is rare tranquility and hospitality that draw guests back year after year. In the evenings you can sit by the flagstone hearth, play parlor games, swap tips on local eateries and "secret" waterfalls, and store up energy for the next day's boating, fishing, and hiking. Doubles, with breakfast, are inexpensive. Major credit cards are accepted. Closed Dec to Apr. Contact Lake Rabun Hotel at 35 Andrea Ln., Lakemont, (706) 782-4946 or (800) 398-5134, www.lakerabunhotel.com.

Fishing boats and canoes can be rented at **Hall's Boat House,** next to the hotel. **Lake Rabun Road,** which twists and turns about 15 miles between US 441 near Tallulah Falls, to GA 197, is a very scenic drive. It curves around Lake Rabun and Seed Lake, with many lovely vistas of the water and woodlands. Ask the proprietors of the Lake Rabun Hotel for directions to **High Branch Falls,** also known as Minnehaha Falls. It's a little tricky to find but well worth the search. During the summer **Rabun Beach Recreation Area** (706-782-3320, www.fs.fed.us/conf) is a relaxing place to swim, have a picnic, and enjoy boating, hiking, and fishing. Campsites have electrical and water hookups.

The Rabun County Visitors Bureau and Welcome Center (232 US 441 North, Clayton, 706-782-4812, www.gamountains.com) can give you further tips on off-the-beaten-path outdoor adventures.

It may be difficult to imagine now, but early in the 20th century, **Tallulah Falls** was one of the South's most popular summer resorts. Honeymooners, families, and other nature-loving city folk came to admire the cataracts of the Tallulah River, which stormed through a gorge 820 feet across and more than 1,200 feet deep. All that ended in the early 1920s, when a series of hydroelectric dams diverted water from the falls but at the same time created Lake Rabun, Lake Burton, and other recreational areas.

Tallulah Gorge State Park invites hikers to explore the depths of the gorge. The parks department and Georgia Power Company periodically open the floodgates and allow kayakers to experience the falls' glorious power. The 2,700-acre park area has a fishing pier and picnic tables on the Tallulah River. Exhibits explain Georgia Power's conservation efforts. Fifty campsites have water and electrical hookups. Phone (800) 864-PARK for reservations. If you'd like to hike the gorge, you'll need to register, free of charge, at the Jane Hurt Yarn Interpretive Center, which has exhibits on the gorge's plant and animal life and a film on the gorge's fascinating ecology. For general information, contact Park Superintendent at 338 Jane Hurt Yarn Dr., Tallulah Falls, (706) 754-7970 or (800) 864-7275, www.gastateparks.org. The most strenuous hike takes you down 400 steep metal stairs to a suspension bridge swaying 80 feet above the river and rocky floor. Another 200 steps go the rest of the way down to the bottom of the gorge. Bring plenty of water and stop for breathers and views of the gorge, the river, and waterfalls. Depending on your physical fitness, going back up can seem two or three times as far. A bit of trivia: 1930s actress Tallulah Bankhead was named for the gorge by her grandparents, who vacationed at the resort in its heyday. There's a $5 parking fee.

Where Wallenda Walked on Air

On July 18, 1970, 65-year-old Karl Wallenda walked across Tallulah Gorge. While 35,000 spectators held their breath, the patriarch of the Flying Wallendas trapeze family stepped onto a thin steel cable strung 700 feet across the 1,200-foot-deep gorge. Balancing a 36-foot pole, he did a pair of handstands before reaching the other side. He earned $10,000 for his 18 minutes of fame, which set a new record for cable height. His luck and pluck ran out on March 22, 1978, when he fell to his death from a cable between two hotels in San Juan, Puerto Rico. You can read about his feat at Tallulah Point Overlook on Historic US 441 in the town of Tallulah Falls (706-754-4318, www.tallulahpoint.com). Just up the highway, the Jane Hurt Yarn Interpretive Center at Tallulah Gorge State Park has a display on Wallenda's walk, with his gold-fringed powder blue costume. In 2012 his grandson Nik Wallenda wowed the world by walking a tightrope across a bigger gorge, the one above Niagara Falls.

Tallulah Gallery (706-754-6020, www.tallulahgallery.biz) has a beautiful selection of paintings, pottery, weaving, and other mountain handicrafts in the parlors of a Victorian mansion built by the president of the now-extinct local railroad. The 2-story home is on Old US 441 Scenic Loop in the center of the small community. Open daily Apr through Dec. Closed in winter.

If you're fond of kitschy local folk arts, stop by the ***Co-op Craft Store,*** on US 441, in the old Tallulah Falls train depot (706-754-6810). They've got a great selection of scenes hand-painted on saw blades and shovel, axe, and hoe heads. They depict hunting dogs, deer, farmhouses, pigs, pastures, tractors, and other rural motifs. While you're there, browse the made-in-Georgia jams and jellies, pottery, wooden toys, patchwork pillows, pot holders, place mats, and other crafts. It's open daily year-round.

Tallulah Gorge Grill, a few steps from the Co-op (110 Main St., 706-782-1065, www.tallulahgrill.com), serves lunch and dinner Thurs through Mon and includes sandwiches, burgers, salads, and local fish. Inexpensive.

If you've read the Foxfire books and magazines or would like to learn more about the vanishing Appalachian Mountain culture, plan a visit to the new ***Foxfire Museum*** complex, up a mountain road from the old museum on US 441. (If you're not familiar with the Foxfire books, they chronicle research by students who scour the mountains to preserve elements of the old, isolated mountain lifestyle.) The complex's more than 20 log structures include an authentic 1820s one-room home that raised three generations; "dog trot" cabins; a chapel; animal barns; a folk art museum; and complete gristmill, blacksmith shop, and working craft shops, where classes are held. The Zurow Wagon is the only existing wagon known to have taken Cherokees to Oklahoma on the 1830s "Trail of Tears." The visitor center/gift store sells Foxfire books and hand-made Appalachian crafts. You can take a self-guided tour or a guided tour with a group of 6 or more. Motor homes and other large vehicles can't negotiate the steep, winding mountain road. Call ahead and someone will come and pick you up on the highway. The museum is at 220 Foxfire Ln., off US 441, Mountain City. Phone (706) 746-5828 or visit www.foxfire.org. Open Mon through Fri 8:30 a.m. to 4:30 p.m. Self-guided tour, $6 for ages 11 and older, $3 for ages 7 to 10, 6 and under free.

Beechwood Inn Bed & Breakfast (PO Box 120, Clayton 30525, 706-782-5485, www.beechwoodinn.ws) has been transformed into one of mountain country's best inns and dining and wining experiences by transplanted Californians David and Gayle Darugh. Gourmet dinners are matched with wines from Georgia and the couple's native Napa and Sonoma. Cooking classes and wine tastings are offered, and package plans are offered for golf, winery tours, white-water rafting, and other activities. On a terraced wooded rise, overlooking

Clayton and the mountains, the 86-year-old former country home has 5 taste-fully appointed guest rooms with private baths, balconies, porches, and work-ing fireplaces. Full breakfast is included in moderate to expensive rates.

Two scenic state parks in Rabun County offer a wealth of outdoor activi-ties and overnight lodgings. *Black Rock Mountain State Park,* 1,500 acres of brawny beauty atop a 3,600-foot elevation of the Blue Ridge Mountains, has an 18-acre lake, many miles of wooded nature trails, waterfalls, 10 cabins and 44 campsites with electrical and water hookups and kitchens. Contact Park Super-intendent: Black Rock Mountain, 3085 Black Rock Mountain Pkwy., Mountain City, (706) 746-2141, (800) 864-PARK, www.gastateparks.org.

Moccasin Creek State Park, on Lake Burton, has a boat ramp and docks, a trout hatchery, hiking trails, and 55 campsites. For reservations, phone (800) 864-PARK. Contact Park Superintendent at Moccasin Creek State Park, 3655 GA 197, Clarkesville, (706) 947-3194, www.gastateparks.org.

For 12 days every August, the normally unhurried Towns County seat of *Hiawassee* (population 1,985) throbs with the energy of the *Georgia Moun-tain Fair.* Against a backdrop of Blue Ridge Mountains, forests, and blue-green lakes, the fair takes Hiawassee and the rest of Georgia's "Little Switzerland" literally by storm.

The fairgrounds resound with the music of bluegrass fiddlers, gospel singers, clog dancers, and some of the very big names of the country music entertainment world. Scores of craftspeople show off their skills at wood-working, pottery, cornshuck and applehead dolls, painting, leatherwork, furniture and toy making, jewelry, basket weaving, needlework, quilting, and macramé.

Pioneer Village is like a walk through a mountain town of yesteryear. You can peruse the canned goods and bolt cloth in the mercantile store, see the hickory switch in the one-room schoolhouse, visit the smokehouse, and stop in at the hand-hewn log cabin. Elsewhere on the 42-acre grounds, you can enjoy midway rides, taste just-squeezed apple cider, and see a "moon-shine" whiskey still up close. "Revenooers" keep a close guard against any free samples. For information contact Georgia Mountain Fair: 1311 Music Hall Rd., Hiawassee, (706) 896-4191, www.georgiamountainfairgrounds.com.

The Rollins Planetarium at Young Harris College (706-379-4312, www.yhc .edu), has seasonal shows on Friday night and free telescope viewings.

Most of the year *Lake Chatuge* is a great place to play. The 7,500-acre Tennessee Valley Authority reservoir on the western edge of Hiawassee is a tranquil retreat for trout and bass anglers, water-skiers, swimmers, and boaters. Several marinas and public boat docks offer easy access to the lake. You'll also find picnic grounds, tennis courts, a sand beach, playgrounds, and camping sites at the 160-acre **Towns County Park** on the lakeside. Contact Lake Chatuge Recreation Area at (706) 745-6928, www.fs.fed.us/conf.

The Ridges Resort & Marina, on the lake, outside Hiawassee, 3499 US 76 West, (706-896-2262, www.theridgesresort.com), has 66 guest rooms in the main hotel, condos and villas, a full-service restaurant and bar, a lakeside pub, a marina with rental fishing boats, ski boats, Jet Skis, a houseboat, kayaks, and tennis courts. Moderate to expensive.

The **Chattahoochee National Forest** blankets much of Towns County with Georgia pines and hardwoods. Sections of four national wilderness areas in the county afford you the opportunity to get well off the beaten track. During certain times of the year, the Appalachian Trail, crossing Towns County near Brasstown Bald Mountain, gets downright busy as hikers test their stamina on the 2,000-mile Maine-to-Georgia route described at the beginning of this chapter.

Brasstown Bald Mountain, 4,784 feet, is Georgia's highest point. A steep, winding road off GA 180 takes you to a parking area a half mile from the top, where you'll find restrooms and a gift shop. You can hike the paved, moderately strenuous trail to the visitor center and observation platform, or take a shuttle van, $3 per person round trip. There's a $4 parking fee in the lot. Be sure your car is up to the task before heading up the mountain. Many a vehicle has been left overheated and steaming by the roadside.

You can follow the 5.5-mile Arkaquah Trail from the crest of Trackrock Gap and the less strenuous 2.5-mile Jack's Trail Knob to the foot of Brasstown. Wagon Train Road meanders 6 miles to a pastoral valley that cradles the pretty town of Young Harris and the campus of Young Harris College.

A short drive from Brasstown Bald Mountain, the **Nottely River Campground** offers a relaxing retreat with fun for the whole family. The secluded campground offers tent and RV sites as well as 4 furnished cabins from which to choose. Fishing, swimming, hiking, and tubing are available on site. The campground is located at 3832 Gainesville Hwy. (706-745-6711, www.notteley rivercampground.com).

Brasstown Valley Resort, opened in 1995 on a scenic 503-acre Blue Ridge mountainscape, has all the upscale resort bells and whistles: 102 attractively appointed guest rooms in the 4-story main lodge and 32 adjacent cottages; 18-hole, 7,000-yard Scottish links–style golf course; and tennis, horseshoes, trout fishing, horseback riding, indoor/outdoor pool, fitness center, and full-service restaurant and lounge. It's a great place to roost for a while and an excellent base while sightseeing in the surrounding mountainlands. Lodge rooms and cottages are moderately to expensively priced. Brasstown Resort is at 6321 US 76 East, Young Harris (706-379-9900 and 800-201-3205, www.brass townvalley.com).

TOP ANNUAL EVENTS

Bear on the Square Mountain Festival
mid-April, Dahlonega
(706) 864-7817
www.bearonthesquare.org

Southworks Arts Festival
late April, Watkinsville
(706) 769-4565

Mountain Laurel Festival
mid-May, Clarkesville
(706) 754-2296

Helen-to-Atlantic Hot Air Balloon Race and Festival
early June
(706) 878-2271
www.helenballoon.com

Blairsville Highland Games
Early June
(706) 745-2161
www.blairsvillescottishfestival.com

Oktoberfest
September and October, Festhalle, Helen
(706) 878-2271
www.helenchamber.com/oktoberfest

Gold Rush Days
late October, Dahlonega
(706) 864-3513
www.dahlonega.org

Sorghum Festival
mid-October, Blairsville
(706) 896-5789
www.sorghum.blairsville.com

Mule Camp Market
mid-October, Gainesville
(770) 532-7714
www.gainesvillejaycees.org

Georgia Mountain Fall Festival
early to mid-October, Hiawassee
www.georgiamountainfairgrounds.com
(706) 896-4191

Toccoa Harvest Festival
early November
(706) 886-2132
www.mainstreettoccoa.com/harvestfest

Alpine Helen Winter Festival
November–January
(706) 865-5356
www.helenga.org

Old Fashioned Christmas
late November through late December, Dahlonega
(706) 864-3513
www.dahlonega.org

Deer Lodge, a hideaway near the junction of GA 66 and I-75, is another heaven-sent place to park awhile and savor the glories of the mountains. In business for 40 years, hospitable proprietors Richard and Willene Haigler serve some of the biggest, best, and lowest-priced steaks and trout anywhere in these parts. Cabins secluded in the nearby woods are inexpensive. Contact Deer Lodge: 7900 S. US 17/I-75, Hiawassee, (706) 896-2726.

The *Richard B. Russell-Brasstown Scenic Highway,* in White and Union Counties, takes you through the heart of some of northeastern Georgia's most spectacular mountain country. Designated as GA 348, the 14-mile paved highway takes you from the outskirts of Georgia's "Alpine Village" of Helen, across the Appalachian Trail, to the state's highest mountain and a picture-perfect state park. Several parking areas and overlooks give you the chance to stop and admire the rugged beauty of the Blue Ridge Mountains. The winding, twisting drive is especially striking in mid-Oct to early Nov, when the hardwoods turn a brilliant orange, yellow, and scarlet.

One of the Scenic Highway's "high points" is 3,137-foot Tesnatee Gap, where the Appalachian Trail crosses on its way between Maine and Springer Mountain, Georgia. You can get out of your car here and mingle a while with the earnest hikers. At its northwestern end the Scenic Highway intersects with GA 180. If you turn right, you can explore 4,784-foot Brasstown Bald. A steep, paved road ends at a parking area 930 feet below the summit. From here either hike to the crest of Georgia's highest peak or take a commercial van up to the view of four states.

A left turn at GA 180 will lead you to US 19 and *Vogel State Park.* Cradled in mountains, beside a pretty lake, Vogel is a delightful place for fishing, boating, warm weather swimming, and year-round hiking on woodland trails. The park's 103 campsites have electricity, water, hot showers, and restrooms; 36 rustic but very snug cottages, by the lake and in the adjacent woodlands, are equipped down to sheets, towels, pots, and pans. For reservations, phone (800) 864-PARK. The park also has a $5 one-time parking fee. The park office is open from 8 a.m. to 5 p.m. Contact Vogel State Park at 7845 Vogel Park Rd., Blairsville, (706) 745-2628, (800) 864-PARK, www.gastateparks.org.

GA 180, which joins US 19 north of Vogel Park, is a 22-mile scenic mountain route to the little community of Suches. Along the way stop at *Sosebee Cove Scenic Area* (706-745-6928, www.fs.fed.us/conf), where a half-mile loop trail takes you through a second-growth forest with wildflowers and rhododendron. Farther along, *Lake Winfield Scott Recreation Area* (770-297-3000, www.fs.fed.us/conf) has a 32-acre, 36-campsite campground with showers and an 18-acre fishing and swimming lake. There is a $5 parking fee for noncampers. A large furnished cabin rents for a 2-night minimum.

Habersham County claims some of northeast Georgia's most photogenic Blue Ridge Mountain country. These mountains and valleys, thousands of acres of Chattahoochee National Forest, and scores of lakes and streams offer limitless opportunities to take a hike, ride a bike, camp out, and fish, swim, and otherwise unwind.

Habersham is one of Georgia's major apple producers. Rich soil and a cool climate encouraged English and Canadian families to initiate the apple-growing arts here in the 1920s. In October, roadside stands overflow with Red Delicious, Stayman Winesaps, dark red Yates, and bright yellow-green Granny Smiths. You can buy 'em by the sackful or the carload and also purchase homemade apple jelly, apple butter, and ice-cold, freshly squeezed sweet apple cider by the glass and gallon jugful. As a rule Habersham owners don't allow visitors to come in and pick their own fruit.

The Big Red Apple, in front of the old train depot in downtown Cornelia, is a tribute to Habersham County's apple industry, which saved the local economy that had been nearly decimated after boll weevils ruined the cotton crop. Weighing in at about 5,200 pounds, the 7-foot-tall Grande Pomme, with a 22-foot "waist," has defied winds, rains, worms, and schoolboy vandals since its dedication in 1926.

Elvis fans who've been to Graceland and think they've seen it all may think again after seeing Joni Mabe's Panoramic Encyclopedia of Everything Elvis at the **Loudermilk Boardinghouse Museum** in Cornelia. An Athens artist, Mabe's 30,000-piece collection includes hundreds of photos, show posters, newspaper and magazine articles, and souvenirs in varying degrees of taste and two rarities: Mabe found the "Maybe Elvis Toenail" in the shag carpeting at Graceland and acquired the "Elvis Wart" from Presley's dermatologist, who removed it before the King was inducted into the army. "The Big E Celebration," honoring his August death anniversary, is the Loudermilk Museum's big day. Impersonators croon his big hits and toast his memory with his favorite food, fried peanut butter and banana sandwiches. The Loudermilk Boardinghouse Museum is at 271 Foreacre St., Cornelia (706-778-2001, www.jonimabe .com). Self-guided tours Fri and Sat, 10 a.m. to 5 p.m., other times by appointment. Closed during winter months. Admission is $5.

Clarkesville, Habersham's snug little county seat, is a happy hunting ground for antiques and mountain handicrafts. Several shops around the courthouse square on US 441 are loaded with handcrafted furniture, pottery, paintings, weaving, leatherwork, handmade baskets and quilts, toys, dolls, jellies, jams, and preserves.

The ***Glen-Ella Springs Hotel*** sits on 17 pastoral acres, off US 441/US 23 between Clarkesville and Tallulah Falls. Owners Ed and Luci Kivett manage the 100-year-old, 16-room country inn, which is full of rustic touches and modern conveniences. In warm weather, enjoy the outdoor swimming pool and explore the 12-acre meadow or hike the creek path. All the rooms have porches with rocking chairs, antiques, and heart-pine paneling. Some have fireplaces and whirlpools. The dining room features fresh mountain trout but varies from traditional mountain fare with veal dishes, pasta, scallops, fresh fish, and other American/continental entrees. Doubles are moderately to expensively priced, including full breakfast. Contact the Kivetts: Route 3, Bear Gap Road, Clarkesville, (706) 754-7295, (888) 455-8786, www .glenella.com.

North 40 Lodge, (15702 GA 197 North, 706-947-1075 or 800-379-6170, www.north40lodge.com) is a true gem. Just a mile from Lake Burton, each of the cozy rooms has its own fireplace and kitchen. The largest has 3 bedrooms. Innkeepers Jinger and Bobby Blackburn keep the lodge open year-round so you can explore the 12-acre property in all seasons. A continental breakfast is included but Bobby is also known for his smokehouse goods. Inexpensively priced.

GA 197, twisting and turning north between Clarkesville and Clayton, is considered one of north Georgia's prettiest drives. The ***Mark of the Potter*** (9982 GA 197, Clarkesville, 9 miles north of Clarkesville, 706-947-3440, www .markofthepotter.com) is a favorite stop for mountain visitors. The weathered old white frame corn-grinding mill, by the rapids of the Soque River, sells some of the finest work of Georgia's most accomplished craftspeople. Shelves are laden with superb pottery, colorful fabrics, metal, and leatherwork.

Browsing inevitably will take you onto the porch overhanging the Soque to throw treats to the fat, pampered trout swimming in the river's pools. Mark of the Potter is open daily. Habersham also shares Tallulah Falls and Tallulah Gorge with Rabun County.

South of Clarkesville, the little town of ***Demorest,*** on US 441, is worth a visit. A couple of antiques shops and a bookstore/coffee shop are on the short main street, and you can stroll through the peaceful campus of Piedmont College.

When your children pose that age-old question—"Where do babies come from?"—take them to ***Cleveland*** and show them. At Cleveland's 70,000-square-foot ***BabyLand General Hospital,*** some very special "babies" come from a cabbage patch.

The soft-sculpted Cabbage Patch Kids were created by White County's own Xavier Roberts. Uniformed "nurses" lead you through the nursery, day-care center, and delivery room. At the magic moment, a "doctor" in surgical garb plucks a newborn Kid from a patch of sculpted cabbage leaves to "oohs" and "aahs" all around. So much detail goes into this "event" that you may find yourself doing some 'splainin' to young children about what the term "Mother Cabbage is dilated" means. You can take home a cuddly Cabbage Patch Kid of your very own. Just remember, they're "babies," not "dolls"; not "bought," but "adopted." Located at 300 N. O. K. Dr. in downtown Cleveland (706-865-2171, www.cabbagepatchkids.com). The "hospital" is open Mon through Sat from 9 a.m. to 5 p.m., Sun from 10 a.m. to 5 p.m. Free admission.

If the sheer granite escarpments of ***Mount Yonah,*** off I-75 north of Cleveland, get your rock-climbing juices flowing, make plans to scale the heights with nearby commercial outfitters ***High Country Wildwood Outfitters*** (6865

Helen Hwy., Helen, 706-865-4451, www.wildwoodoutfitters.com). They will put you in the proper climbing gear and send you up Yonah's 150- to 300-foot cliffs with experienced guides. Mount Yonah is also one of Georgia's best and most popular hang-gliding points.

Driving up to the rustic-looking *Old Sautee Store* (706-878-2281, 888-463-9853, www.oldsauteestore.com) at the junction of US 17 and GA 255, Sautee, you might imagine an old-time mercantile stocked with bolts of cloth, seeds, farm implements, and sacks of cornmeal. After greeting the big-nose Norwegian troll on the front porch, inside you'll see a small museum's worth of yesteryear merchandise. Farther along you'll be tempted by high-quality sweaters and jackets, caps, gloves, T-shirts, cheeses, jams and jellies, specialty foods, and gifts. The adjacent Old Sautee Market is a cozy deli with sandwiches, salads, coffee, cookies, and cold drinks. The store and market are open Mon through Sat from 10 a.m. to 5:30 p.m., Sun noon to 5:30 p.m. Around the US 17/GA 255 junction you can also browse a Native American store, a furniture and home accessories store, and other businesses. The nearby *Northeast Georgia Folk Pottery Museum* illuminates two centuries of pottery making by Georgia's mountain artists. The 3,200-square-foot exhibition hall is a centerpiece of the Sautee-Nacoochee Center, a former mountain school that houses a local history museum, art studio, gallery, and theater. Constructed of heavy timbers with soaring windows overlooking the Sautee-Nacoochee Valley's rolling countryside, the Folk Pottery Museum features farm churns, kitchenwares, and other utilitarian pottery, as well as face jugs and other decorative pieces by such acclaimed pottery makers as the Meaders, Hewell, and Ferguson families and newer generations of pottery artists. The museum is located at 283 GA 255, Sautee-Nacoochee. Call (706) 878-3300 or visit www.folkpotterymuseum.com for more information. Open Mon through Fri from 10 a.m. to 5 p.m., Sat and Sun noon to 5 p.m. Admission is $4 for adults, $2 for seniors and children.

Michael Crocker, who was instrumental in the museum's creation—his large pottery piece is in the lobby—is one of more than 15 artists with studios on the *Folk Potters Trail of Northeast Georgia.* For information on the trail, visit the Folk Pottery Museum's website. At Crocker's studio (6345 W. County Line Rd., Lula, off US 23/GA 365 north of Gainesville, 770-869-3160) you can watch him create face and snake jugs, vases, pots, and utilitarian wares and take home the finished products. He's open Mon through Fri from 9 a.m. to 5 p.m. and Sat by appointment. You can spread a picnic by the *Stovall Covered Bridge,* in a small park by Chickamauga Creek on GA 255, between Helen and Batesville. Only 33 feet long, it's the shortest covered bridge anywhere in Georgia and legend has it—it's haunted. If you dare to go at night, you may hear horse-drawn carriages crossing or babies crying.

The *Stovall House,* nearby on GA 255, is one of the nicest country inns anywhere in the state. Built in 1837, the handsome 2-story frame house is in the heart of the scenic Sautee Nacoochee Valley. Five guest rooms are decorated with country antiques and all the modern comforts. The dining room features Southern and continental cooking and is one of the best anywhere in the mountains. For pure, sweet relaxation, settle yourself into a porch swing and listen to the absolute peace of this lovely countryside. Moderate rates; all rooms with private bath and breakfast. Contact the Stovall House at 1526 GA 255 North, Sautee, (706) 878-3355, www.stovallhouse.com.

US 17 cuts a most picturesque path through the Sautee-Nacoochee Valley as it meanders westerly toward Helen. You may want to stop for a picture—or attend Sunday services—at *Crescent Hill Baptist Church,* on a wooded hillock near the intersection of US 17 and I-75. The pretty Carpenter Gothic church was built in the 1870s by the same well-off gentleman who built the grand Victorian house and gazebo atop the Indian mound at US 17 and I-75.

Going north on combined US 17/I-75, stop off at *Nora Mill Granary & Store* (706-878-1280, 800-927-2375, www.noramill.com). Founded in 1876 on the banks of the Chattahoochee River, the mill's current owners still grind corn into meal and grits in the tried-and-true old-fashioned way. You can watch it being ground and take home a sackful. It's open daily, free.

Habersham Winery, across I-75 from Nora Mill, is Georgia's second-largest wine producer. In their attractive red-roofed winery, (706-878-9463, www.habershamwinery.com), you can free-sample their many varieties, which have won 150 national and international awards; shop for your favorite gourmet foods and wine accessories in the gift shop. It's in Nacoochee Village, a half mile south of Alpine Helen. In Nacoochee Village, you can shop for antiques, fishing, and boating gear, and enjoy lunch and dinner at the Nacoochee Grill. See details in "Where to Eat in Northeast Georgia," p. 215.

Don't try to pinch yourself awake as you drive by the WILKOMMEN signs of *Alpine Helen.* You haven't wandered onto a Disney film set. In an effort to boost tourism back in 1969, this then-humble mountain logging hamlet underwent a wholesale transformation into a make-believe Alpine village. Nowadays, the red-tile roofs, flower boxes, biergartens, and stucco-fronted shops selling cuckoo clocks, Christmas ornaments, Tyrolean hats, and loden coats put the once-quiet village very much on the well-beaten path. Outlet stores, with all the usual suspects, are amassed on the south end of town.

Like it or disdain it, Helen's worth at least a short stroll and a browse. The many inns and "hofs" around town are good bases for more off-the-beaten-path adventures, such as the Appalachian Trail, Richard B. Russell-Brasstown

Scenic Highway, and Chattahoochee National Forest. In trout season, you can don your waders and cast in the Chattahoochee River, which rises near here and wends its bonny way through the middle of town.

More Blue Ridge than Bavarian, *Betty's Country Store* (Main Street, Helen, 706-878-2943, www.bettysinhelen.com), on the north end of town, has grown into a full-blown supermarket. The modern store with some rustic ambience is loaded with jams and jellies, fresh vegetables, gourds, cookbooks, canned goods, cheeses, fresh meat and fish, gourmet coffee, apple cider, and other goods.

Hofer's of Helen, across from Betty's (8758 N. Main St., 706-878-8200, www.hofers.com), fits tongue-in-groove with Helen's Bavarian motif. Walk in the door and you'll be intoxicated by the aromas of fresh-baked breads, cakes, cookies, and strudels. In the cozy dining room, treat yourselves to Belgian waffles with maple syrup and whipped cream, Alpine French toast, and a variety of bountiful omelets; the lunch menu includes bratwurst and sauerkraut, German-style meat loaf, smoked pork chops, and grilled and deli sandwiches. Breakfast and lunch daily.

At *Troll Tavern* (Castle Inn, Main Street, Helen, 706-878-3181, www.troll tavern.com), sit on an outdoor terrace by the Chattahoochee and watch the tubers float gently through Helen. The menu includes bratwurst, smoked pork chops, chicken, fish, deli sandwiches, Mexican and Italian food, German beer, and wine. Lunch and dinner are served daily.

If you've never made it to Munich for Oktoberfest, *Helen* has a scaled-down replica. In mid-Sept through Oct, the town's Festhalle pavilion resounds to oompah bands and thousands of folk-dancing feet. After a lager or two, you'll be out on the floor flapping your arms to the hypnotic beat of "The Chicken Dance." In late Oct and early Nov, the mountain hardwoods change their colors as brilliantly as those in New England, making this an especially worthwhile time to visit. It's also prime season for freshly squeezed apple cider and boiled peanuts. Simmered in brine in huge iron kettles, the goobers are warm, salty, sticky, and a special mountain delicacy that not everyone goes for, but that should at least be experienced. Contact Helen-White County Visitors Bureau at 726 Brucken Strasse, Helen, (706) 878-2181, (800) 858-8027, www .helenga.org.

Unicoi State Park, just north of Helen, is a treat that everyone can enjoy. With 1,050 acres of highlands and woodlands, threaded by streams, lakes, and waterfalls, there's plenty of off-the-beaten-path solitude.

Swimming, canoeing, and fishing focus on a picture-postcard 53-acre lake. You can take solitary walks on 12 miles of trails and take part in nature walks led by park naturalists. Craftspeople share the secrets of pottery, quilting, dulcimer and furniture making, and other mountain arts. The handicraft shop in the Unicoi Lodge sells an array of beautiful items.

Also in the lodge the cafeteria-style dining room serves excellent breakfast, lunch, and dinner at extremely low prices. The park's accommodations include 82 camping sites, with water, electricity, nearby showers, and restrooms; and 30 2- and 3-bedroom, completely furnished cottages. For reservations, call (800) 864-7275. Contact Park Superintendent: 1788 GA 356, Helen, (706) 878-2201, (800) 864-PARK, www.gastateparks.org.

Anna Ruby Falls is the awesome showpiece of a 1,600-acre Chatta-hoochee National Forest recreation area that neighbors Unicoi. You actually get there by going through Unicoi. From the parking area follow a moderately strenuous half-mile trail through the woodlands bordering a swift-flowing stream. An observation platform sits at the base of Anna Ruby's two cascades, which drop dramatically 153 and 50 feet over the edge of Tray Mountain. Back at the parking area, restore your energy with a picnic by the water's edge. A handsome visitor center has an excellent gift shop and a porch from which you can toss treats to some of creation's fattest trout. A Trail for the Blind identifies trees and plants in Braille. There is a $5 per car parking fee.

The *Lodge at Smithgall Woods,* west of Helen, is a peaceful counterpoint to the hyper Alpine village. In 1994 north Georgia publisher Charles Smithgall made his pristine 5,600 acres of woodlands and streams a gift-purchase to the state. Although it's administered by the state park system, the similarities to other parks are few. Virtually no car traffic is allowed. Visitors who wish to hike the preserve's 3 wilderness trails and catch-and-release trout in 4-mile Dukes Creek sign in at the visitor center and take a free shuttle bus to their destinations. Mountain bikers can use 12 miles of improved roads. On the Martin's Mine Historic Trail, hikers can stop at the site of an 1893 gold mine, with a 125-foot-deep shaft and a 900-foot-long tunnel. Guests have full access to Dukes Creek trout fishing, rated in the top 100 by Trout Unlimited. In order to give everybody casting room, only 15 are allowed on the creek at the same time. A $5 parking pass is the only charge.

Overnight guests stay in 5 deluxe cottages, including Charles Smithgall's former Montana lodgepole pine retreat. Nudged alongside Dukes Creek's rush-ing waters, the cottages are furnished with plush sofas and chairs, fieldstone fireplaces, twin and queen-size beds, stocked kitchens, open porches, TVs, phones, computers, and Internet access. The staff prepares 3 full meals daily, with wine. Rainbow and brown trout, fresh from the creek, are the kitchen's tour de force. Naturalists lead waterfall and wildflower hikes. Double occu-pancy rates include all meals and activities. Open daily, it's located at I-75-Alt, 3 miles west of Helen, and just south of the Richard B. Russell Scenic Highway

(GA 348). The lodge is at 61 Tsalaki Trail, Helen. Call (706) 878-3087 or (800) 864-7275 or log on to www.smithgallwoods.com. Expensive.

The Nacoochee Valley gets its name from a Native American version of *Romeo and Juliet*. According to legend, Cherokee Princess Nacoochee fell in love with a warrior from an enemy tribe. Her father captured the suitor and had him executed. In her grief, Nacoochee leaped to her death from Mount Yonah on the western end of the valley. Some say her tearful laments can still be heard on moonlit nights.

In 1828 a trapper named Benjamin Parks allegedly stubbed his toe on a rock in **Dahlonega** and shouted the Georgia version of "Eureka!" as he gazed at a vein of gold that soon sent prospectors streaming into these hills. Dahlonega is a Cherokee Indian word "tahlonega" meaning "golden," and until the War Between the States, the substance flowed into a major US Mint right here. Although it's no longer a major industry, enough gold is still mined here to periodically releaf the dome of Georgia's state capitol building and intrigue visitors who pan for it at reconstructed camps. The Dahlonega-Lumpkin County Visitors Center on the square has restrooms and information on anything you could possibly be interested in. It's at 13 S. Park St., Dahlonega. Phone (706) 864-3711 or (800) 231-5543 or access www.dahlonega.org.

True to its heritage, the **Dahlonega Courthouse Gold Museum State Historic Site** (1 Public Sq., Dahlonega, 706-864-2257, 800-864-PARK, www .gastateparks.org), in the center of the little town of 2,800, chronicles the gold rush and the numerous mines that flourished in these parts. A 28-minute film upstairs in the old courtroom is especially worthwhile. Operated by the Georgia Department of Natural Resources, the Gold Museum is open Tues through Sat from 9 a.m. to 5 p.m., Sun from 10 a.m. to 5:30 p.m. Admission is $6 for adults, $3.50 for seniors and children 6 to 18; free for children 5 and under.

"thar's gold . . ."

"Thar's gold in them there hills," was purportedly first shouted in 1849 by a civic-minded citizen of Dahlonega, who was trying to discourage miners from abandoning the northeast Georgia hills for the newer and richer gold fields of California.

Buildings around the square have a rustic frontier look. Shops purvey gold-panning equipment, ice cream, fudge, mountain handicrafts, gold jewelry, and antiques. Many people make the 70-mile drive north from Atlanta just to feast at the famous **Smith House.** It's off the square at 202 S. Chestatee St., Dahlonega (706-867-7000, 800-852-9577, www.smithhouse.com). The Smith House puts out huge family-style spreads with fried chicken, chicken and dumplings, beef stew, shrimp, numerous vegetables, biscuits, relishes, and dessert for a moderate price. They also serve breakfast and have a cafeteria line for those not up to the full board. It's open daily except Mon.

You can stay close to the chow line in the Smith House Inn's 16 guest rooms, all with private baths. Inexpensive to moderate. Many other restaurants, inns, and motels are close to the square.

The **Worley Homestead Inn** (410 W. Main St., Dahlonega, 706-864-7002, 800-348-8094, www.bbonline.com/ga/worley) is a short stroll from the Gold Museum, restaurants, and shops on Dahlonega's square. Seven guest rooms in the mid-19th-century Victorian house are full of antiques and pictures of Worley family ancestors. Each has a private bath, some with claw-foot tubs. There are even rumors of a friendly resident ghost. The moderate tariff qualifies you for a huge country breakfast.

Gold Rush Days, the third weekend of Oct, celebrates the gilded heritage with arts and crafts, clog dancing, and lots of bluegrass fiddling and singing. You can pan for gold year-round at **Crisson's Gold Mine** (2736 Morrison Moore Pkwy., Dahlonega, 706-864-6363, www.crissongoldmine.com). You'll feel some of old Benjamin Parks's excitement and might even whoop out "Eureka!" when you spot a few grains gleaming amid the mud in your pan.

You can also take a guided walk through the tunnels of the old **Consolidated Mine.** In the early 1900s it was the largest and richest gold mine in the eastern United States. It went mysteriously bankrupt in 1906, and much of the old equipment is still in place. Phone (706) 864-8473 or go to www.consolidatedgoldmine.com. Open daily 10 a.m. to 5 p.m. Adults $15, ages 4 to 14 $9, and that includes free gold panning. Located off GA 60, 3.7 miles south of Dahlonega. Dahlonega is a popular gateway to the northeastern Georgia mountain vacation areas. From here US 19 snakes north toward Vogel State Park, while other roads aim toward Helen, Cleveland, and Amicalola State Park.

One of northern Georgia's most interesting and unusual dining and lodging places is off the beaten path among the green hills and marble quarries of Pickens County. The **Woodbridge Restaurant and Inn** at Jasper departs joyously and deliciously from the culinary path most often trod in rural Georgia.

German-born Joe Rueffert and his Georgia-born wife, Brenda, have been the hospitable proprietors of the Woodbridge Restaurant and Inn since 1967. On the surface, the rustic pre–Civil War inn, with the checkered tablecloths and big windows with panoramic views of the mountains, gives few hints of surprises.

Specialties include grilled swordfish steaks, fresh grouper, and mahi mahi with rich creamy sauces; chateaubriand forestière and steak au poivre; veal dishes with silken béarnaise and hollandaise sauces; roast duckling with orange sauce; and bananas Foster and other luscious desserts.

You may select American or European wines and beers—there is also a full bar—from the Woodbridge list. After your feast, you're only a few steps from your lodgings in the inn's moderately priced guest rooms and cabins. Comfortably furnished and air-conditioned, the 18 large rooms come with complimentary mountain views. The dining room serves lunch on Wed, Sat, and Sun and dinner Tues through Sat. Prices are moderate to expensive, and major credit cards are accepted. Contact Woodbridge Inn at 411 Chambers St., Jasper, (706) 253-6293, www.woodbridgeinn.net. Moderate to expensive.

The inn is, true to its name, across a wooden bridge, at the northern edge of the bucolic town of Jasper. If you've forgotten how sweet and peaceful a town of 5,000 can be, take a leisurely constitutional on Jasper's main street, and chat with the folks in the stores and around the Pickens County Courthouse. The Ruefferts don't serve breakfast, so you may wish to indulge in the grits and eggs at one of Jasper's hometown cafes.

Amicalola Falls State Park and the *Appalachian Trail approach trail* are a scenic half-hour drive from Jasper, in neighboring Dawson County. The 400-acre park, centered on a majestic 729-foot waterfall, has hiking trails above and below the falls, picnic areas, fishing, campsites—with electricity, water, hot showers, and restrooms—and 14 furnished cottages with fireplaces. The rustic-contemporary mountaintop *Amicalola Falls Lodge* has 56 guest rooms with spectacular views and all the modern comforts. For reservations phone (800) 864-PARK or visit www.gastateparks.org. Contact the park at 418 Amicalola Falls Lodge Rd., Dawsonville, (706) 265-8888. The Appalachian Trail is described at the beginning of this chapter.

As its name suggests, the secluded *Hike Inn,* operated by Georgia State Parks, is accessible only by a moderately strenuous 5-mile hike through woodlands and hilly terrain that begins at Amicalola Falls State Park. Twenty rooms with bunk beds open onto a wraparound porch. A common room looks east into a spectacular sunrise. The inn furnishes bed linens and towels, rib-sticking family-style meals, trail lunches, and snacks. Rooms have no electrical outlets or TV. Phone (706) 265-4703 or (800) 581-8032 or access www.hike-inn.com. Inexpensive.

The mountain may not have come to Muhammad, as the old saying goes, but in 1957, an inland sea came to northeastern Georgia's Hall County. The US Army Corps of Engineers closed the Buford Dam on the Chattahoochee River and created Lake Sidney Lanier. Nowadays about 25,000 of the lake's 38,000 acres and some 380 miles of its green and hilly 550-mile shoreline cover former Hall County farmlands and forests.

Lake Lanier Islands is the huge waterway's biggest recreational package. Developed by the state on wooded hilltops that bobbed above the water after the dam was closed, the islands have a life-guarded, Florida-sand swimming beach; an 850,000-gallon wave pool; mild and hair-raising water slides; miniature golf and championship golf; all kinds of rental boats, such as houseboats, pontoon boats, sport boats, ski boats, sailboats, fishing boats, and paddleboats; horseback riding; picnic grounds; campgrounds; and a deluxe resort hotel.

The islands' 300 lakeside campsites are equipped with water, electricity, and some sewer hookups. Campers also have their own fishing pier, outdoor pavilion, and boat launch ramp. For reservations, phone (770) 932-7200 or (800) 840-5253 or log on to www.lakelanierislands.com. The water park side of the 1,500-acre resort, which includes the wave pool, water slides, and beach, is appropriately named *Lanier World.* Admission is $34.99 for adults and $19.99 for children 42 inches and under; children 2 and under are free. Lanier World is open daily 10 a.m. to 8 p.m. For information, contact Lake Lanier Islands at 6950 Holiday Rd., Lake Lanier Islands, (770) 932-7200 or (800) 840-5253; and Gainesville-Hall County Convention and Visitors Bureau at 117 Jesse Jewell Pkwy., Gainesville, (770) 536-5209, (888) 536-0005, www.hallcounty.org/tourism/attractions.asp.

Gainesville, the Hall County seat (population about 34,000; Hall County, 180,000), is a popular gateway to northeastern Georgia vacationlands. Mexicans and other Hispanics who work in the city's poultry industry have fostered a number of Latino cafes, stores, a Spanish-language radio station, and other amenities. Before heading for the hills, enjoy a leisurely stroll through the *Green Street Historical District.* The wide, tree-lined thoroughfare, also designated as US 129, holds a wealth of late 19th- and early 20th-century Victorian and neoclassical Revival residences.

Also in the Green Street Historical District, the *Quinlan Visual Arts Center* (514 Green St., Northeast, Gainesville, 770-536-2575, www.quinlanarts center.org) shows the works of state, regional, and national artists. The Quinlan doubled its space in 2004, enabling it to present more than half a dozen special exhibits annually, showcasing realism, folk art, abstracts, landscapes, still life,

"My Old War Horse"

General James Longstreet, the Confederate hero whom Robert E. Lee called "My Old War Horse," survived his numerous Civil War battles and retired to Gainesville, where he lived from 1875 until his peaceful death in 1904. After he hung up his uniform and sidearms, Longstreet ran a hotel, a farm, and a vineyard and became a leader of the Republican Party. He and his family are buried in Gainesville's Alta Vista Cemetery.

portraits, photography, and other forms. Classes are offered in several fields. It's open Mon through Sat from 10 a.m. to 4 p.m., Sun from 2 to 5 p.m. at no charge but there is a suggested donation of $10.

Gainesvillians don't have to go to Atlanta for live theater. The **Gainesville Theatre Alliance** (770-718-3624, www.gainesvilletheatrealliance.org) produces 4 annual plays at Brenau University and Gainesville State College from Feb through Nov. They include fully staged comedy, drama, children's plays, and musicals.

The **Northeast Georgia History Center** (322 Academy St., Gainesville, 770-297-5900, www.negahc.org) features a permanent exhibit that details the history and culture of Northeast Georgia. One of the most popular exhibits is the "Ed Dodd Room," dedicated to the Gainesville native son who created the "Mark Trail" comic strip adventurer mentioned in the Metro Atlanta chapter (p. 19). You'll also see excellent displays on Native Americans, black history, textiles, Gainesville's vital poultry industry, spinning, weaving, pioneer life, and the April 1936 tornado that devastated downtown Gainesville and killed more than 200 people. Open Tues through Sat 10 a.m. to 4 p.m. Free admission.

Elachee Nature Science Center (2125 Elachee Dr., Gainesville, 770-535-1976, www.elachee.org) is a great place to get lost in the woods for a while and learn something about the world around us. Located on the heavily wooded, 1,500-acre Chicopee Woods Nature Preserve, Elachee's many fascinating experiences include please-touch fish, amphibians, reptiles, and a 300-gallon trout tank. The interactive, computer and contemporary music–enhanced "If Everyone Lived Like Me" exhibit looks at the effects of our lifestyles on our environment. The Chicopee Woods Nature Preserve includes 13 miles of nature trails and Chicopee Lake, where you can take a close look at animal and plant habitats. Open Mon through Sat from 10 a.m. to 5 p.m. Admission is $5 for adults, $3 for children aged 2 to 12.

The **Interactive Neighborhood for Kids** (I.N.K.) is a wonderful place for small fry and big fry to climb on a 1927 LaFrance fire truck and a pretend train, shop, and check out "groceries" in a mini-mart, look at X-rays in the Radiology Department, delve into a book in the library, and spend a day doing a lot of other fun, educational things. It's at 999 Chestnut St., Gainesville (770-536-1900, www.inkfun.org). Open Mon through Sat from 10 a.m. to 5 p.m., Sun 1 to 5 p.m. Admission is $8, free for ages 2 and under.

If you enjoy unusual monuments, bring your camera to **Poultry Park,** where a rooster atop a 25-foot granite obelisk hails Gainesville's distinction as "Poultry Capital of the World." Some 2.6 million broilers leave here every week for kitchens around the world.

The Big Rabbit commemorates a time when the small community of Rabbittown on the north side of Gainesville owed its livelihood to the commercial farming of bunnies. In 1993 residents of the "Hoppin' Little Place" chipped in for the 20-foot stone rabbit that waves a hospitable "Howdy" in front of the ***Rabbit-town Cafe*** (2415 Old Cornelia Hwy., I-985 exit 24, 770-287-3695), which serves first-rate Southern breakfast, lunch, and dinner daily. Open 5:30 a.m. until 10 p.m. daily except Sun when they close at 2 p.m. The Rabbittown Celebration, Saturday the week before Easter, starts with breakfast at the cafe, followed by an Easter parade, Easter egg hunt, gospel singing, and clog dancing.

Jaemor Farm Market (5340 I-985/GA 365, Alto, 770-869-3999, www .jamsjellies.com) is the one-stop place for Georgia apples, peaches, pumpkins, sweet potatoes, green vegetables, melons, jams and jellies, folk art, furniture, flowers, seeds, bedding plants, gifts, and souvenirs. It's open daily year-round but in the fall has a huge corn maze to delight and confound.

As Scarlett O'Hara's Aunt Pittypat might exclaim: "Kangaroos in Georgia! However did they get here?" The answer's simple: Debbie and Roger Nelson brought their 'roos and other Down Under and African critters to ***Kangaroo Conservation Center,*** an 87-acre Dawson County "Outback," in the 1990s. The Nelsons breed the largest collection of the hip-hopping marsupials outside of Australia—200 and counting—and exotic birds and animals for zoos and sanctuaries as far away as China including African and Asian antelope. Still if you drive by the center, you can get some great views of the 'roos hopping or lounging on the hillside. For a time, the center was open for public tours, but the Nelsons felt it distracted from their real goal of conservation. Kangaroo Conservation Center is at 222 Bailey-Waters Rd., Dawsonville (706-265-6100, www.kangaroocenter.com).

Wineries & Big Lakes

Created by US Army Corps of Engineers impoundments of the Savannah River, ***Lake Hartwell*** is a vast inland sea whose 55,000 acres offer limitless off-the-beaten-path opportunities for fishing, boating, swimming, and nature hikes. You can headquarter at 2 state parks on the lake and play another park's 9-hole golf course. While meandering the green, hilly back roads of Hart, Stephens, and Franklin Counties, you can rest awhile at an 18th-century stagecoach inn and reminisce with old-timers who still remember baseball's "Georgia Peach," Ty Cobb.

Hart State Park (330 Hart Park Rd., Hartwell, 706-376-8756, reservations 800-864-PARK, www.gastateparks.org) spreads 417 acres along the lakeshore. Set up housekeeping in 78 camping sites, with utility hookups, adjacent restrooms, and showers, and in furnished cottages. Enjoy swimming, boating, waterskiing, hiking, and fishing for largemouth bass, bream, black crappie, walleye, pike, and rainbow trout.

Tugaloo State Park, on a wooded peninsula jutting into Lake Hartwell (1763 Tugaloo State Park Rd., Lavonia, 706-356-4362, 800-864-PARK, www .gastatepark.org) is another mother lode of bass and other fish fry favorites. Nonfisherfolk can play tennis and miniature golf, swim, and water-ski from a sand beach, and hike and bike on trails threading through the woodlands. Lodgings include 20 furnished cottages and 113 tent and camper sites.

After driving all day, are you tantalized by thoughts of a round of golf, a swim, maybe some late-afternoon fishing? *Victoria Bryant State Park* (off I-85 near Royston, 1105 Bryant Park Rd., Royston, 706-245-6270, 800-864-PARK, or 706-245-6770, www.gastateparks.org) may be the answer to your search. The park's 5,421-yard, 18-hole course is hardly a monster, but clusters of Georgia pines, hills, and plenty of water hazards will keep you on your toes. Rental clubs and pull carts are available at the clubhouse, which also has showers, changing rooms, and a snack bar.

Nongolfers can enjoy the swimming pool and angle for bass, bream, and catfish in stocked ponds. The park's 35 camping sites have utility hookups, with access to restrooms and showers.

The *Ty Cobb Museum,* in his hometown of Royston (population 2,700), honors baseball legend Tyrus Raymond "Ty" Cobb. From the early 1900s to the 1920s, the "Georgia Peach" was one of Major League Baseball's most exceptional players. While he led the Detroit Tigers to American League and World Series championships, his fierce competitiveness earned him a lifetime batting average of .367, the highest in baseball history. He won a record 12 batting titles, hit safely 4,191 times, scored a major-league-record 2,245 runs, and stole 894 bases.

He may have been ruthless on the field, but Cobb was a humanitarian. He helped fund the Cobb Memorial Hospital in Royston, dedicated to his parents, and the Cobb Health Care System, with facilities in three northeast Georgia counties. The museum, in the Joe A. Adams Professional Building, exhibits vintage photos, artwork, uniforms, and equipment, and a film with rare action footage and interviews. It's at 461 Cook St., Royston (706-245-1825, www .tycobbmuseum.org). Open Mon through Fri from 9 a.m. to 4 p.m., Sat 10 a.m. to 4 p.m. Adults $5, seniors $4, students $3, ages 5 and under and military free.

In the 1830s and 1840s—more than a century before Ty Cobb headed to the majors—travelers enduring the bone-jarring stagecoach trip through the northern Georgia wilderness took solace in the thought that by and by they'd reach *Travelers Rest* (8162 Riverdale Rd., Toccoa, off US 123, 6 miles northeast of Toccoa, 706-886-2256, 800-864-PARK, www.gastateparks.org).

The sturdy, 14-room plank structure was built in 1833 as the plantation home of wealthy planter Devereaux Jarrett. As more and more travelers streamed through the region, the enterprising Jarrett turned his home into a

NORTH GEORGIA'S WINERIES

Before Prohibition turned the state bone-dry, Georgia ranked sixth among the nation's wine-producing states. With Château Élan leading the way, a dozen North Georgia wineries now produce a variety of vintages. Most of them welcome visitors for tours and tastings.

Blackstock Vineyards
5452 Town Creek Rd.
Dahlonega
(770) 983-1371
www.bsvw.com

Crane Creek Vineyards
916 Crane Creek Rd.
Young Harris
(706) 379-1236
www.cranecreekvineyards.com

Fox Vineyards and Winery
225 US 11
Social Circle
(770) 787-5402
www.foxvineyardswinery.com

Frogtown Cellars
330 Damascus Church Rd.
Dahlonega
(706) 865-0687
www.frogtownwine.com

Georgia Winery Taste Center
I-75 exit 350/Battlefield Parkway
Ringgold
(706) 937-2177
www.georgiawines.com

Habersham Winery
7025 South Main St.
Helen
(706) 878-9463
www.habershamwinery.com

Monta Luce
501 Hightower Church Rd.
Dahlonega
(706) 867-4060
www.monteluce.com

Persimmon Creek Vineyards
28 East Savannah St.
Clayton
(706) 212-7380
www.persimmoncreekwine.com

Three Sisters Vineyards and Winery
439 Vineyard Way
Dahlonega
(706) 865-9463
www.threesistersvineyards.com

Tiger Mountain Vineyard and Winery
2592 Old US 441
Tiger
(706) 782-9256
www.tigerwine.com

Wolf Mountain Vineyards
180 Wolf Mountain Trail
Dahlonega
(770) 992-4120
www.wolfmountainvineyards.com

19th-century B&B. South Carolina statesman John C. Calhoun was a guest, and Joseph E. Brown, Georgia's Civil War governor, spent his honeymoon here.

Now a state historic site maintained by the Georgia Department of Natural Resources, the 14 rooms are furnished with four-poster beds, rocking chairs, vanities, marble-topped tables, goose feather mattresses, spinning wheels, china, cutlery, glassware, and memorabilia of Travelers Rest's days as a post office. The grounds are shaded by a huge white oak tree, believed to be well into its third century, and several century-old crape myrtle trees. Open Tues through Sat from 9 a.m. to 5 p.m. Admission is $4 for adults, $2.75 for children 6 to 18; free for children under 6.

Approaching the Winder/Chestnut Mountain exit (126) on I-85, 30 miles north of Metro Atlanta's I-285 Perimeter Highway, what appears to be a 16th-century French castle, surrounded by vineyards, rises from the piney landscape. It's no mirage. ***Château Élan Winery & Resort*** (100 Rue Charlemagne, Braselton, 678-425-0900 or 800-233-WINE [9563], www.chateauelan.com) was established in 1982 as Georgia's first major winery since the end of Prohibition. Inside the Château's "castle," you're welcome to stroll around a movie-set French marketplace and purchase jams, mustards, wine guides, cookbooks, picnic hampers, and other gourmet foods and gifts. Before purchasing the Château's grape, take the winery tour, followed by a free tasting. In a short time, cabernet sauvignon, chardonnay, Riesling, pinot noir, zinfandel, and other varieties bearing the Château Élan label have won more than 65 awards in national competitions. Southerners are partial to the sweet, fruity Summerwine, a blend of peaches and muscadine grapes. Wines are about $10 to $20.

Seven restaurants include Cafe Élan with quiche, pâté, chicken breast, salads, cheeses, and other light luncheon fare. Candlelit Le Closs serves a 5-course dinner with appropriate wines (and appropriate prices). For a taste of another old country, stop in the Château's Paddy's Irish Pub. Constructed in Ireland, dismantled, and shipped to Georgia, it was reassembled by Irish craftsmen and staffed with smiling young lasses and laddies. The rough-hewn timber ceiling, beer barrel tables, slate floors, and stacked stone fireplace—and a menu that includes

AUTHOR'S FAVORITES

Hike Inn

Lake Burton

Brasstown Bald Mountain

Boiled peanuts

Brasstown Valley Resort

Vogel State Park

Unicoi State Park

Anna Ruby Falls

Lodge at Smithgall Woods

Dahlonega's town square and Gold Museum

Amicalola Falls State Park

Tallulah Gorge

Mark of the Potter

Northeast Georgia Folk Pottery Museum

Helen's Oktoberfest

Downtown Athens dining

Irish lamb stew, Irish whiskey mousse, and Irish ales, stouts, and whiskeys—
make the pub seem like a cozy corner of Eire transplanted to the Georgia hills.

The 3,100-acre resort also has 3 championship golf courses with 63 stem-
winding holes, tennis, and an indoor heated pool. You can overnight in the
deluxe 275-room Château Élan Inn or in furnished *Golf Villas.* The *Château
Élan Spa* has diet and nutrition services, smoking cessation programs, massages, mineral baths, herbal wraps, saunas, and even couples treatments.

Fort Yargo State Park, on GA 81 at nearby Winder, takes its name from
a still-standing log blockhouse that white settlers built in 1792 as protection
against hostile Creeks and Cherokees. The park's big green lake is an inviting
place to swim and fish and to rent paddleboats, rowboats, and canoes. You can
also enjoy tennis and miniature golf, hike nature trails, and set the youngsters
loose on the playground. *Will-A-Way Recreation Area,* inside the park, has
facilities for persons with disabilities, including specially equipped, furnished
cottages. There are also 3 furnished cottages, 5 yurts, and 40 campsites not so
equipped. For reservations, call (800) 864-PARK. Contact Park Superintendent
at PO Box 764, Winder 30680, (770) 867-3489, www.gastateparks.org.

At Christmas, many people bring their holiday mail to the post office in the
nearby little community of Bethlehem for that special postmark. Bethlehem is
located on GA 11, 4 miles south of Winder (www.bethlehem.org).

The *Crawford W. Long Museum* (28 College St., Jefferson, 706-367-5307,
www.crawfordlong.org) in Jefferson honors the physician who first used ether
for surgical anesthesia. Dr. Long, then a young Jackson County practitioner,
performed the first painless surgery on March 30, 1842. The museum displays
his personal papers and a diorama depicting the first operation. An 1840s doctor's office and apothecary and a general store are also part of the museum.
The outdoor herb garden grows many plants commonly used in 19th-century
medicine. Open Tues through Fri 10 a.m. to 5 p.m. and Sat 10 a.m. to 4 p.m.
Adults $5, seniors $4, students and military $3.

Bulldog Country

Ever wonder where all the tombstones come from? The answer is *Elbert
County.* "The Granite Capital of the World" is home to more than 40 quarries
and 150 finishing plants, which produce hundreds of tons of blue-gray stone
shipped to all 50 states and several foreign countries. The multimillion-dollar
Elberton granite industry had a simple, bizarre birth in 1898, when the first
finishing plant was built expressly to create a Confederate soldier for Elberton's
Public Square. But when the 7-foot "Johnny Reb," on a 15-foot-tall pedestal,
was unveiled, townsfolks' Rebel Yells turned to jeers and tears.

With his round face, squat legs, and a uniform that looked suspiciously Union, wiseacres said he was "a cross between a Pennsylvania Dutchman and a hippopotamus" and dubbed him "Dutchy." Resentment grew and in 1900 Dutchy was pulled from his perch, "lynched," and buried face down, a military sign of disgrace.

Fearing for his own life, the sculptor, who apparently didn't know a Reb from a Yank, fled town and never returned. But from "Dutchy's" seed, Elberton granite grew dramatically.

Forgotten for eight decades, Dutchy was exhumed from the public square in 1982, pressure washed, and in recognition of his pioneering status, given a place of honor in the *Elberton Granite Museum & Exhibit.*

Georgia Guidestones, a sort of Elbert County Stonehenge, is granite country's most curious landmark. In 1979 a mysterious stranger calling himself "R. C. Christian," commissioned the monument on a hilltop 7 miles north of Elberton. He told the president of an Elberton granite finishing company that what he called the "Georgia Guidestones" would be "for the conservation of the world and to herald a new Age of Reason." He also said his name wasn't really Christian, but he was a patriotic Christian who represented a group outside of Georgia that shared his beliefs. Only the Elberton banker who handled "Mr. Christian's" substantial deposit ever knew his true identity. The banker reportedly took the secret to his grave, and no group has ever taken responsibility.

Quarrying, cutting, and etching the stones and putting them in place took nearly a year. Fewer than 100 people came for the March 1980 dedication. A minister denounced it as a potential shrine for devil-worshippers. Perhaps to calm his fears, a self-proclaimed witch twice drew pentagrams around each stone, once to drive away negative forces, the second to invoke positive forces.

Like the 4,000-year-old original on England's Salisbury Plain, the Guidestones are arranged in a circle. The central stone, which weighs 20,957 pounds, is 16 feet, 4 inches high, 3 feet by 3 feet wide, and about 1.5 feet thick. It's surrounded by 4 upright slabs radiating from it like spokes on a wagon wheel. Each slab weighs 42,437 pounds and measures 16 feet, 4 inches high and 6.5 feet wide. A 9-foot, 8-inch capstone is across the top. Slots drilled in the center stone allow visitors to track summer and winter solstices and other celestial events.

On the 4 upright slabs, "Guides to the Age of Reason," etched in 4,000 4-inch letters, in English, Spanish, Russian, Hebrew, Hindi, Chinese, and Swahili, read like New Age Ten Commandments:

- Maintain humanity under 500 million in perpetual balance with nature.

- Guide reproduction wisely, improving fitness and diversity.

- Unite humanity with a new living language.

- Rule passion, faith, tradition, and all things with tempered reason.

- Protect people and nations with fair laws and just courts.

- Let all nations rule internally, resolving external disputes in a world court.

- Avoid petty laws and useless officials.

- Balance personal rights and social duties.

- Prize truth, beauty, love, seeking harmony with the infinite.

- Be not a cancer on the earth, leave room for nature.

While some who speak the living languages may find their way to this isolated monument adjoining a northeast Georgia cow pasture, only a scholar of dead languages will be able to read the admonition, "Let these be Guidestones to an Age of Reason," etched on the capstone. It's written in Egyptian hieroglyphics, Sanskrit, Babylonian cuneiform, and classical Greek.

Elberton is on US 17, 36 miles south of I-85 Lavonia exit 173. The Elberton Granite Museum and Exhibit (on College Avenue, 1 Granite Plaza, Elberton, 0.5 mile west of downtown, 706-283-2551, www.egaonline.com) is open from 2 to 5 p.m. Mon through Sat. You can see Dutchy, a model of the Guidestones, and a film and exhibits about the granite industry. Free admission. Georgia Guidestones is on GA 77, 7.2 miles north of town. Free admission. You can walk right up to it.

Two state parks on the Savannah River's big reservoirs are happy hunting grounds for bass and trout fishing. **Bobby Brown State Park** (GA 72, 21 miles southeast of Elberton, Box 232, Elberton, 706-213-2046, 800-864-PARK, www.gastateparks.org) has boat ramps, picnic areas, a swimming pool, and 61 campsites on 70,000-acre Clarks Hill Lake. Just upriver, **Richard B. Russell State Park** (GA 77, 8 miles northeast of Elberton, Box 118, Elberton, 706-213-2045, 800-864-PARK, www.gastateparks.org) also has campsites, cottages, a swimming beach, boat ramps, an 18-hole golf course, and fish that aim to please. Both parks have a $5 per visit parking fee.

Athens throbs with the vitality of 30,000 **University of Georgia** (UGA) students, who almost balance "The Classic City's" 45,000 townies. Founded in 1785, America's oldest chartered state university existed only on paper for 16 years before the legislature provided funds for land and academic buildings in 1800. The first classes met in 1801. That same year Athens was founded on hills above the Oconee River—hopeful of Olympian inspiration, the rude little settlement was named for Greece's hub of classical learning. Planters and literati embellished the campus and Athens's elm- and oak-lined thoroughfares with

Greek Revival, Georgian, and Federal architecture. Over the ensuing decades, "town and gown" have coexisted in peace and harmony only seriously disrupted when 85,000 Bulldog football fanatics shake the skies over Sanford Stadium with exhortations of "Go-oooo Dawgs!"

Stop first at the Athens Welcome Center in the **Church-Waddel-Brumby House** (280 E. Dougherty St., Athens, 706-353-1820, 800-653-0603, www .visitathensga.com). The fine Federalist house was built in 1820 for Alonzo Church, who became one of UGA's early presidents. Dr. Moses Waddel, who succeeded him in the president's chair, also lived in the house, believed to be the city's oldest surviving residence. You may view the lovely rooms and pick up walking and driving tours of the Athens Historic District and information about other attractions.

As Athens and the university have grown, much of the city's antebellum heritage has been lost. Many antebellum homes have been torn down, others turned into UGA sorority and frat houses, funeral homes, commercial offices, and academic buildings. Only the **Taylor-Grady House** (634 Prince Ave., Athens, 706-549-8688) is open as a museum. It was built in 1845 by General Robert Taylor. In 1863 Major William S. Grady purchased the house and his son, Henry W. Grady, lived in it while studying journalism at UGA. Grady went on to become the nationally renowned editor of *The Atlanta Constitution* and spokesman for the post–Civil War "New South." UGA's journalism school is named for him. Open Mon through Fri 9 a.m. to 5 p.m. Donations appreciated.

The **State Botanical Garden** (2450 S. Milledge Ave., Athens, 706-542-1244, www.botgarden.uga.edu) is a serene oasis 3 miles from UGA's high-energy campus. The 3-story glass and steel Visitors Center and Conservatory is the gateway to the 313-acre sanctuary, which UGA created in 1968 as a "living laboratory" for the study and enjoyment of plants and nature.

"Just in Case"

If you fancy Civil War oddities, don't miss the "Double-Barreled Cannon," a whimsical piece of memorabilia that was a spectacular failure. Cast in Athens in 1862, each barrel was to be loaded with cannonballs connected to each other by an 8-foot chain. When fired, the missiles were supposed to exit together, pull the chain tight, and sweep the cannon across the battlefield like a scythe. In reality, the barrels weren't synchronized, and instead of devastating Yankees, the errant shots went in different directions, plowing up a cornfield, knocking down a tree and a log cabin chimney, and killing a cow. It was permanently retired and rests today on the City Hall grounds, pointing north, "just in case."

After a 10-minute audiovisual introduction, stroll among orchids, ferns, bamboo, bougainvillea, birds of paradise, and other lush tropical and semi-tropical plants that flourish along man-made streams and ponds. You can have lunch in the sunny indoor/outdoor *Gardenside Cafe* and browse among plants, books, and gardening paraphernalia in the gift shop. Revolving exhibits highlight botanical and horticultural paintings by regional and national artists.

Five miles of color-coded trails wind through hardwood forests and along ravines of the Middle Oconee River. As you admire azaleas, wildflowers, rhododendron, 125-year-old beech trees, and other plants and trees native to the Georgia piedmont, you might spot white-tailed deer, rabbits, foxes, opossum, and a remarkable variety of birds.

Theme gardens display roses, dahlias, mums, camellias, hollies, ornamentals, and other seasonal plants. There are plenty of spots for quiet musings. Eleven collections in the 3-acre International Garden follow the history and culture of botany back to the beginnings of civilization. Grounds are open daily from 8 a.m. to sunset. Visitors Center hours are 9 a.m. to 4:30 p.m. Tues through Sat and 11:30 a.m. to 4:30 p.m. Sun. Free admission.

UGA's contemporary vitality is a dichotomy with antebellum Athens. Stop at the *UGA Visitors Center* (Four Towers Building, 405 College Station Rd., Athens, 706-542-0842, www.uga.edu/visctr), in a refurbished dairy barn on the edge of UGA's new East Campus, for information about campus landmarks and activities. Open Mon through Sat from 9 a.m. to 5 p.m. and Sun from 1 to 5 p.m. The campus is a crazy quilt of classical and modern architecture. According to tradition, freshmen may not walk under the three-columned University Arch, which was forged in cast iron in 1857 and is the centerpiece of Georgia's Great Seal, representing wisdom, justice, and moderation. Walk under it and you're on the historic *North Campus.* Listed on the National Register of Historic Places, "Old North's" landmarks include Phi Kappa Hall, an 1836 Greek Revival; Federal-style Waddel Hall, 1820; Palladian-style Demosthenian Hall, 1824; Greek Revival University Chapel, whose bells clamor joyously when the Bulldogs win one on the gridiron; and Old College, where Crawford W. Long, a Georgian who pioneered the use of anesthesia for surgery, was the 1832 roommate of Alexander Hamilton Stephens, who became vice president of the Confederacy.

The *Georgia Museum of Art* (90 Carlton St., Athens, 706-542-4662, www.uga.edu/gamuseum) exhibits more than 7,000 paintings, sculptures, and other works by regional, national, and international artists. It hosts more than 20 annual special exhibits and educational programs and film series. Open Wed, Fri, and Sat from 12 to 5 p.m., Thur 10 a.m. to 9 p.m., and Sun from 1 to 5 p.m. Free admission.

Georgia's Many Symbols

From its official state bird (brown thrasher) to official state wildflower (azalea), Georgia has more than a dozen official state symbols. Some of the others are butterfly, tiger swallowtail; fish, largemouth bass; fossil, shark's tooth; fruit, peach; game bird, bobwhite quail; gem, quartz; insect, honeybee; marine mammal, right whale; mineral, staurolite; reptile, gopher tortoise; seashell, knobbed whelk; character, "Pogo" Possum; tree, live oak; vegetable, Vidalia onion; and two official state songs, "Our Georgia," a waltz, and "Georgia on My Mind," by Albany native Ray Charles.

With its thousands of perpetually ravenous students, finding a place to eat in Athens is no problem. Restaurants, casual cafes, coffeehouses, and snack bars line Broad Street across from the University Arch and spill over onto adjacent streets.

When it comes to music, Athens is a spawning ground for modern rock groups. The *40 Watt Club* (285 W. Washington St., Athens, 706-549-7879, www .40watt.com) still lives on its reputation as the launching pad for R.E.M. and the B-52s back in the 1970s. Widespread Panic is the latest Athens group to make the big time. Local bands and touring groups play at the early 1900s *Morton Theater* (199 W. Washington St., 706-613-3770, www.mortontheatre.com). Built in 1910, the Morton was once the state's most famous black vaudeville theater. It has been restored to its former glory.

Oconee County

Knock on a farmhouse door down a rutted dirt road in the backwoods of Oconee County, or stop by a tidy house on a shady street in *Watkinsville,* the 200-year-old county seat, and don't be surprised when an artist invites you in. The rural but rapidly suburbanizing county of 25,000, just south of Athens, boasts what people here proudly claim is one of Georgia's most extraordinary congregations of creative talent. From Watkinsville (population 2,100) down pasture roads and in the woods around Farmington, Bishop, and Bogart, 100 or more virtuosos are painting, throwing pottery, and making jewelry; metal, marble, and papier-mâché sculptures; decorative woodcraft; calligraphy; ceramics; woven rugs; forged iron; folk art; custom furniture; and blown and fused glass and fabric wall hangings that sell in shops from here to Alaska.

The *Oconee Cultural Arts Foundation* (OCAF) fosters many of the county's visual and performing arts programs. With the enthusiastic support of local governments and a wellspring of donated time, labor, and money, a

1902 redbrick school building has been regeared as a setting for exhibitions, plays, and educational workshops. Located 34 School St. (706-769-4565, www .ocaf.com).

Works by Oconee's artists span the spectrum from representational to anarchic, folkloric to contemporary. There are Christmas ornaments that would fit in your pocket and steel and marble sculptures that would require an army to move—and a philosopher to interpret. Some artists are homegrown, but many move here initially to study in the University of Georgia's nationally respected visual arts programs.

A few artists work in close communities, but most prefer to labor alone in barns, cabins, old industrial buildings, and refitted farmhouses around the county. You can search for them by riding through the rolling piedmont countryside, a patchwork of pecan and peach orchards, cornfields, covered bridges, pine forests, and cattle farms, but many artists live and work hidden away on isolated roads, with no clue to the creative endeavors transpiring behind the trees.

The surest way to locate them is to stop first at the *Eagle Tavern Welcome Center* (across from the courthouse on Watkinsville's 1-block, back-in-time Main Street, Watkinsville, 706-769-5197, www.oconeecounty.com). The tavern has been a landmark since 1820, when it was a frontier stagecoach stop. "The Oconee County Guide to the Arts," a free foldout guide, lists more than 50 artists, and the staff will point you in the right directions.

Most people trace the arts community's birth to 1970, when Jerry and Kathy Chappelle came down from Minnesota to teach pottery at the University of Georgia. The Chappelle's *Happy Valley Pottery,* a collection of old farm buildings and workshops 9 miles south of Watkinsville (1210 Carson Graves Rd., Watkinsville, 706-769-5922), is one of the county's largest one-stop arts

Gotcha Covered

There are almost 80 covered bridges across the state of Georgia, but the longest one is the Watson Mill Bridge near Comer. Measuring 228.6 feet long, it was built in 1885 by celebrated black bridge builder Washington W. King. The bridge is still in use and is at the heart of Watson Mill State Park in Oglethorpe County, just off Route 22 north of Athens. Washington King was the son of freed slave Horace King, also a noted bridge builder. The last remaining covered bridge in Georgia built by Horace King is Red Oak Creek Bridge in Meriwether County. Washington has several bridges remaining including the Euharlee Creek Bridge near Cartersville and the Stone Mountain Covered Bridge.

sources and one of the few that keep regular hours. Their high-fire stoneware is characterized by colorful fruit, flowers, and mountainscapes. ***The Chappelle Gallery,*** a beautiful shop in the historic Haygood House in downtown Watkinsville (25 S. Main St., 706-310-0985, www.chappellegallery.net), carries the work of dozens of artists in painting, pottery, photography, wood, fabric, copper, pewter, and other media.

Places to Stay in Northeast Georgia

YOUNG HARRIS

Brasstown Valley Resort
6321 US 76
(706) 379-9900
(800) 201-3205
www.brasstownvalley.com
Moderate to Expensive
See p. 187 for details.

CLAYTON

Beechwood Inn Bed & Breakfast
220 Beechwood Dr.
(706) 782-5485
www.beechwoodinn.ws
Moderate to Expensive,
includes full breakfast
See p. 185 for details.

DAHLONEGA

Cavender Creek Cabins
220 Beaver Dam Rd.
(866) 373-6307
(706) 864-7221
www.cavendercreek.com
Moderate to Expensive
On 25 woodsy acres, 4 miles from the Dahlonega square, Cavender Creek's 8 1- to 3-bedroom cabins are rustic on the outside, deluxe on the inside, equipped with full kitchens, wood-burning fireplaces, wireless Internet, hot tubs, and gas grills on the covered deck. Guests fish in a stocked pond and enjoy the recreation lodge.

Forrest Hills Mountain Resort & Conference
135 Forrest Hills Rd.
(800) 654-6313
(706) 864-6456
www.foresths.com
Expensive
It's worth a visit just to hear David Kraft tell how he and his sisters came from Florida as teens 40 years ago and built the mountain resort's first cabins with their own hands, with no building experience and only a few hand tools. Now the resort, in Dawson County, east of Dahlonega, has 111 rooms, a day spa, fitness center, conference rooms, horse-drawn carriage rides, and plenty of wooded nature to explore.

Lily Creek Lodge
2608 Auraria Rd.
(706) 864-6848
www.lilycreeklodge.com
Expensive
Each of the 13 guest suites in the deluxe European-style mountain lodge near Dahlonega has a different decorative theme, including Bavarian, Greek, Asian, Argentine, African, Venetian, Antarctic, and American West. Amenities include 7 acres of gardens, an adult tree house, bocce court, outdoor pool and hot tub, wireless Internet, and a full American/European breakfast.

Park Place Hotel
27 Park St.
(706) 864-0021
www.parkplacedahlonega
.com
Inexpensive to Moderate
On the Dahlonega Square, around restaurants, shopping, the visitor center, and attractions, the new Park Place Hotel has large guest rooms and 2-room suites, with flat panel TV, wireless Internet, complimentary Starbucks coffee, and wine.

Worley Homestead Inn
410 W. Main St.
(706) 864-7002
(800) 384-8094
www.bbonline.com/ga/
worley
Moderate, includes full
country breakfast
See p. 197 for details.

LAKE RABUN

Lake Rabun Hotel
35 Andrea Dr.
Lakemont
(706) 782-4946
www.lakerabunhotel.com
Inexpensive, includes
breakfast
See p. 183 for details.

SAUTEE

Stovall House
1526 Georgia 255
(706) 878-3355
www.stovallhouse.com
Moderate, includes
breakfast
See p. 193 for details.

GAINESVILLE

**Holiday Inn Lanier Centre
Hotel**
400 E. E. Butler Pkwy.
(770) 531-0907
(877) 270-6397
www.laniercentrehotel.com
Moderate to Expensive
In downtown Gainesville,
a short walk from the
square's shops, restau-
rants, and government
offices, the Holiday Inn
is in a prime location to
take advantage of historic
downtown Gainesville as
well as nearby attractions.
Lanier Centre is a modern

motor hotel with 122 guest
rooms. The hotel offers a
full-service restaurant and
bar.

FLOWERY BRANCH

**Whitworth Inn Bed &
Breakfast**
6593 McEver Rd.
(770) 967-2386
www.whitworthinn.com
Inexpensive
The inn has 10 light, airy
guest rooms, all with private baths, a few minutes
from Lake Lanier. Enjoy the
cool mountain air on open
porches. Innkeepers Ken
and Christine Jonick send
you off in the morning with
a full country breakfast.

ATHENS

**The Colonels Bed and
Breakfast**
3890 Barnett Shoals Rd.
(706) 559-9595
www.thecolonels.net
Moderate to Expensive
Located on 30 acres on
the outskirts of town in a
columned 1860 mansion,
the Colonels provides 7
bedrooms and 3 suites.
Your hosts are Marc and
Beth, both retired lieutenant colonels.

Foundry Park Inn & Spa
295 E. Dougherty St.
(706) 549-7020
(800) 9ATHENS
www.foundryparkinn.com
Expensive
Downtown Athens's only
boutique-style hotel has
119 deluxe guest rooms
and suites in buildings

that replicate 1820s row
houses. Full-service res-
taurant, pub, spa, and
conference center are a
short walk to restaurants,
shops, and the University
of Georgia.

HELEN

**Helendorf Inn & Confer-
ence Center**
33 Munichstrasse
(706) 878-2271
(800) 445-2271
www.helendorf.com
Inexpensive to Moderate
On the Chattahoochee
River in downtown Helen,
the hotel has standard riverfront rooms with fridges,
microwaves, and private
balconies. Jacuzzi suites
have wood-burning fire-
places, wet bar kitchen,
and balconies. Amenities
include a heated pool and
laundromat.

**Lodge at Smithgall
Woods**
61 Tsalaki Trail
(706) 878-3087
(800) 318-5848
www.smithgallwoods.com
Expensive
See p. 195 for details.

WATKINSVILLE

**Ashford Manor Bed-and-
Breakfast**
5 Harden Hill Rd.
(706) 769-2633
www.ambedandbreakfast
.com
Moderate, includes break-
fast
This homey B&B was
opened in 1997 by two

Chicago brothers and a partner. They've beautifully decorated and furnished 7 rooms in an 1893 Victorian mansion, which sits on 5 acres of lawns, gardens, and woods within walking distance of downtown shops. Pets are welcome at an adjacent cottage.

Watson Mill Bridge State Park

on GA 22, 6 miles south of Comer
(706) 783-5349
(800) 864-PARK for camping reservations
www.gastateparks.org
Inexpensive
The site of Georgia's longest covered bridge. The century-old bridge's 4 spans stretch 236 feet over the South Fork of the Broad River. It's an idyllic place for a picnic, canoeing, and an overnight stay in the campgrounds.

HIAWASSEE

Bed and Breakfast at Swan Lake

2650 Upper Bell Creek Rd.
(706) 896-1582
www.bbswanlake.com
Moderate
With stunning views of Eagle Mountain as well as Swan Lake, this bed and breakfast has 3 rooms and a cottage available. Gourmet breakfast served.

Deer Lodge

7466 GA 17
(706) 896-2726
Inexpensive
See p. 188 for details.

The Ridges Resort & Marina

3499 US 76
Hiawassee
(706) 896-2262
www.theridgesresort.com
Moderate to Expensive
See p. 187 for details.

TOCCOA

Simmons-Bond Inn Bed and Breakfast

74 W. Tugalo St.
(706) 282-5183
www.simmons-bond.com
Moderate
This beautifully restored Queen Anne Victorian mansion in downtown Toccoa has 5 rooms with private baths. Beautifully restored, it is furnished with antiques including a writing desk once owned by journalist Nelly Bly. Gourmet breakfast each morning.

Places to Eat in Northeast Georgia

DAHLONEGA

Back Porch Oyster Bar

19 Chestatee St.
(706) 864-8623
www.backporchoysterbar.net
Inexpensive to Moderate
The Outer Banks have come to Dahlonega. Former coastal North Carolinians Trish and Lee Creef's snug dining room and bar has everything

Cape Hatteras except a sea breeze. Locals and tourists pack the place for cold water oysters, ahi tuna seared and sushi, crab cakes, calamari, tilapia tacos, soft-shell crab, seafood gumbo, fried grouper, shrimp and oyster sammies, and other dishes as rare as trout's teeth in mountain country. Full bar and an outdoor deck. Dinner Wed to Fri, lunch and dinner Sat and Sun.

Corkscrew Cafe

51 Main St.
(706) 867-8551
www.thecorkscrewcafe.com
Moderate to Expensive
The urbane dining room, with an outdoor terrace, near Dahlonega's Public Square, prepares a varied menu, from bistro sandwiches and paninis, soups, and salads, to rack of lamb, duck, beef, and seafood. Large wine list. Lunch and dinner Tues through Sun.

The Crimson Moon Cafe & Gallery

24 N. Park St.
Public Square, downtown
(706) 864-3982
www.thecrimsonmoon.com
Inexpensive
A coffeehouse and sandwich, salad, and dessert shop by day, featuring organic and locally grown products, this long, narrow 1858 storefront across from the Dahlonega Gold Museum turns into an energy-buzzing acoustic

music venue after the sun goes down, with performances by local and visiting groups playing a variety of styles. The gallery sells pottery, paintings, and other mountain crafts. Specialty coffees, beer, and wine are served. Open daily.

Smith House
202 S. Chestatee St.
(706) 867-7000
(800) 852-9577
www.smithhouse.com
Moderate
See p. 196 for details.

Wolf Mountain Vineyards
180 Wolf Mountain Trail
(706) 867-9862
www.wolfmountainvine
yards.com
Moderate to Expensive
One of northeast Georgia's new breed of small wineries, Wolf Mountain, 5 miles up a winding mountain highway north of Dahlonega, serves its wines with an elaborate Sunday blues and jazz buffet from Mar until Oct. Dine inside or on the outdoor patio with Blue Ridge Mountain vistas. The multicourse buffet is complemented by a tasting of Wolf Mountain wines. Tours and tastings are conducted Thurs through Sun from Mar to Dec, and food and wine pairings are available on Fri and Sat from noon to 3 p.m.

GAINESVILLE

2Dog
317 Spring St.
(770) 287-8382
www.2dogrestaurant.com
Moderate
Call it "Rustic-Euro-Soul food"—2Dog prides itself on using local foods from local suppliers. The food is fresh and creative. Everything from food to beer and wine changes with the season. The menu is unique and innovative. You'll find things you've never tasted before and will want again.

Luna's
200 Main St.
(770) 531-0848
www.lunas.com
Moderate to Expensive
Juan and Frankie Luna's restaurant and piano lounge, on the downtown Gainesville Square, is the finest dining and wining experience in town. The lunch menu ranges from soups, salads, hamburgers, and Cuban sandwiches to plates with tilapia, salmon, oysters, chicken, and steak. For dinner, the choice includes crab cakes, Spanish paella, lamb chops, calamari, and filet mignon, with complementing wines and a full bar. The kids' menu has pizza and burgers. Lunch Mon through Fri. Dinner nightly except Sun.

HELEN

Hofer's of Helen
8758 N. Main St.
(706) 878-8200
www.hofers.com
Moderate
See p. 194 for details.

Nacoochee Grill
7277 South Main St.
(706) 878-8020
www.nacoocheegrill.com
Inexpensive to Moderate
In the new Nacoochee Village development, a half mile south of Alpine Helen, the grill serves a full menu of soups, salads, sandwiches, fish, steak, pasta, and vegetarian dishes, with wine and a full bar. Open for lunch and dinner daily.

Troll Tavern
Castle Inn, Main Street
(706) 878-3181
www.trolltavern.com
Moderate
See p. 194 for details.

JASPER

Woodbridge Restaurant and Inn
411 Chambers St.
(706) 253-6293
www.woodbridgeinn.net
Moderate to Expensive
See p. 197 for details.

ATHENS

East West Bistro
351 E. Broad St.
(706) 546-4240
www.eastwestbistro.com
Moderate to Expensive
Athens's first fusion restaurant prepares

HELPFUL WEBSITES

Athens Welcome Center
www.visitathensga.com

State Botanical Garden of Georgia
www.botgarden.uga.edu

University of Georgia Performing Arts Center
www.uga.edu/pac

Dahlonega-Lumpkin County Chamber of Commerce
www.dahlonega.org

Union County Chamber of Commerce
www.blairsvillechamber.com

Towns County Tourism
www.mountaintopga.com

Helen and White County Information
www.helenga.org

Mediterranean and Asian cuisines in a 2-story downtown building. Full bar with a large wine list. Lunch and dinner Mon through Sat, Sunday brunch.

Five & Ten
1653 S. Lumpkin St.
(706) 546-7300
www.fiveandten.com
Moderate to Expensive
Canada native Hugh Acheson, who has cheffed at some of San Francisco's finest restaurants, came to Athens when his wife, Mary, enrolled in UGA's graduate school. At Five & Ten, a white-tablecloth restaurant in the Five Points neighborhood, he combines classical French and traditional Southern cooking. He introduced Athens to red grouper wrapped in peanut beurre blanc, plantation quail on a bed of Red Mule cheese grits, New Orleans–style "dirty rice" with maple-brined pork, and Canada's

Jackson-Triggs ice wines for dessert. Dinner nightly.

The Grit
199 Prince Ave.
(706) 543-6592
www.thegrit.com
Inexpensive
R.E.M.'s Michael Stipe owns the building, but native Brit Mark Dalling rules the kitchen of this "renegade vegetarian" restaurant that's so good even nonvegans wait in line for tofu chicken salad, lentil and roasted garlic soup, and other specialties. It must be good. It's been here more than 20 years. Lunch and dinner daily.

Last Resort
184 W. Clayton St.
(706) 549-0810
www.lastresortgrill.com
Moderate
Considered one of the finest restaurants in the South, the Last Resort opened originally as a music club in 1966. That music history is preserved

as patrons munch on innovative Southern cuisine that includes pork belly and fried green tomatoes as well as shrimp and grits.

Weaver D's
1016 E. Broad St.
(706) 353-7797
Inexpensive
Dexter Weaver's white cinder-block diner on the edge of downtown Athens serves classic African-American soul food: crisp chicken straight from the fryer basket, nutmeg-spiked sweet potato soufflé, collard greens swimming in fatback potlik-ker, and squash casserole enriched with cheddar. Weaver admonishes UGA students skipping their veggies: "How about some greens? Come on, make your mama proud!" His motto, "Automatic for the People," inspired R.E.M.'s hit album. Lunch Mon through Sat.

Index

A

Acworth, 29
Aging Gracefully
　Antiques, 25
Agrirama, 68
A. H. Stephens State
　Historic Park, 135
AJ's Dockside, 176
Albany, 57
Albany Civil Rights
　Institute, 59
Albany Museum of Art, 59
Alexandria, 139
Alice Walker Driving
　Tour, 132
Alliance Theater, 5
Alpine Helen, 193
Alpine Helen Winter
　Festival, 188
Altamaha River, 85
Altamaha River
　Campground, 85
American Camellia
　Society, 61
American Roadhouse, 37
Americus, 64
Americus Garden Inn, 72
Americus-Sumter County
　Tourism Council, 74
Amicalola Falls Lodge, 198
Amicalola Falls State
　Park, 198
Andalusia, 130
Andersonville, 63
Andersonville Antiques
　and Civil War Artifacts
　Fair, 63
Andersonville Antiques,
　Crafts and Civil War
　Artifacts Fair, 48
Andersonville Historic
　Fair, 63
Andersonville National
　Cemetery and Historic
　Site, 62
Anna Ruby Falls, 195
Annual Lewis Grizzard
　Storytelling and
　Barbecue, 26
Ansley Park, 7

Antebellum and Victorian
　Newnan Driving Tour
　of Homes, 26
Antebellum Inn, 132, 145
Antebellum Trail, 129
Antique Griffin at
　Dovedown, 25
Appalachian Grill, 117
Appalachian Trail, 179
Appalachian Trail
　approach trail, 198
Appling Country Club, 86
Archibald Smith
　Plantation, 13
Armstrong's Cricket
　Farm, 85
ART Station, 18
Ashford Manor Bed-and-
　Breakfast, 213
Ashley-Slater House, 92
Athens, 207
Athens Welcome
　Center, 216
Atlanta Botanical
　Garden, 7
Atlanta Braves Baseball, 37
Atlanta Convention &
　Visitors Bureau, 37
Atlanta Dogwood
　Festival, 30
Atlanta Gay Pride Parade
　and Festival, 30
Atlanta History Center, 8
Atlanta, Metro, 1
Atlanta Preservation
　Center, 6
Atlanta Steeplechase, 115
Atlanta Symphony
　Orchestra, 5
Augusta, 139
Augusta Canal National
　Heritage Area, 141
Augusta Convention &
　Visitors Bureau, 146
Augusta Museum of
　History, 140
Augusta National Golf
　Club, 143
Aurora Theatre, 20

B

BabyLand General
　Hospital, 191
Back Porch Oyster
　Bar, 214
Baldwin County
　Courthouse, 131
Bamboo Farm and Coastal
　Gardens, 157
Barbara Jean's, 177
Barnsley Gardens
　Resort, 111
Baxley-Appling County
　Tourism Board, 97
Baxley Tree Festival, 93
Bear on the Square
　Mountain Festival, 188
Beaver House Inn &
　Restaurant, 84, 97
Beaver Kreek Golf
　Club, 92
Bed-and-Breakfast
　Atlanta, 34
Bed and Breakfast at
　Swan Lake, 214
Bed & Breakfast Inn, 172
Bed & Breakfast
　Reservations of
　Savannah, 173
Bedingfield Inn on the
　Square, 53
Beechwood Inn Bed &
　Breakfast, 185, 212
Belford's, 175
Bell, Book and Candle, 24
Belle Meade Fox
　Hunt, 139
Bellevue Avenue, 82
Bellevue Mansion, 41
Bennie's Red Barn, 178
Berry College, 104
Betty's Country Store, 194
Between the Rivers
　Walking Tour, 101
Big, Bang, Boom, 76
Big Chicken, The, 31
Big House, The, 123
Big Pig Jig, 79, 93
Billiard Academy, The, 74
Birthday House, 21
Blackbeard's, 177

Black History
Museum, 155
Black Rock Mountain State
Park, 186
Blackstock Vineyards, 203
Blairsville Highland
Games, 188
Blanton Creek Park, 47
Blind Willie McTell Blues
Festival, 131
Blind Willie's, 37
Blue and Gray
Museum, 93
Blue Jeans Pizza and Pasta
Factory, 116
Blue Ridge Mountains, 182
Blue Ridge Scenic
Railroad, 116
Blue Willow Inn
Restaurant, 128
Blue Willow Village, 128
Bobby Brown State
Park, 207
Boll Weevil
Plantation, 144
Bonnie Castle Bed &
Breakfast, 34
Booth Western Art
Museum, 113
Botanical Gardens, 84
Brady Inn, 134
Brasstown Bald
Mountain, 187
Brasstown Valley Resort,
187, 212
Brick Store Pub, The,
16, 39
Broad Street Antique
Mall, 16
Broad Street Artist
Row, 143
Broxton Rocks
Preserve, 92
Brunswick, 163
Brunswick–Golden Isles
Convention & Visitors
Bureau, 164
Brunswick Manor, 173
Buckhead neighborhood
(Atlanta), 8
Buford Highway, 15
Bulloch Hall, 13
Bulloch House, The, 74
Bull Street, 151
Burr, Aaron, 171
Buzzard Day, 91, 93

C
Caboose, The, 135
Cafe Alsace, 39
Cafe Solterra, 177
Callaway Brothers Azalea
Bowl, 46
Callaway Gardens, 46
Callaway Gardens Spring
Celebration, 48
Callaway Plantation, 137
Calvary, 61
Candles & Carols of
Christmases Past, 115
Cannonball House, 122
Cannon Brewpub, The, 73
Capitoline Wolf, 101
Carriage and Horses
Restaurant, 73
Carter, Jimmy, 64
Cartersville-Bartow County
Convention & Visitors
Bureau, 119
Cassville, 112
Castleberry Hill, 3
Cavender Creek
Cabins, 212
Cave Spring, 105
Cave Spring Arts
Festival, 105
Cedar Creek Park, 117
Cedar Valley Arts
Festival, 115
Celebration of Lights and
Winter Wonderland, 93
Centennial Olympic
Games Museum, 9
Centennial Olympic
Park, 1
Center for Puppetry
Arts, 11
Center for Wildlife
Education, 83
Chappelle Gallery, 212
Charles, Ray, 58
Charlie Joseph's, 45
Charlie's Original Oyster
King, 29
Château Élan Spa, 205
Château Élan Winery &
Resort, 204
Chattahoochee National
Forest, 187
Chattahoochee Nature
Center, 12

Chattahoochee River
National Recreation
Area, 12
Chattahoochee
Riverwalk, 47
Chattahoochee Trace, 41
Chattanooga and
Chickamauga National
Military Park, 106
Chattooga River
rafting, 182
Cheatham Hill, 29
Chehaw National Indian
Festival, 59
Cherokee County Indian
Festival, 115
Cherokee Fall Festival, 111
Cherry Blossom
Festival, 124
Cherry Blossom Trail, 125
Chesser Island
Homestead, 89
Chiaha Harvest Fair, 115
Chieftains Museum, 103
Chipley Murrah Bed and
Breakfast, 72
Chipley's Family
Restaurant, 73
Chippewa Square, 152
Christ Church, 167
Christmas at Bulloch
Hall, 30
Christmas at
Callanwolde, 30
Christmas at Callaway
Plantation, 131
Christmas Festival of
Lights, 48
Christmas in
Savannah, 163
Christmas in
Thomasville, 48
Christ's Memory
Chapel, 161
Church-Waddel-Brumby
House, 208
City Cafe, The, 91
City Cellar and Loft, 118
City Market, 156
Claremont House Bed &
Breakfast, 117
Clarkesville, 190
Claxton, 84
Cleveland, 191
Climax Swine Time, 48, 60

Cloudland Canyon State
   Park, 98
CNN Center, 3
Cobb, 28
Coca-Cola, 22
Coca-Cola Space Science
   Center, 49
Cohutta National
   Wilderness, 110
Coleman House, 82
Colonels Bed and
   Breakfast, The, 213
Col. Oscar Poole's Pig Hill
   of Fame, 116
Columbus, 47
Columbus Black Heritage
   Tour, 49
Columbus Convention &
   Visitors Bureau, 47, 74
Columbus Museum, 51
Confederate Museum, 135
Consolidated Mine, 197
Conyers Cherry Blossom
   Festival, 30
Co-op Craft Store, 185
Corkscrew Cafe, 214
Country's BBQ, 73
Court Square, 16
Covington, 23
Crab Shack, The, 176
Crane Creek
   Vineyards, 203
Crawford W. Long
   Museum, 205
Creative Arts Guild, 108
Crescent Hill Baptist
   Church, 193
Crescent, The, 90
Cricket's Restaurant, 74
Crime and Punishment
   Museum, 94
Crimson Moon Cafe &
   Gallery, The, 214
Crisson's Gold Mine, 197
Crooked River State
   Park, 174
Crown Gardens and
   Archives, 108
Culpepper House, 27
Cumberland Island
   National Seashore, 169
Cumberland Island
   National Seashore
   Museum, 171
Cumberland Queen, 169
Cyclorama, 10

D
Dahlonega, 196
Dahlonega Courthouse
   Gold Museum State
   Historic Site, 196
Dahlonega-Lumpkin
   County Chamber of
   Commerce, 216
Dalton, 107
Dalton carpet outlets, 107
Dalton Convention &
   Visitors Bureau, 119
Dalton Depot Restaurant
   & Trackside Cafe,
   108, 118
Daphne Lodge, 67
Darlington School, 104
Day Butterfly Center at
   Callaway Gardens, 45
Days Inn, 174
Decatur, 16
Deer Lodge, 188, 214
DeKalb County, 15
DeKalb County
   Convention & Visitors
   Bureau, 37
Demorest, 191
Depot Museum, 66
Dinglewood Pharmacy, 69
D Morgan's, 118
Doc Chey's Noodle
   House, 37
Dodge Hill Inn, 95
Dominick's Little Italy,
   20, 40
Douglas, 92
Douglas Community Golf
   Course, 92
Douglass Theatre, 124
Downtown Macon Historic
   District, 120
Downtown Tifton, 68
Drummer Boy
   Museum, 63
Dublin-Laurens County
   Welcome Center, 97
Dunaway Gardens, 27

E
Eagle Tavern Welcome
   Center, 211
Earl, The, 9
Early County
   Courthouse, 54
Earth Day Nature
   Trail, 164

Earthlodge, 124
East Atlanta Village, 9
East Dublin's Redneck
   Games, 82
East West Bistro, 215
Eats, 37
Edenfield House Inn, 82
Edwin L. Hatch Nuclear
   Plant Visitors
   Center, 86
1884 Paxton House
   Inn, 72
1842 Inn, 124, 145
Elachee Nature Science
   Center, 200
Elbert County, 205
Elberton Granite Museum
   & Exhibit, 206
Elijah Clark State Park, 144
Ellijay, 115
Ellijay's Georgia Apple
   Festival, 115
Elliott Street Deli and Pub,
   The, 4
Ellis Hotel, The, 33
Emma's Bed &
   Breakfast, 174
Epworth-by-the-Sea, 174
Etowah Indian Mounds
   Historic Site, 112
Ezekiel Harris House, 142

F
Fair Oaks Inn, 71
Fannie's on the
   Beach, 176
Farmhouse Inn, 134
FDR Memorial
   Museum, 55
Federal Reserve Bank
   of Atlanta's Monetary
   Museum, 10
Fern Bank Bar & Grill,
   92, 96
Fernbank Museum of
   Natural History, 17
Fernbank Science
   Center, 17
Fire Ant Festival, 94
Fitzgerald, 92
Fitzpatrick Hotel, 145
Five Rings Fountain, 1
Five & Ten, 216
Flannery O'Connor
   Room, 130

Flint River Outdoor
Center, 56
Flint RiverQuarium, 57
Florence Marina State
Park, 52
Foley House, 172
Folk Potters Trail of
Northeast Georgia, 192
Folkston, 90
Folkston Funnel, 90
Folkston/Okefenokee
Chamber of
Commerce, 97
Forrest Hills
Mountain Resort &
Conference, 212
Fort Frederica National
Monument, 166
Fort King George State
Historic Site, 161
Fort McAllister State
Historic Park, 159
Fort Morris State Historic
Site, 160
Fort Mountain State
Park, 110
Fort Pulaski National
Monument, 157
Fort Yargo State Park, 205
40 Watt Club, 210
Foundry Park Inn &
Spa, 213
Fourth of May Cafe &
Deli, 178
4-Way Lunch, 114
Foxfire Museum, 185
Fox Theatre, 6
Fox Vineyards and
Winery, 203
Franklin D. Roosevelt
State Park, 56
French Market Grille, 146
Fresh Air Bar-B-Que, 127
Frogtown Cellars, 203
Frontier Village, 53
fruitcake plant tours, 85
Fulton County, 1
Funk Heritage Center, 113
Fusco's Via Roma, 29

G
Gainesville, 199
Gainesville Theatre
Alliance, 200
Gallery Espresso, 153
Garcia's, 109, 118

Gardenside Cafe, 209
Garibaldi Cafe, 175
Gastonian, The, 172
Gates House, 71
General Coffee State
Park, 92
Geneva's Restaurant, 100
George & Louie's, 74
George L. Smith State
Park, 82
George's Restaurant, 37
George T. Bagby State
Park, 53
Georgia Apple
Festival, 115
Georgia Aquarium, 3
Georgia Cotton
Museum, 80
Georgia Department of
Natural Resources,
Parks and Historic Sites
Division, x
Georgia Dept.
of Economic
Development, Tourist
Division, x
Georgia Guidestones, 206
Georgia Mountain
Fair, 186
Georgia Mountain Fall
Festival, 188
Georgia Museum of
Agriculture and
Historic Village, 68
Georgia Museum of
Art, 209
Georgia National Fair,
76, 93
Georgia National
Fairgrounds &
Agricenter, 76
Georgia National Junior
Livestock Show and
Rodeo, 76
Georgia Peach Festival, 61
Georgia Pig, The, 177
Georgia Renaissance
Festival, 30
Georgia Rural Telephone
Museum, 66
Georgia Sea Turtle
Center, 166
Georgia Sports Hall of
Fame, 124
Georgia State Parks, 37

Georgia Tourist
Division, 37
Georgia Veterans
Memorial State Park, 67
Georgia Winery Taste
Center, 203
Geranium Festival, 25
Geranium House, 24
Gertrude Herbert Institute
of Art, 142
Ghost Talk, Ghost
Walk, 150
Gilmer County, 115
Glen-Ella Springs
Hotel, 190
Glenn Hotel, The, 33
Global Village and
Discovery Center, 64
Glover Park, 31
Golden Isles, 162
Gold Rush Days, 188, 197
Golf Villas, 205
Gone With the Wind, 19
Goodbread House Bed
and Breakfast, 174
Goode Feathers, 175
Gordonia-Altamaha State
Park, 85
Gordon-Lee Mansion, 106
Grand Dining Room,
The, 177
Great Golden Easter Egg
Hunt, 163
Great Southern Carriage
and Wagon Auction, 63
Great Temple Mound, 124
Green Meldrim
House, 152
Green Street Historical
District, 199
Green Tomato
Festival, 131
Greenwood's, 36
Greyfield Inn, 170
Griffin, 25
Grit, The, 216
Gritz, 24
Gryphon Tea Room, 175
Gwinnett, 19

H
Habersham County, 189
Habersham Winery,
193, 203
Hahira, 91

Hahira Honeybee Festival, 91
Hall's Boat House, 183
Hampton Square, 116
Happy Valley Pottery, 211
Hard Labor Creek State Park, 134
Hard Rock Cafe, 5
Hardy, Oliver, 125
Harness Racing Festival, 80, 93
Hart State Park, 201
Havana Restaurant, 38
Hawkinsville, 80
Hawkinsville-Pulaski County Chamber of Commerce, 81
Hay House, 120
Hayward, Susan, 105
Hearn Inn, 105
Hearn Inn Bed and Breakfast, 117
Hearthstone Lodge, The, 117
Helen, 194
Helen and White County Information, 216
Helendorf Inn & Conference Center, 213
Helen-to-Atlantic Hot Air Balloon Race and Festival, 188
Helmstead, The, 96
Henderson Village, 79, 96
Henry County, 24
Henry's Louisiana Grill, 29
Heritage Corner Tours, 48
Heritage Hall, 134
Heritage Station Museum, 92
Heritage Trail, 102
Herndon Home, 11
Hiawassee, 186
Hidden Hollow Country Inn, 100, 117
High Branch Falls, 183
High Country Wildwood Outfitters, 191
High Falls State Park, 127
High Museum of Art, 5, 37
Hike Inn, 198
Hill Manor Bed & Breakfast, 34
Hills & Dales Estate, 43
Hilton Garden Inn, 58, 71
Historic Banning Mills, 28

Historic DeSoto Theater, 104
Historic House & Garden Pilgrimage, 115
Historic Roswell Convention & Visitors Bureau, 37
Historic St. Marys Christmas Tour, 163
Hofer's of Helen, 194, 215
Hofwyl-Broadfield Plantation State Historic Site, 162
Holiday Inn Lanier Centre Hotel, 213
Holly Ridge Country Inn, 145
Homecoming, The, 75
Hotel Indigo, 33
Hotel Warm Springs Bed & Breakfast Inn, 55
House on Seventh, The, 71
Houston County, 76
Hummingbird's Perch Bed & Breakfast, 72

I
Imagine It! The Children's Museum of Atlanta, 3
Indian Museum, 127
Indian Springs State Park, 126
Inman Park Spring Festival and Tour of Homes, 30
Inn at Folkston, The, 95
Inn at Still Pond, The, 96
Inside CNN Tour, 3
Interactive Neighborhood for Kids, 200
Iron Horse, The, 129
Isaiah Davenport House, 154
Isle of Hope, 159

J
Jack Hadley Black History Museum, 70
Jaemor Farm Market, 201
James Earl Carter Library, 64
James H. (Sloppy) Floyd State Park, 101
Jarrell 1920 House, The, 145

Jarrell Plantation State Historic Site, 125
Jay Bird Springs Ministries, 81
Jaycee Landing Bait and Tackle and Campground, 86
J. Christopher's, 14
Jefferson Davis Memorial State Historic Site, 91
Jekyll Island, 164
Jekyll Island Arts Festival, 163
Jekyll Island Campground, 173
Jekyll Island Club Hotel, 165, 173
Jekyll Island Historic District, 165
Jepson Center for the Arts, 154
Jessye Norman Amphitheater, 140
Jesup, 86
Jimmy Carter Boyhood Home, 66
Jimmy Carter National Historic Site, 65
J. Mac's Island Restaurant & Bistro, 178
Joe's East Atlanta Coffee House, 9
John A. Sibley Horticultural Center, 46
John Tanner State Park, 105
Jo Jo's Biscuits and Burgers, 96
Jomax Barbecue, 97
Jonah's Fish and Grits, 75
Jones Creek Course, 144
Juliette Gordon Low Girl Scout National Center, 151
Just What I Like!, 20

K
Kangaroo Conservation Center, 201
Kennesaw Mountain, 26
Kennesaw Mountain National Battlefield Park, 29
Kettle Creek Battleground, 138

Kimbrough Brothers
General Store, 47
King-Keith House Bed &
Breakfast, 34
King & Prince Beach &
Golf Resort, 174
Kingston Confederate
Memorial Day, 115
King-Tisdell Cottage, 155
Knight's 1889, 118
Koffee Klutch, 24
Kolb's Farm, 29
Kolomoki Mounds State
Historic Park, 53

L
Lady and Sons, The, 175
Lafayette Manor Inn, 145
LaGrange, 41
LaGrange Art Museum, 43
Lake Blackshear Resort &
Golf Club, 67, 71
Lake Chatuge, 186
Lake Grace, 85
Lake Hartwell, 201
Lake Lanier Islands, 198
Lake Mayers, 86
Lake Oconee, 128
Lake Rabun, 183
Lake Rabun Hotel,
183, 213
Lake Rabun Road, 183
Lake Seminole, 54
Lake Sinclair, 132
Lake Winfield Scott
Recreation Area, 189
La Maison, 147
Lamar Dodd Art
Center, 41
Lamar Q. Ball Jr. Raptor
Center, 83
Landis, Kenesaw
Mountain, 26
Lane Packing
Company, 61
Lanier World, 199
Lapham-Patterson House
State Historic Site, 69
La Scala Restaurant &
Bar, 118
Last Resort, 216
Laura S. Walker State Park
and Golf Course, 88
Lawrenceville, 20
Lawrenceville Female
Seminary, 20

Lewis Grizzard Memorial
Museum, 26
Lighthouse Inn Bed &
Breakfast, 172
Lily Creek Lodge, 212
Limerick Junction, 37
Little Five Points, 9
Little Manse, The, 27
Little Ocmulgee State
Park, 95
Little St. Simons
Island, 168
Little White House, 47, 54
Lock and Dam Park, 102
Lodge at Smithgall Woods,
195, 213
Lodge, The, 46, 169
Longstreet, James, 199
Lookout Mountain, 107
Loudermilk Boardinghouse
Museum, 190
Lowndes County, 90
Luckie Food Lounge, 35
Lucy Craft Laney Museum
of Black History, 142
Luigi's, 143, 147
Lulu's Chocolate Bar, 175
Lumpkin, 53
Luna's, 215

M
Machu Picchu, 38
Macon-Bibb County
Convention and
Visitors Bureau, 120
Macon Cherry Blossom
Festival, 131
Macon Confederate
Museum, 122
Macon Convention &
Visitors Bureau, 146
Macon County, 62
Macon Marriott City
Center, 145
Madison, 132
Madison–Morgan
County Chamber of
Commerce, 146
Madison–Morgan County
Chamber of Commerce
Welcome Center, 133
Madison–Morgan County
Cultural Center, 133
Madison National Historic
District, 133

Madison Oaks Inn and
Gardens, 134
Madison's Spring Tour of
Homes, 131
Magnolia Springs State
Park, 83
Major Ridge Home, 103
Male Academy
Museum, 26
Mama Mia's, 18
Mansion on Forsyth
Park, 172
Manuel's Tavern, 38
Margaret Mitchell House
and *Gone With the
Wind* Museum, 6
Marietta *Gone With the
Wind* Museum, 32
Marietta Museum of
History, 32
Marietta Welcome
Center, 37
Maritime Center at the
Historic Coast Guard
Station, 168
Market Diner, 75
Mark of the Potter, 191
Mark Trail, 19
Marlin Monroes, 177
Marriott Columbus, 72
Marshall Forest, 104
Marshes of Glynn
Overlook Park, 164
MARTA, 7
Martha Berry Museum and
Art Gallery, 104
Martin Luther King, Jr.
Center for Nonviolent
Social Change, 5
Martin Luther King, Jr
National Historic
District, 5
Mary Mac's Tea Room, 38
Mary's, 9
Mary Willis Library, 138
Massee Lane Camellia
Society Gardens, 74
Massengale Park, 168
Masters Golf Tournament,
131, 143
Masters Practice
Rounds, 143
Matilda's Enchanted
Cottage, 15
Max Lager's American
Grill and Brewpub, 36

Mayhaw Festival, 59
McIntosh County, 161
McKinnon House, 173
McRae, 95
Meadow Garden, 142
Mercer Williams House
  Museum, 153
Meritage Cafe and
  Gallery, 73
Michael C. Carlos
  Emory University
  Museum of Art and
  Archaeology, 16
Michael Guido
  Gardens, 82
Michelle's of
  Georgetown, 73
Midtown neighborhood
  (Atlanta), 5
Midway Church, 160
Midway Museum, 160
Mighty Eighth Air Force
  Museum, 156
Milledgeville, 129
Milledgeville Grits, 131
Milledgeville Trolley
  Tour, 131
Milledgeville Visitors
  Center, 146
Minnie's Uptown
  Restaurant, 73
Missionary Ridge, 107
Mistletoe State Park, 144
Mittie's Tea Room Cafe, 36
Moccasin Creek State
  Park, 186
Mom & Dad's Italian
  Restaurant, 75
Monastery of the Holy
  Ghost, 23
Monta Luce, 203
Monterey Square, 153
Montezuma, 62
Moody Forest Natural
  Area, 86
Moosebreath Trading
  Company, 16
Morgan County African-
  American Museum, 133
Morgan County
  Courthouse, 134
Morris Museum of Art, 140
Mossy Creek Barnyard
  Festival, 93
Mountain Crossing/
  Walasi-Yi Center, 179

Mountain Laurel
  Festival, 188
Mount Yonah, 191
Mrs. Wilkes Dining
  Room, 176
Mulberry Inn, 172
Mule Camp Market, 188
Mule Day, 48, 61
Museum of Aviation and
  Georgia Aviation Hall
  of Fame, 79
Museum of Coastal
  History, 167
Myrtle Hill Cemetery, 102
Myrtlewood Plantation, 70

N
Nacho Mama's, 143
Nacoochee Grill, 215
Natalia's, 146
National Grits Festival,
  48, 60
National Infantry
  Museum, 49
National Mayhaw
  Festival, 48
National Prisoner of War
  Museum, 63
Neptune Park, 167
New Echota State Historic
  Site, 110
New Manchester
  Manufacturing
  Company, 28
Newnan, 25
New Perry Hotel, 78, 96
N.O.G.S. Tour of Hidden
  Gardens, 163
Nora Mill Granary &
  Store, 193
Norcross's Historic Old
  Town, 19
Norcross Station Cafe,
  20, 40
North 40 Lodge, 191
North Beach Grill, 176
North Campus, 209
Northeast Georgia Folk
  Pottery Museum, 192
Northeast Georgia History
  Center, 200
Northwest Georgia Travel
  Association, 119
Nottely River
  Campground, 187

O
Oak Hill, 104
Oakland Cemetery, 11
Oakwood Cafe, The, 118
Oatland Island Education
  Center, 157
Obediah's Okefenok, 88
Ocmulgee Indian
  Celebration, 131
Ocmulgee National
  Monument, 123
Oconee Cultural Arts
  Foundation, 210
Okefenokee
  Adventures, 88
Okefenokee Art
  Festival & Earth Day
  Celebration, 93
Okefenokee Heritage
  Center, 88
Okefenokee Restaurant, 96
Okefenokee Swamp
  National Wildlife
  Refuge, 88
Okefenokee Swamp
  Park, 86
Oktoberfest, 188
Olde Pink House,
  The, 176
Old Fashioned
  Christmas, 188
Old Fort Jackson, 156
Old Governor's
  Mansion, 130
Old Havana Cigar
  Company, 104
Old Market House, 139
Old Opera House, 81
Old Rock Gaol, 129
Old Sautee Store, 192
Old South Farm Days, 93
Oliver Hardy Festival, 131
Olympic Stadium, 14
"Original City Tours," 49
Orphans Cemetery, 81
Oscar Poole's Real Pit Bar
  B-Q, 119
Owens-Thomas
  House, 154
Oxbow Meadows
  Environmental Learning
  Center, 49
Oxford College of Emory
  University, 23
Oyster Shak, 177

P

Panola Mountain State Conservation Park, 23
Park Place Hotel, 212
Parks at Chehaw, 58
Partridge Inn, 146
Pasaquan Folk Art Compound, 56
Pastis, 36
Pauly's Cafe, 178
Peach County, 61
Peachtree Center, 5
Peachtree Road Race 10K, 30
Pebble Hill Plantation, 69, 74
Persimmon Creek Vineyards, 203
Pete Phillips Lodge and Convention Center, 95
Peter Bonner's *Gone With the Wind* Tour, 18
Phinizy Swamp Nature Park, 143
Pickett's Mill Battlefield Historic Site, 33
Piedmont National Wildlife Refuge, 126
Piedmont Park, 7
Pierpont, James Lord, 155
Pine Lake Campground, 85
Pine Mountain's Main Street, 47
Pine Mountain Trail, 56
Pine Mountain Wild Animal Safari, 47
Pioneer Village, 186
PJ's Cafe, 24
Place Away, A, 63
Plains Inn, 72
Plains Inn and Antique Shop, 66
Planter's Walk Antique Mall, 24
Plant Vogtle Whale, 83
Plaza, The, 75
Pleasant Peasant, 36
Pope Dickson & Son Antique Funeral Museum, 18
Port Columbus National Civil War Naval Museum, 50
Poultry Park, 200

Prater's Mill Country Fair, 108, 115
President's Quarters, The, 172
Priester's Pecans, Candy Kitchen, and Restaurant, 78
Providence Canyon State Park, 51
Providence Spring, 63

Q

Queen Anne Inn, 146
Quilt Plaza, 1
Quinlan Visual Arts Center, 199

R

Rabbittown Cafe, 201
Rabun Beach Recreation Area, 183
Raiford Gallery, 15
Rainbow Grocery, 17
Ralph Mark Gilbert Civil Rights Museum, 155
Rattlesnake Roundup, 48, 60, 85
Red Door Studio, 135
Red Hat Lane, 20
Redneck Games, 93
Redneck Gourmet, The, 39
Red Peppers, 29
Red Top Mountain State Park, 114
Reed Bingham State Park, 91
Reese-Bourgeois Cottage, 134
Resources Room, 123
Richard B. Russell-Brasstown Scenic Highway, 188
Richard B. Russell State Park, 207
Richard S. Bolt Visitors Center, 89
Ridges Resort & Marina, The, 187, 214
Rising Fawn, 100
Ritz-Carlton Lodge at Reynolds Plantation, 128
RiverCenter for the Performing Arts, 51
Riverfest Weekend, 48

River Street, 151
Riverwalk Augusta, 140
Riverwalk Bluegrass Festival, 131
R. L.'s Off the Square, 24
Road to Tara Museum, 18
Robert C. Williams American Museum of Papermaking, 10
Robert Toombs House State Historic Site, 137
Rock Eagle, 132
Rock House, 139
Rocky Mountain Recreation and Public Fishing Area, 103
Rolater Park, 105
Rome, 101
Rome Area History Museum, 103
Rome Braves' State Mutual Stadium, 102
Rome Convention & Visitors Bureau, 119
Rome–Floyd County Public Library, 102
Roscoe, 27
Rose Cottage, 74
Rose Festival, 70
Rose Hill Cemetery, 123
Ross's Diner, 118
Roswell, 13
Roswell Visitors Center, 15
Rothschild-Pound House, 72
Rusty's Downtown Grill and Bar, 97
Ruth Ann's, 73
Rutledge, 135
Rutledge antiques and craft stores, 135
Rutledge Hardware, 135
Rylander Theater, 64

S

Saint Charles Inn, The, 33
Sapelo Island Cultural Festival, 163
Sapelo Island Tours, 162
Savannah, 148
Savannah-Americus-Montgomery Shortline, 67
Savannah History Museum, 151

Savannah Music
Festival, 163
Savannah National Historic
District, 150
Savannah Tour of Homes
& Gardens, 163
Scarlett's Retreat and Day
Spa, 24
Scotland Yard
Antiques, 20
Scott's Book, 26
Seabrook Village, 160
Sea Island, 169
SeaJay's Waterfront Cafe &
Pub, 177
2nd Friday Art strolls, 3
Seminole State Park, 54
Senoia, 27
Sen. Sam Nunn Library, 76
Seoul Garden, 38
Shellmont Inn, 34
Ships of the Sea Maritime
Museum, 155
Shorter College, 104
Sidney Lanier Cottage, 123
Sign of the Dove Bed
& Breakfast and
Restaurant, 57, 71
Silver Comet Trail, 32
Simons-Bond Inn Bed and
Breakfast, 214
Sitton Creek Gulch, 98
Six Pence Pub, 153, 176
Skate Escape, 8
Skidaway Island State
Park, 158
Smith House, 196, 215
Social Circle, 128
Sorghum Festival, 188
Sosebee Cove Scenic
Area, 189
Southeastern Flower
Show, 30
Southeastern Railway
Museum, 22
Southern Belles &
Whistles Tour, 18
Southern Cross Guest
Ranch B&B, 134
Southern Elegance Bed
and Breakfast, 145
Southern Forest World
Museum, 87
Southern Museum of Civil
War and Locomotive
History, 30

Southworks Arts
Festival, 188
Spalding Hosiery
Shoppe, 25
Spanish moss, 159, 170
Spanky's Beachside, 177
Spencer House Inn, 175
Springer Mountain, 179
Springer Opera House, 48
Stanley House, The, 35
Starr's Mill, 28
State Botanical
Garden, 208
State Botanical Garden of
Georgia, 216
Statesboro, 83
Statesboro Inn and
Restaurant, 84, 96
Statesboro Tourism
Office, 97
St. Cyprian's Episcopal
Church, 161
Steffen Thomas Museum
and Archives, 134
Stephen C. Foster State
Park, 89
St. Marys Submarine
Museum, 170
Stonebridge Golf
Club, 103
Stone Mountain Park, 17
Stone Mountain Village, 17
Stone Mountain Village
Arts Festival, 30
Stovall Covered
Bridge, 192
Stovall House, 193, 213
St. Patrick's
Celebration, 163
St. Patrick's Day Festival,
82, 93
St. Simons Inn by the
Lighthouse, 174
St. Simons Island, 166
St. Simons Lighthouse, 167
Sugar Hill Bed &
Breakfast, 96
Sugar Hill Municipal Golf
Course, 21
Sumter County, 62
Sunbury Crab
Company, 177
Sunflower Festival, 136
Surin of Thailand, 38
Suwannee Canal
Recreation Area, 88

Swallow at the Hollow,
The, 36
"Swamp Gravy," 59
Swanson, The, 97
Sweetwater Creek
Conservation Park, 28
Swheat Market Deli, 118

T
Tallulah Falls, 184
Tallulah Gallery, 185
Tallulah Gorge, 184
Tallulah Gorge State
Park, 184
Taqueria del Sol, 39
Tarrer Inn, The, 60, 71
Taste of Britain, 19
Taylor-Grady House, 208
Teaching Museum
North, 13
Teacup Cottage, 29
Ted's Montana Grill, 35
Telfair Academy of Arts &
Sciences, 154
Tellus: the Northwest
Georgia Science
Museum, 114
Temple Mickve Israel, 153
10 East Washington, 40
Ten-Fifty Canton Street
Bed & Breakfast, 95
Theatre in the Square, 31
Thomas County Historical
Museum, 69
Thomasville, 68
Thomasville Antiques
Show and Sale, 48
Thomasville Black
Heritage Trail, 69
Thomasville Rose Festival,
48, 68
Thomasville Rose
Garden, 70
Three Sisters Vineyards
and Winery, 203
Thronateeska Heritage
Foundation, 59
Thyme Away Bed and
Breakfast, 71
Tic Toc Room, 146
Tiger Mountain Vineyard
and Winery, 203
Toccoa Harvest
Festival, 188
Tour of Homes and Arts
and Crafts Show, 26

Towaliga River, 127
Town Clock, 102
Towns County Park, 187
Towns County
    Tourism, 216
Trader Vic's, 36
Trattoria Il Localino, 38
Travelers Rest, 202
Troll Tavern, 194, 215
Tubman African American
    Museum, 123
Tugaloo State Park, 202
Tumlin House Bed &
    Breakfast, 117
Tunnel Hill Heritage
    Center, 109
Turner Field, 14
Twelve Days of
    Christmas, 131
Twila Faye's Tea Room &
    Soda Fountain, 125
2Dog, 215
Tybee Island, 157
Tybee Island Inn, 173
Tybee Lighthouse and
    Museum, 158
Ty Cobb Museum, 202

U
UGA Marine Education
    Center and
    Aquarium, 158
UGA Visitors Center, 209
Uncle Remus
    Museum, 132
Unicoi State Park, 194
Union County Chamber of
    Commerce, 216
University Museum, 83
University of Georgia, 207
University of Georgia
    Performing Arts
    Center, 216

V
Valdosta, 90
Valdosta-Lowndes
    Convention & Visitors
    Bureau, 97
Vandy's Barbecue, 84, 97
Vann House, 109
Varsity, The, 36

Victoria Bryant State
    Park, 202
Victorian Tea Room,
    The, 74
Vidalia Onion Festival, 93
Vidalia sweet onion, 84
Village Inn and Pub, 174
Village Inn Bed &
    Breakfast, The, 35
Villas by the Sea
    Resort, 173
Virginia Hand Callaway
    Discovery Center, 46
Virginia-Highland
    neighborhood, 8
Vogel State Park, 189
Vortex Bar & Grill,
    The, 38

W
Wahoo! A Decatur
    Grill, 39
Wallenda, Karl, 184
Warm Springs, 55
Warm Springs Welcome
    Center, 55
Washington, 137
Washington Historical
    Museum, 137
Washington Jockey
    Club, 139
Washington Plantation
    Bed and Breakfast, 145
Washington–Wilkes
    Chamber of
    Commerce, 146
Washington–Wilkes Tour
    of Homes, 131, 139
Watermelon Festival,
    48, 67
Watershed, 39
Watkinsville, 210
Watson Mill Bridge, 211
Watson Mill Bridge State
    Park, 214
Waycross/Ware County
    Tourism Bureau, 97
Weaver D's, 216
Wesley, John, 153
West-Holt Family
    Farm, 136
West Point Lake, 45

Westville, 52
Whipporwill Co., 16
Whistle Stop Cafe, 31, 126
Whitlock Inn Bed &
    Breakfast, 35
Whitworth Inn Bed &
    Breakfast, 213
Wild Adventures Theme
    Park, 91
Wild Chicken Festival,
    93, 94
Will-A-Way Recreation
    Area, 205
William Breman Jewish
    Heritage Museum, 11
Williams, Jim, 138
Windsor Hotel, 65, 72
Winn Park, 7
Wolf Mountain Vineyards,
    203, 215
Woodall House, 139
Woodbine Crawfish
    Festival, 171
Woodbridge Restaurant
    and Inn, 197, 215
Woodrow Wilson's
    Boyhood Home, 141
Woodruff Arts Center, 5
Woodruff Arts Center/
    High Museum of Art, 7
Woodruff Park, 5
World of Coca-Cola, 3
Worley Homestead Inn,
    197, 213
Wormsloe State Historic
    Site, 159
Wren's Nest, 11

Y
Yellow River Wildlife
    Game Ranch, 21
Ye Olde Colonial,
    134, 147
Yesterday Cafe, The,
    129, 147
Yesterday's Cafe, 135
Yoder's Deitsch Haus, 62

Z
Zoo Atlanta, 10